Health Cooperatives

In the era of complex healthcare challenges, the question arises: Can health cooperatives be the catalysts for transformation in the healthcare system? This research monograph delves into this thought-provoking query, exploring the potential of health cooperatives as influential entities in the future of healthcare. Despite advancements, healthcare systems still need help with sustainability, equality, costly therapies, and various other segments.

This monograph aims to dissect the notion of "Healthy lives and well-being for everyone," protracted by policymakers and proponents of the existing healthcare setup. Researchers, cooperative professionals, healthcare practitioners, decision-makers, patients, policy developers, librarians, and booksellers will find this book relevant and interesting to read. The captivating narrative is supported by analysing 20 countries across five continents, explaining their historical and modern notion of the context and health cooperatives' development. It also sheds light on the significance of modern cooperatives in the current healthcare landscape. In addition, the monograph offers insights into multiple case studies of health-oriented cooperatives showing their diversity and flexibility in operations.

This research monograph paves the way for envisioning a future where health cooperatives have the potential to play an important role in addressing various challenges affecting positive societal changes.

Milorad Stamenovic is a multi-disciplinary professional with a diverse educational background. He obtained his bachelor's degree in economics from the Faculty of International Economics in Belgrade, Serbia. Building upon this foundation, Milorad pursued a master's degree in International Business and Management, which he completed through a joint program between the Faculty of Organisational Sciences in Belgrade and Middlesex University in London. His academic journey continued by obtaining the Doctor of Economic Sciences title from Belgrade's Faculty of Business Studies. He has completed multiple management and regulatory-oriented courses offered by esteemed organisations in the area of Public Health. His research aptitude led to his selection as a Research Fellow by Serbia's Ministry of Science, Education, and Technological Development.

Routledge Advances in Management and Business Studies

Corporate Social Hypocrisy
CSR in the Era of Global Crises
Dalia Streimikiene, Asta Mikalauskiene and Gabija Stanislovaityte

Information, Security and Society in the COVID-19 Pandemic
Edited by Natalia Moch, Wioletta Wereda and Jerzy Stańczyk

Technologies and Trends in the Halal Industry
Edited by Nor Aida Abdul Rahman, Kamran Mahroof and Azizul Hassan

Digital Transformation, Perspective Development, and Value Creation
Research Case Studies
Edited by Małgorzata Pańkowska

Responsible Management and Sustainable Consumption
Creating a Consumer and Enterprise Social Responsibility Index
Edited by Piotr Wachowiak, Anna Dąbrowska, Monika Zajkowska and Celina Sołek-Borowska

Co-operative and Mutual Enterprises Research
A Comprehensive Overview
Tim Mazzarol

Health Cooperatives
Historical Developments and Future Challenges for Global Healthcare
Milorad Stamenovic

For more information about this series, please visit: www.routledge.com/Routledge-Advances-in-Management-and-Business-Studies/book-series/SE0305

Health Cooperatives

Historical Developments and Future
Challenges for Global Healthcare

Milorad Stamenovic

Routledge
Taylor & Francis Group
NEW YORK AND LONDON

First published 2024
by Routledge
605 Third Avenue, New York, NY 10158

and by Routledge
4 Park Square, Milton Park, Abingdon, Oxon, OX14 4RN

Routledge is an imprint of the Taylor & Francis Group, an informa business

ISBN: 978-1-032-02362-5 (hbk)
ISBN: 978-1-032-02363-2 (pbk)
ISBN: 978-1-003-18306-8 (ebk)

DOI: 10.4324/9781003183068

Typeset in Times New Roman
by Newgen Publishing UK

*With heartfelt gratitude to my family and a special acknowledge-
ment to Branislav Gulan and Jose Pérez, who played a vital role
in fuelling my passion for health cooperatives, this research monograph is dedicated to them, inspiring the pursuit of transformative
healthcare solutions.*

Contents

Illustrations

Figures

Images

Tables

About the author

Dr Milorad Stamenovic is a multi-disciplinary professional with a diverse educational background. He obtained his bachelor's degree in economics from the Faculty of International Economics in Belgrade, Serbia. Building upon this foundation, Milorad pursued a master's degree in International Business and Management, which he completed through a joint program between the Faculty of Organisational Sciences in Belgrade and Middlesex University in London. His academic journey continued by obtaining the Doctor of Economic Sciences title from Belgrade's Faculty of Business Studies. While his expertise lies in economics, Milorad's activities led him to pursue a medical bachelor's degree and obtain a master's degree in health sanitary engineering. Milorad embarked on an academic program at the Universite Cote D'Azur in Nice, France, focusing on Innovation Management and academic research. He has completed multiple management and regulatory-oriented courses offered by esteemed organisations in the area of Public Health. His research aptitude led to his selection as a Research Fellow by Serbia's Ministry of Science, Education, and Technological Development.

Additionally, Milorad has experience as an editor for scientific journals and conferences. Professionally, Milorad has been actively involved in clinical research since 2007, working with prominent pharmaceutical and biotechnology companies. His contributions to over 50 academic and commercial medical

Image 0.1 Photography of Dr Milorad Stamenovic, created by the author.

research projects have paved the way for developing and introducing new drugs and medical devices into the market. He visited around 30 state health institutions having insights into their organisation and medical research.

Milorad Stamenovic has authored several research monographs, among which is "The World Trade Organization – Environment and Health Care System" (published by the Institute of International Politics and Economics, Serbia), as an outcome of the scientific project funded by the Ministry of Education, Science, and Technological Development of the Government of the Republic of Serbia. Milorad has also authored other research monographs, such as "Economy of Serbia and EU" (2016, published by BKC, Serbia), "Serbia Today – Contemporary Aspects of Neoliberalism, Economy, Demography, and Healthcare" (2017, published by Prometej, Serbia), "Globalization – Contemporary Aspects of Trade, Economy, and Healthcare" (2018, published by the Economics Faculty, University of Nis, Serbia), and "Health Cooperatives – Serbian Roots for Global Development" (2020, published by Prometej, Serbia). Milorad has also contributed numerous scientific articles in the field of health cooperatives and has been invited to speak at various conferences and scientific discussions. He initiated the Initiative for Reopening Health Cooperatives in the Republic of Serbia in 2020. As a result of his research advocacy, the new state strategy of rural development in Serbia considered health cooperatives for the first time since 1949. Multiple newspaper texts were written by Milorad and published in major Serbian journals, resulting in the book collection issued in 2022 under the title "44 Views – Proposals for Development of Economic and Healthcare System." Beyond his professional pursuits, Milorad Stamenovic is a devoted father of two and currently resides in Nice, France.

1   Introduction

Centuries ago, Thomas Hobbes explained that if individuals lack the knowledge or ability to live following ethical principles, they should step aside and yield their position to those who are capable. This notion emphasises the importance of ethical integrity and implies that those with the necessary understanding should assume leadership roles or positions of influence. By doing so, it is believed that society can benefit from the guidance and actions of individuals who possess the competence and moral compass to make informed decisions and act in the best interest of the collective.

Using pragmatism as a philosophical viewpoint in this research, we still consider that Hobbes' concept, guided by core humanitarian principles addressing morality for society leaders, can be applied to tackle the challenges in modern healthcare systems and emphasise the importance of responding to those in contemporary society. Furthermore, the quote can be understood within the broader context of cooperative values we are dealing with in the monograph, as cooperatives are founded on ethical principles and democratic participation. By upholding these principles, cooperatives ensure that their members operate fairly and transparently, benefiting both the cooperative and society. Additionally, by advocating for economic democracy and collaboration, cooperatives offer an alternative or complement to the traditional capitalist economic system, promoting more equitable and sustainable economic development. The principles underlying cooperatives emphasise the significance of ethical conduct and democratic decision-making in creating a fair and just society.

Driven by these ideas, the research monograph explores health cooperatives' history and modern aspects. We aim to analyse the historical development of these organisations and shed light on their contemporary perspectives, uncovering the narratives of these distinctive organisational forms within the global healthcare landscape. Recognising that comprehending the current state of health cooperatives necessitates an examination of their historical evolution, our research encompasses the historical evolution of health cooperatives in 20 countries across five continents, encompassing Europe, North and South

DOI: 10.4324/9781003183068-1

America, and Asia, supplemented by examples from African countries. This overview also reveals whether health cooperatives have undergone growth throughout their historical timeline and could be deemed emerging organisational forms from a historical standpoint.

To evaluate developmental aspects over time, we examined the development of healthcare systems, the evolution of cooperatives, and the progress of health cooperatives in each of the 20 observed countries, identifying correlations among these aspects. Our investigation encompasses the period preceding the 19th century, focusing on the 19th and 20th centuries leading up to the present era. We employ a multidimensional approach, delving into medical history-related knowledge and legal, sociological, and economic perspectives. By incorporating various disciplines, we offer a comprehensive understanding of the intricate interplay between health cooperatives and their environments.

Additionally, we highlighted numerous pioneering health cooperatives among the observed countries, illuminating the visionary individuals who spearheaded their development and facilitated knowledge transfer among nations. The monograph emphasises the indispensable contributions and cooperative efforts of international organisations such as the International Labour Organization (ILO), World Health Organization (WHO), United Nations (UN), International Cooperative Alliance (ICA), and International Health Cooperative Organisation (IHCO), unveiling their roles in the establishment and ongoing operations of health cooperatives worldwide. Through our research, we identify contributing factors that led to the geographical dispersion of initial health cooperatives, revealing the significance of pivotal historical landmarks and how these cooperatives spread across diverse regions, forming geographical clusters with similar developmental patterns. The monograph provides case studies examining the characteristics of health cooperatives, including their organisational structures, governance frameworks, financial models, and unique identities, indicating their potential and adaptability as organisational forms.

By exploring the challenges faced by historical and contemporary healthcare systems and providing a detailed understanding of these issues, we investigate how health cooperatives can contribute to resolving these complex problems. We also propose potential solutions for the future of healthcare delivery based on the models presented in the text. The monograph recognises the rigidity of current healthcare systems in adapting to changing needs, as demonstrated by the Covid-19 pandemic. It argues that health cooperatives, with their focus on community involvement, participatory decision-making, and ethical principles, have the potential to offer innovative solutions and address the limitations of traditional healthcare models. Through its research and analysis, the monograph aims to offer insights and recommendations for healthcare professionals and a variety of stakeholders interested in transforming the healthcare system. It highlights the role of health cooperatives in promoting a fairer, more responsive, and patient-centric approach to healthcare delivery. Acknowledging the challenges modern healthcare systems face highlights the importance of shedding more light on health cooperatives from historical and contemporary perspectives.

The complexity of healthcare provision and the involvement of health cooperatives and mutual aid societies have identified various typologies of healthcare systems. These typologies aim to clarify the roles of different service providers within public healthcare systems, including for-profit, non-profit, and cooperative organisations, although the latter often play a marginal role. Universal healthcare systems integrate pre-existing private mutual and non-profit organisations, while some healthcare systems strive for universal public coverage but struggle to ensure access to health services for all population groups. Mixed healthcare systems guarantee essential health services through public policies targeting low-income groups. Mutual aid societies and cooperatives tend to play an increasingly significant role across these healthcare system typologies, reflecting the growing challenges faced by these systems over time.

When considering crisis, health cooperatives also should be considered, and further research should be done on the possibilities for mitigating crisis events, including the long-term goals, as with the climate crisis, to shorter-term goals related to conflict-related crises. The WHO has identified the climate crisis as a significant threat to the planet and human health. Emissions from the climate crisis contribute to approximately seven million premature deaths yearly, accounting for over a quarter of deaths caused by heart attacks, strokes, and lung cancer. Extreme weather events, such as droughts and floods, worsen malnutrition rates and facilitate the spread of infectious diseases like malaria. Therefore, addressing the climate crisis is crucial for safeguarding the environment and public health.

In addition to the climate crisis, healthcare delivery faces specific difficulties in conflict-affected regions. Countries experiencing conflicts often witness numerous attacks on healthcare workers and facilities, resulting in casualties and hindering disease containment efforts. Displaced populations also struggle to access healthcare services, exacerbating their health challenges. Bridging the gap between socioeconomic groups and improving healthcare access, particularly for marginalised populations, are essential to ensure health equity. Expanding the availability and affordability of medicines is equally important, as many individuals worldwide lack access to essential medications. Also, efforts to combat substandard and counterfeit medical products are necessary to save lives and instil trust in healthcare systems.

Health cooperatives had their role in multiple conflicts globally, with many casualties due to their devotion to population health support in crisis times. There are historical examples from different regions globally confirming it, which might be seen when multiple health cooperatives were burnt, leaving no health protection behind at the beginning of WWI in Serbia, or during the

Indo-Pakistani war, when a significant impact was present in the work and development of health cooperatives contributing to the population health. We further argue that the flexibility of the cooperative model, as demonstrated by historical perspectives, may offer viable solutions to these challenges. We can strive towards a healthier and more equitable future by addressing these issues, promoting health in the face of climate change, and improving healthcare access.

Considering the flexibility of the model, one of the advantages is associated with flexibility in financing. Health cooperatives have diverse business models and sources of revenue, depending on their relationship with the state and prospective users, taking into account the presence or absence of a third-party payer. One of the examples where health cooperatives showed such flexibility was seen in Argentina at the beginning of the 21st century (see chapter related to South American countries). Within cooperatives, funding for healthcare activities can come from various sources, such as contracts or service agreements with the state or public bodies, individual payments (out-of-pocket or insurance covered), provider billing (charging fees to healthcare professionals), insurance system payments (user fees or reimbursements), and donations or grants. Regarding health insurance, cooperatives and mutuals have made significant progress over the past two centuries, aligning with the development of the welfare state. Health insurance schemes can be categorised as compulsory or voluntary within national welfare systems, providing primary coverage through a national health service or health insurance funds. The role of mutuals in health insurance varies depending on the country and the type of insurance scheme.

The cooperative model is also crucial in achieving sustainable development goals. One area where cooperatives excel is poverty and exclusion reduction, as recognised by various actors such as the UN, the ILO, and the ICA. Cooperatives contribute to poverty reduction by identifying economic opportunities for their members, empowering the disadvantaged, providing security through collective risk-sharing, and facilitating member access to assets for livelihoods. For example, savings and credit cooperatives enable financial access, agricultural cooperatives provide inputs and market access for farmers, and consumer cooperatives ensure affordable household supplies. Such services help lift members out of poverty.

Furthermore, cooperatives play a significant role in promoting gender equality. Women's participation in cooperatives enhances their economic and social engagement in local economies and societies worldwide. Women also demonstrate a strong presence in consumer and worker cooperatives, holding directorial positions and other leadership positions. Women's participation in financial and agricultural cooperatives is on the rise in many regions globally, with an increasing number of women joining and assuming leadership roles contributing to social inclusion and empowerment.

Examining the history of the development of health cooperatives, in the 19th century, cooperative and mutual involvement primarily focused on social security initiatives, including limited healthcare and social care provisions. These initiatives were driven by the cooperative consumer movement in Western, Northern, and Central Europe. The ICA plays a crucial global role as the custodian of the Cooperative Identity statement, which encompasses the values and principles of the cooperative movement. In 1995, the ICA adopted a revised version of this statement, which includes the definition of a cooperative, the values that underlie cooperatives, and the seven cooperative principles. The ICA also offers detailed guidance through the Guidance Notes on the Cooperative Principles and Values to assist cooperative enterprises in their practical implementation.

In the 1920s and 1930s, cooperative engagement in health service delivery was expanded worldwide. In Japan, both agricultural and consumer cooperative movements were involved in providing health services. Early modern health cooperatives were developed in Serbia, representing the model for many other countries globally. Farmers' organisations played a crucial role in early experiments with user-owned cooperatives in the United States. Canada's agricultural cooperative movements supported community-based health services, while joint trade unions and cooperative enterprise-based health services were integral to Jewish settlement in Palestine. Rural user-owned and community-based health cooperative systems also emerged and expanded significantly in Eastern Europe, particularly in former Yugoslavia and later in Poland. Countries like India, Sri Lanka, and China conducted various rural community-based experiments in cooperative health service delivery, following the model established in former Yugoslavia which was initiated in Serbia. During the same period, government-cooperative/mutual partnerships continued to grow, especially in European countries where elements of the welfare state were gradually established.

Today, health cooperatives are widely present in many countries worldwide with a high diversity level in healthcare services provided, structure and financing. By combining all the historical data for numerous countries globally and considering the long timeline explored, we have concluded the rising trend from the historical perspective of the health cooperatives and their flexibility to adapt to different ideologies, politics and economic models on national levels. We are fascinated by the multitude of global applications within highly diversified models, showing great potential.

2 Historical and modern aspects of health cooperatives development in Western Europe (UK, Spain, Italy, France, Belgium, and Sweden)

United Kingdom (UK)

Healthcare system development in the United Kingdom

The United Kingdom has a long history of providing healthcare through different options, rooting back to the 15th century (Borsay & Hunter, 2014). Socially endangered categories in today's sense (i.e. poor, old, and infirm) received certain forms of healthcare through religious formations, such as monasteries. That is a generally known approach, which took root in numerous countries where religious organisations provided healthcare and had specific knowledge but also the capacity to implement healthcare into reality (Brown, 2001). There was an exciting event that occurred in England in 1543 when the Church of England was forced to excommunication when King Henry VIII wanted to formalise his second marriage with Anne Boleyn, which unfortunately affected both monastery medicine and healthcare as that was the basic model of healthcare protection for vulnerable social groups of that time. In 1601, Queen Elizabeth I passed a law enabling home treatment (through almshouses) for people experiencing poverty. Moreover, that type of "outdoor relief" was in operation until the 19th century (Borsay & Hunter, 2014). In addition, insurance appeared in the 1700s in the United Kingdom, and its development influenced the global understanding of insurance. Initially, it did not include health insurance but represented a good "base" for developing private health insurance. That refers primarily to the beginnings of doctor insurance models. The Napoleonic wars stimulated the need for life insurance, affecting both war insurance and terminal illness. However, it took work to calculate benefits for insurance companies. During the 19th century, awareness of the need for better-organised healthcare slowly changed. Local and municipal authorities became involved, especially in mental illnesses and personal types of handicaps. During the 19th century, many cooperative insurance organisations in the United Kingdom dealt with healthcare. Before the National Health Service (NHS) was created in the United Kingdom, the National Health Insurance System (NHIS) was formed,

DOI: 10.4324/9781003183068-2

which started operating in 1911 (Compton & Schlackman, 1998). Voluntary organisations were also founded and provided healthcare. However, there was also private health practice that was rather lucrative. Further private practice development also led to family doctors, who became famous at the beginning of the 20th century through various insurance programs. Until then, community care was under the supervision of local municipalities until the subsequent development of the National Health System. That was contributed to by the expansion of the insurance scheme initiated by Lloyd George in 1911, which then included all employees.

The establishment of the NHS resulted from increasing financial pressure, unequal access to health services, and the conversion of popular attitudes towards the role of government. Later, the Beveridge Report in 1942 promoted social reforms, and the development of major social policy reforms was supported by the election of the Labour Government at the end of WWII. The NHS was established in 1948 and provided free, universal, and comprehensive healthcare in England and Wales, with Scotland having its own health system. Moving forward through the 20th-century timeline in the United Kingdom, most healthcare was provided by NHS, a public healthcare system funded by general taxation. It offered healthcare to all permanent residents free of charge at the point of delivery. The NHS is overseen by policymakers who distribute funds and supervise the delivery of services, with Scotland, Wales, and Northern Ireland having their health policies, while in England, the UK government is in charge. Some services are organised across the United Kingdom referring to the NHS' work area.

The growth of the public sector as a direct service provider continued until the 1970s when an economic crisis led to the election of the "New Right" Thatcher-led Conservative Government. Policies of the "New Right" affected the healthcare sector and led to the establishment of a competitive mechanism for the "contracting out" of services and the creation of internal "quasi-markets" through the purchaser/provider split, which created a favourable environment for third-sector organisations to provide services. Later, with the NHS and Community Care Act of 1990, the government introduced general practitioner fund-holding, which allowed practices serving over 11,000 patients to apply for their health system budgets to cover their staff costs, prescriptions, outpatient care, and a defined range of hospital services. Fundholders became purchasers of health services on behalf of their patients (Cylus et al., 2015).

In 1997, a reform was implemented that allowed the four countries of the United Kingdom to have the power to organise their health services and financing. While that led to differences in national implementations, all four countries maintained an NHS that provided universal access to comprehensive services, primarily free of charge. The NHSs across the United Kingdom were founded on the same ground. The priorities of this system have been set, as well as the periods for the process, through the implementation of strategies such as "The

Health of the Nation" since 1991. In 1989, the publication "Caring for People" adopted a set of community healthcare principles proposals. This was primarily related to mental illnesses and ways of accessing healthcare in which the non-profit sector and local governments were promoted in providing this type of healthcare (Greengross et al., 1999). Despite changes in the ruling party of the government of Scotland, there has been significant continuity in healthcare policy since the first Scottish Health White Paper in 1999 (Scottish Office Department of Health, 1999). Under the Health Act (2006), the Secretary of State is legally obliged to promote a comprehensive health service that provides services free of charge to those eligible for the NHS, without discrimination and within certain time limits (Egdell & Dutton, 2016). In 2000, the UK government committed unprecedented funding towards increasing healthcare spending for the whole United Kingdom. Scotland, Wales, and Northern Ireland received significant increases in allotment due to devolution. Since then, each country has taken its own approach to healthcare. For example, England has focused on decentralisation, reinforcement of the internal market, and localised decision-making. At the same time, Scotland and Wales have moved towards a more consistent and consensual approach, promoting social policies that prioritise greater social integration, inclusion, fairness, and solidarity. Today, the NHS functions as a whole of state-owned hospitals, general practitioners network, community health services, and other sections of the UK's healthcare system.

Even though it is globally one of the better-organised health systems, NHS is facing multiple challenges that might sound to the reader similar to once discovered in the other national health systems within this monograph. British Medical Association identified some of the major challenges in resourcing, financing, governance, and use of new technologies. For years, the NHS has noted chronic understaffing and poor retention, leading to a growing crisis. Insufficient workforce planning, government accountability, and inadequate funding and infrastructure for training new doctors have contributed to staff shortages. Retaining existing doctors has become even more challenging. That pressure has become unsustainable, with a significant number of doctors expressing their intention to retire early or work fewer hours after the pandemic. The strain of delivering care amid persistent shortages has resulted in chronic unease, leading to issues like stress, fatigue, burnout, moral injury, and declining mental health and well-being. General practice faces growing pressure as it manages the needs of an ageing and expanding population while experiencing stagnation in the growth of the GP workforce. Insufficient funding and outdated infrastructure further exacerbate the challenges faced by the NHS. Recent funding injections have not fully addressed the need to manage the pandemic, clear the care backlog, or upgrade facilities for future challenges. Inadequate space, deteriorating estates, outdated IT systems, and falling bed numbers add to the strain. The NHS struggles to meet the increasing demand for hospital treatment, resulting in long delays and growing waiting lists for emergency, routine, and cancer care, pushing the system beyond safe operational standards.

In 2021, the NHS in England is facing unprecedented challenges, requiring an equally unprecedented and long-term response from the government. Addressing the backlog of physical and mental healthcare caused by the pandemic and creating a healthcare system that tackles health inequalities and other weaknesses exposed by Covid-19 were the major challenges. The NHS is simultaneously tasked with implementing the most extensive vaccine campaign in its history and developing services for patients with chronic Covid-19 (Ham, 2020). Staff absence due to infections and self-isolation affects the NHS' ability to care for Covid and non-Covid patients. Social care and public health have also been exposed as weak points. Social care has been neglected by successive governments, lacking sustainable reform, while public health budgets have faced cuts, exacerbating health inequalities. The pandemic's disproportionate impact on ethnic minority groups and deprived communities highlights the need for comprehensive action to address health disparities (Toh & Haynes, 2022).

To address these challenges, a more ambitious vision is required, building on the innovative solutions developed by NHS staff recently. An adequately resourced workforce strategy should be a national priority, accompanied by an updated long-term plan for the NHS. The government must also make credible commitments to social care and health inequalities, including increased public spending and closer integration with the NHS. Addressing health inequalities requires a whole-government approach, focusing on early years, fair employment, living standards, prevention, and rebuilding the public health system. Although some may argue that these reforms are unaffordable given the government debt, mere tinkering or restoring the pre-Covid status quo is inadequate. Only an ambitious program that matches the scale of the current challenge will enable the NHS to manage immediate pressures and build a better future.

Health cooperatives and mutuals development in the United Kingdom

The early development of agricultural and semi-industrial communities in the United Kingdom was conceptually developed through the doctrines of Robert Owen (1771–1858) and more pragmatic Dr William King (1757–1865) (among others, also the creator of *The Cooperator* magazine). The beginning was similar to organisations like Friendly societies and mutual funds, which had a long history in the United Kingdom. We can also mention The Fenwick Weavers' Society, a professional organisation and cooperative formed as early as 1761 in Scotland (a consumer cooperative). Also, the early developments of health insurance among miners served as life insurance but also for certain forms of health insurance. Those models were also transferred to other countries, such as the United States, in the early periods (Brown, 2001).

Health cooperatives and mutuals have a historical presence in the United Kingdom, but the growth of for-profit private providers has curbed their role in providing health and social care services. The legal form of health cooperatives is mainly adopted by general practitioners, who provide out-of-hours care through cooperatives or specialised providers. Mutuals still have a role in the health system as providers of voluntary insurance schemes. Social enterprises, including those that emerged from the cooperative tradition, have played an increasingly active part in providing health and social care in recent years through increasing government initiatives for supply in the healthcare sector (Allen, 2009). Considering health-related cooperatives and varieties of the model, including mutuals, they have a long history in different parts of the United Kingdom (Borsay & Hunter, 2014).

These types of organisations have existed for hundreds of years, and through the formation of social networks, they enabled their users to meet particular needs they had, including healthcare. Those organisations began to gain momentum in exercising the rights of their members practically from the 18th century. In the early stages, they organised mutual aid and social events. In addition, they also provided support to legitimate guilds (e.g. The Company of Barber-Surgeons, founded as early as 1540 by Thomas Vickary, Henry VIII surgeon). Finally, temperance societies should be mentioned as those providing healthcare, although slightly different, mainly reflected in a healthier way of life (e.g. alcohol prevention).

During the 19th century, cooperative societies primarily focused on providing benefits such as unemployment support and old age pensions to their members. They also offered limited medical coverage, usually partial payments for doctors, surgeons, or apothecary fees. Members had limited access to hospital services, mainly relying on philanthropic agencies or the poor law guardians, which were part of the local government system at the time.

Cooperatives emerged as a specialised form of friendly societies in the early 19th century. For instance, the Rochdale Pioneers considered their society an extension of the friendly society tradition and registered under the Friendly Societies Act of that period. While consumer cooperatives and trade unions provided certain benefits to their members, direct provision of health insurance and healthcare services by the cooperative movement was relatively limited compared to friendly societies. Cooperative enterprises dedicated to providing health services were not established during that time. However, the cooperative movement had a significant indirect impact on health through improvements in nutrition, poverty reduction, and the provision of holidays and sanatoriums (UN, 1997, pp. 51–66).

Modern cooperative organisations can be traced back to the Rochdale Pioneers (1844), although model variations existed earlier. However, those early organisations pointed to the need to adopt certain principles of the work of those organisations, which were established through the cooperative principles donated at the Congress in Rochedel. Poverty and the need to exercise one's rights in various areas during the 18th and 19th centuries contributed to developing various organisational forms of cooperatives, having a foothold, and developing in parallel with mutual societies and through social networking. The Industrial Revolution had numerous impacts on society, and one of those impacts was the greater flywheel of cooperatives. Early cooperatives that had services (in a broad sense) to provide healthcare and insurance were the Cooperative Group (founded in 1844) and the Lincolnshire (founded in 1861), which also provided pharmaceutical services and products. Community shops were also developed earlier and should not be made an excessive distinction with food-oriented coops, being the fact that those early cooperatives were mainly located and are found today in rural areas (examples of early cooperatives are Allendale [founded in 1862], Central England [founded in 1854], and Channel Islands [founded in 1919]).

With the British Cooperative Congress held as early as 1865 in London, the importance of cooperatives was levelled to the international context. The United Kingdom also significantly impacted the development of the International Cooperative Organization (ICA), where the first sector of the International Health Cooperative Organization (IHCO) was later formed. Namely, in 1895, the First International Cooperative Congress was held in London as a continuation of earlier initiatives from 1865 (Hopton & Heaney, 1999).

At the First International Cooperative Congress held in London in 1895, health-related discussions were among the topics addressed. One of the key issues discussed was the establishment of cooperative societies to provide affordable access to healthcare services for working-class people. The idea was to protect cooperative members against sickness and death, which were considered as significant livelihood risks. The congress recognised the importance of cooperative health organisations and encouraged the formation of mutual aid societies that could pool resources to provide healthcare services to their members. That laid the foundation for developing cooperative health organisations, which were crucial in providing healthcare services to vulnerable populations in the following decades (International Cooperative Alliance, 2021).

Later, during the 20th century, cooperatives in the health sector had more propagators in the United Kingdom. In the early 20th century, the government introduced the NHIS, which provided primary healthcare to workers and their families through contributions from employers, employees, and the government, which led to the formation of a number of cooperatives that focused on providing additional healthcare services to their members, such as dental and optical care. Guild Socialism from the 1920s should be mentioned here, which focused on trade unions and cooperatives and was primarily promoted by George Douglas Howard Cole (Cylus et al., 2015). In the later decades of the 20th century, Margaret Thatcher also supported such initiatives, looking back on Rotarians and other voluntary services. In contrast, those oriented to

R.EPORT

OF THE

FIRST INTERNATIONAL

CO-OPERATIVE CONGRESS·

HELD IN THE

HALL OF THE SOCIETY OF ARTS,

ON

19th, 20th, 22nd, and 23rd AUGUST 1895.

LONDON :
P. S. KING & SON,
12 & 14 KING STREET, WESTMINSTER, S.W.

THE INTERNATIONAL CO-OPERATIVE ALLIANCE,
15 SOUTHAMPTON ROW, LONDON, W.C.

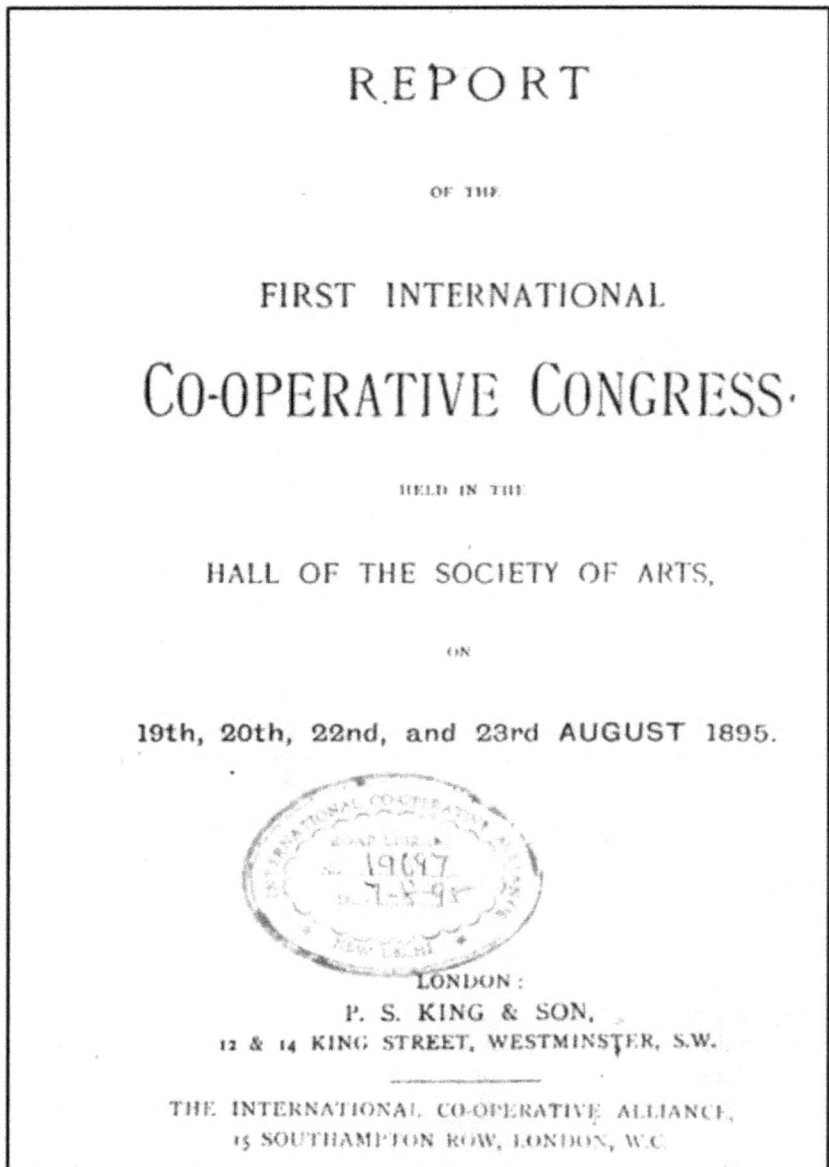

Image 2.1 Front page of the Cooperative Congress Report, 1895.

Source: ICA (1895).

the left on the political spectrum and neoliberals believed that friendly societies and cooperatives prove that individual interests can be subordinated to the collective interest (Thatcher, 1985). On the other hand, during the 1980s and 1990s, the Thatcher government's policies of privatisation and marketisation led to the growth of for-profit healthcare providers and a decline in the number of health cooperatives. However, there has been a resurgence of interest in health cooperatives in recent years, driven by concerns about the quality and affordability of healthcare services and the need to empower patients and care workers.

In the United Kingdom, considering early development, there is a good example of National Cooperative Chemists as a secondary cooperative founded in 1945 and owned by approximately 25 primary consumer-owned retail cooperatives. Together, they operate a network of 230 pharmacy outlets across the United Kingdom. In 1994, the net sales of National Cooperative Chemists surpassed 86.8 million pounds sterling, and by 1995, the sales further increased to 91.5 million pounds sterling, also operating today (UN, 1997, pp. 51–66). The establishment of the welfare state in the late 1940s disrupted previous arrangements made by both the cooperative sector and friendly societies. As a result, there is little continuity between those historical organisations and contemporary initiatives in developing health and social care cooperatives, whether user-owned or provider-owned. Nevertheless, these modern cooperatives aim to address similar needs using similar organisational structures. They have emerged in response to health service and community care reforms implemented in the late 1980s, which created opportunities for new service delivery models. These cooperative enterprises rely heavily on state funding, such as through the NHS in case of healthcare and income support payments for elderly care. They are characterised by democratic control by users and potential users, prioritising the needs of both users and providers in setting objectives and overseeing operations, and fostering a commitment to service quality. In this new context, various types of provider-owned health cooperatives have emerged.

One of the oldest forms is the general practitioner cooperative, where family doctors (general practitioners) practising in the community under the NHS collaborate through a cooperative structure. These cooperatives operate as extended rota systems, with members collectively responsible for providing after-hours coverage and care to each other's patients and their own. Certain worker-owned cooperatives deliberately decided to implement an integrated employment policy, wherein they actively hired individuals with mental, physical, or social disabilities as part of their workforce (in some cases, up to half of the workforce consisted of such individuals). Those cooperatives operated regularly and maintained their viability in the market through effective business practices. They produced various goods, including wooden murals, bulk-quality foods, and bakery products. The inclusive workforce of those cooperatives encompassed individuals with various disabilities, such as physical or mental impairments, as well as those facing social challenges, such as former prisoners, individuals struggling with drug or alcohol addiction, single parents, victims of domestic violence, homeless individuals, and long-term unemployed individuals. Within those cooperatives, employees with disabilities participated in management and decision-making processes, with the cooperative policy fostering their self-confidence and avoiding unnecessary restrictions compared to other employees. The worker-owned cooperatives also maintained a flexible approach to operations, enabling individuals with disabilities to carry out their work effectively. While the number of such cooperatives was relatively small then, they had successfully integrated individuals with disabilities into the labour force. The concept of provider-owned health cooperatives involves the collaboration of healthcare providers to fulfil specific obligations within the NHS. By combining their efforts, these cooperatives aim to reduce individual costs and effectively meet the needs of their clients. One type of provider-owned health cooperative is the multi-practice or multi-fund cooperative. In this model, member practices consist of multiple general practitioners who receive an annual fund-holding management allowance from the Family Health Service Authority. With this allowance, they have the autonomy to purchase medical and other services as needed. While retaining control over their own budgets, member practices contribute a portion of their allowance to the cooperative. The cooperative is administered by a committee comprising representatives from all member practices, supported by professional staff. Its purpose is to coordinate member activities; facilitate contract negotiations, joint purchasing, and information sharing; provide general support; and serve as a platform for implementing and developing the NHS in all aspects.

Another type of provider-owned health cooperative in the United Kingdom comprises practitioners specialising in complementary or alternative therapies. These cooperatives, known as complementary therapy health cooperatives, bring together practitioners such as hypnotherapists, aromatherapists, and acupuncturists. The cooperative helps reduce individual practice overheads by providing shared premises, receptionists, booking services, and mutual insurance. By lowering costs, these cooperatives enable more affordable access to complementary therapies for a larger population.

In 1995, the United Kingdom had approximately 40 to 50 social employment cooperatives specifically offering employment opportunities to individuals with disabilities or those recovering from mental illness (UN, 1997, pp. 51–52). Several well-known examples included Daily Bread, a wholefood retailer and wholesaler employing individuals in recovery; Pedlar Sandwiches, a catering cooperative for people with mental illnesses; Adept Press, a printing business employing individuals with hearing impairments; Rowanwood, a producer of wooden panelling products providing jobs for individuals with learning disabilities; Gillygate Wholefood Bakery, employing individuals with learning

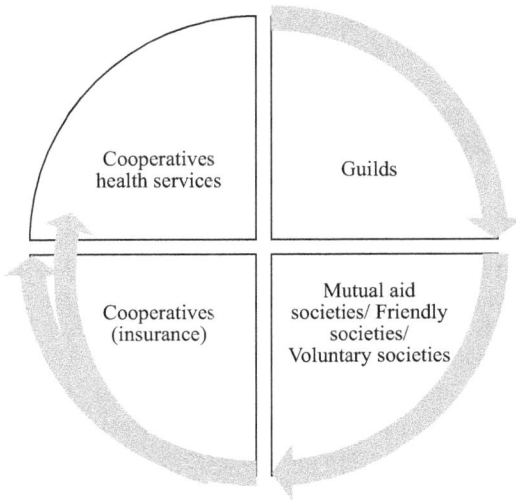

Figure 2.1 Historical development of health cooperatives in the United Kingdom through the organisational prism, created by the author.

disabilities; and Teddington Wholefood Co-op, which had recently evolved from a daycare centre and employed individuals with learning disabilities.

Today, examples of modern health cooperatives in the United Kingdom include various types such as the Equal Care Co-op, which provides digital platform-based social care services in West Yorkshire, and the Greenwich Cooperative Development Agency, which supports the development of health and social care cooperatives in South East London.

There are several reasons why people might decide to establish or join a health cooperative. In some cases, this may be because of the level of care they receive from the NHS and want to take more control of their health. In other cases, it may be because they want to pool their resources to access better quality care than they could afford individually. Also, there are different health cooperative models, but they all share the same basic principle of people coming together to pool their resources. One standard model is for a group to buy health insurance collectively. This can often result in cheaper premiums than if everyone bought the insurance individually. Another model is for a group of people to pool their money to invest in a specific healthcare project or service. This type of cooperative can often be seen as a way of bridging the gap between the public and private healthcare systems. Many different healthcare cooperatives are operating in the United Kingdom, and they are often able to offer a more personalised service than larger healthcare organisations. This can be particularly useful for people with complex health needs navigating to the NHS. Also, health cooperatives can offer numerous benefits to patients and caregivers. For example, they can provide longer appointments and more flexible appointment times than GP surgeries. They can also offer a more personalised service, as members are usually more involved in running the cooperative. In addition, health cooperatives may offer various other services, such as home visits and community programs.

Case study – Equal Care Co-op

Equal Care Co-op (Eccoop) is a UK-based social enterprise that seeks to challenge the traditional model of social care provision by offering an alternative approach that empowers both care workers and those receiving care. Eccoop was founded in 2018 by a group of social entrepreneurs who sought to create a new social care provision model based on the principles of equality and cooperation. The cooperative founders were motivated by their personal experiences working in the care sector and their challenges as care workers. They recognised that the current system of social care provision was failing both care workers and those receiving care and that a new approach was needed. Established in 2018, it is a pioneering digital platform social care cooperative in the Upper Calder Valley in Calderdale, West Yorkshire (Equal Care Co-op, n.d.). It is owned and run by care and support workers and individuals needing assistance. Eccoop connects those seeking care with local care and support workers and trained volunteers. Individuals who require care can choose who provides their support, how they receive it while controlling their data, and who is granted access. This social enterprise offers an alternative to conventional care agencies that prioritise profits, often paying minimum wage and providing limited autonomy to their workers regarding their hours or job security. Eccoop raised over £400,000 through a pioneering community share offer in June 2019 and acquired over 150 new investor members. These funds are intended to enhance the platform software that will digitise reports, care plans, appointments, and training, resulting in removing administrative costs and more money directed towards workers (Equal Care Co-op: A UK Social Care Platform, 2019).

The cooperative is structured as a worker-owned cooperative, which means that care workers have control over their work and the decisions that affect it. This structure enables care workers to work cooperatively, sharing knowledge, skills, and resources to provide high-quality care to those in need. In addition, they offer their members various services such as personal care, domestic tasks, social and emotional support, and companionship. The cooperative also strongly emphasises using technology to enable care workers to work more efficiently and effectively. Using digital platforms enables care workers to communicate with each other, manage their schedules, and access training and support. This platform also enables those receiving care to communicate directly with their care workers, giving them greater control over their care. The potential impact of the work of the Eccoop, as well as the other digital-based platforms for health provision, is significant. By empowering care workers and enabling them to work together cooperatively, Eccoop is challenging the traditional model of social care provision.

Case study – Benenden

Healthcare Mutual Benenden was founded in 1905, more than 40 years before the UK's NHS. It was founded by a group of postal workers who wanted to support each other in times of ill health. When founded, the primary goal was to meet the population's health needs due to the tuberculosis epidemic. Since then, it has grown into a national provider with over 900,000 members. As a mutual society, its members own Benenden, and any profit gets reinvested into the organisation. Members can access various health services, including consultations with medical professionals, diagnostics, and private treatment.

Benenden is a non-profit organisation that provides a wide range of services, and today they have large capacities (Benenden Health, n.d.). In 2020, the *Times* voted this organisation one of the "Top 100 Best Places to Work." It is interesting that often in different countries, which is also the case in the United Kingdom, it is considered that cooperatives arose from health systems. This organisation has undergone numerous transformational changes since its inception until today (Roberts, 2016). The changes in modern times are based on the satisfaction of users and employees, which is a function of market growth and the offer of better services. As this organisation has more than 900,000 members, attention must be paid to the diversification of services to maintain the users' attention and ensure that the users receive all the necessary services of the appropriate level of quality.

Benenden Health's model of mutual healthcare has received recognition for its focus on delivering affordable and accessible care. In 2021, it was awarded the prestigious Queen's Award for Enterprise in the innovation category, highlighting its role in improving the UK's healthcare landscape. The mutual model allows Benenden to prioritise its members' needs and offer services tailored to their specific requirements. This approach has proved popular, with high member satisfaction and retention rates.

In recent years, Benenden has expanded its services to include digital health and well-being solutions, such as its online GP service and mental health support platform (Marshall, 2020). This move reflects a growing trend in the United Kingdom towards digital healthcare, as patients seek more convenient and accessible ways to manage their health (Benenden Health, n.d.).

This organisation provides a significant range of health services for just under £9 a month. These services are not preconditioned by the previous health condition of the user, and today they deliver slightly more than 60 million pounds of health services for their members annually. In the future, the Benenden intentions are to transition to the cooperative. Through the additional branch of Benenden Wellbeing, this organisation entered the insurance business, and the business has multiplied with other, not strictly medical, services. Therefore, the market has more significant growth by making the functions more complex.

Cooperation between health cooperatives and national health systems is feasible and could be considered a hybrid model. This is exemplified by Benenden's consideration of extending their services to non-acute diseases or chronic illnesses through mutual societies. The idea is to provide better quality healthcare for taxpayers while relieving the burden on the public healthcare system. Such proposals have been launched in other countries like the Republic of Serbia, where the initiative for the re-establishment of health cooperatives has been proposed (Stamenovic, 2020, pp. 1–7). The main challenge for these proposals is the need for more legal framework and regulation, which makes it difficult to find practical solutions. Additionally, there needs to be more understanding of health cooperative organisations, their organisational structures, and ownership concepts. Universities need to further promote the literature on the social economy to achieve a better understanding of cooperatives. When users are owners and patients, cooperative decision-making ensures a patient-centred model, making it a unique and democratic approach to health service provision.

Presented UK Mutual has 47 branches across the country, with a democratic decision-making process (decentralised) involving everyone in the branch. Today, professional management and corporate governance practices have brought innovations to cooperatives and mutuals. CEOs and CFOs are democratically elected, and they also visit branches to gather insight into emerging user needs and any strategic changes that need to be made. There are also various incentives for employees, like recognition and sharing of successful business practices. In academic circles, the management of human resources and the leader–manager relationship in the modern context are being questioned, and health cooperatives provide an alternative perspective to these discussions.

One of the challenges that cooperative and mutual societies face is their perceived need for more efficiency in current market conditions, which can limit their stability compared to private organisations in the form of a public limited company (PLC). However, during crisis periods and in their aftermath, mutual societies and cooperatives have seen a growth in membership and participation. That was particularly evident after the 2008 financial crisis when those organisations experienced increased revenue, employees, and membership. Despite concerns about capitalisation, mutual societies and cooperatives are increasingly focused on socially essential goals, such as contributing to GDP growth and improving society's overall health and well-being. They reinvest their profits into development and do not owe any debt to investors or shareholders (Preston, 2018). In contrast, PLCs often prioritise the interests of shareholders over those of other stakeholders, which can lead to a focus on short-term profit maximisation rather than long-term growth and development. Therefore, the cooperative and mutual society model is increasingly being recognised as a valuable and sustainable alternative to the PLC model in many sectors of the economy. Hence, while mutual societies and cooperatives may face specific challenges, their commitment to social goals, reinvestment of profits, and democratic decision-making processes make them an attractive model for businesses and organisations that prioritise the long-term well-being of their members and society as a whole. As such, they are becoming an increasingly important part of the modern economy, with their benefits being recognised by academic circles and industry professionals.

Spain

Healthcare system development in Spain

The history of the Spanish health system can be divided into two phases. Early healthcare in Spain was significantly influenced by Al Andalus Muslims and, later, Jewish culture. After the Reconquista (finishing in the 15th century), healthcare was defined for the area of Spain and areas of the colonial territories. Later, the experiences of the overseas colonies, where there was a significant development of the public health sector as it is defined today, contributed to the development of Spanish healthcare. The year 1855 (after the unsuccessful initiative of the Cortes of Cadiz to implement a sanitary code) marked the beginning of a more modern healthcare system established in Spain through the Direccion General de Sanidad, approved in 1904. The first phase began in 1942, adopting a centralised and bureaucratised system based on the Bismarckian model. That system had non-universal coverage and was funded through social insurance linked to wages. The second phase started with reforms in 1974 and 1986, leading to the current health system. Health insurance was not mandatory until 1944 when, after the Spanish Civil War, it was established based on tax for employees. It functioned until the end of Franco's regime, when it was modified and much more complex, including different types of diseases and accompanying treatments. The National Health System in Spain, which encompasses universal coverage, was established through significant reforms in 1978 and further modifications in 1986 ((EU) 2021/522 of the European Parliament and of the Council of March 24, 2021). Although there have been numerous attempts to improve this health system by introducing new policies, laws, or organisation methods within institutions, in general, the evolution of the Spanish health system has not been very dynamic during the last decades. The pivotal moment was the enactment of the General Health Law 14/1986, which shifted the system towards a Beveridgean model with universal care funded through general taxes. That laid the foundation for the National Health System, where autonomous communities were responsible for creating their health services and delivering medical care through regional units in health districts. A significant milestone towards achieving universal coverage occurred in 2003 with the approval of the Law on the Cohesion and Quality of the National Health System (Law 16/2003). Its objective was to ensure equal access to healthcare for all Spanish citizens under the same conditions, promoting coordination and cooperation among the autonomous communities. Another crucial step was taken with the General Law 33/2011 on Public Health, which solidified the connection between universal entitlement to health protection and free public healthcare. In 2011, a notable change was made to financing the national health system. Previously, funds primarily came from social contributions, national budgets, local taxes, and fees for specific services. However, the General Law on Public Health 16/2013 established that the National Health System should be funded through taxes, severing its link to social security contributions. The current Spanish health system follows a decentralised approach, with regional governments responsible for health services and coordination at the national level through the Ministry for Health and Social Services. The national government uses collaboration agreements with private institutions to provide certain services. Each regional government has its own administrative and management body overseeing health centres, services, and facilities within its jurisdiction. The central government retains healthcare management in the autonomous cities of Ceuta and Melilla through the National Health Management Institute – INGESA.

Today, healthcare in Spain is generally of good quality, although there are still some areas where improvement is needed. This process has been quite progressive regarding public funding and legislation, especially regarding medical management and care facilities. In this sense, it is worth mentioning the Health Information System (SIS), which has been successfully implemented throughout the country and which today is an essential primary tool for managing information and documentation from the central part of the health administration. The public administration also introduced a co-management system with community participation to improve the quality of services and ensure better accessibility of health facilities in isolated areas and promote prevention. In addition, some recent studies suggest the need to rethink traditional concepts of health and disease to promote a more appropriate concept of health and integrate social determinants of health into health policy and public health practice. In this regard, the "Health for All Program" of the European Union is worth mentioning, which promotes better coordination of health services in the European Union to facilitate access to efficient and affordable health services and promote public health through health promotion activities ((EU) 2021/522 of the European Parliament and of the Council of March 24, 2021). These and similar programs attempt to reform the traditional conceptualisation of health and reduce inequality based on the principles of solidarity and collectivism.

Spain has many cooperatives active in the health sector and others working to develop and implement new effective programs to help employees and the quality of life of their families. The Government of Catalonia has also developed a new strategy to encourage citizens to create their communities. Under the leadership of President Arturo Mas, the Catalan government embarked on an ambitious initiative to promote the creation of healthy shared communities and enhance the accessibility of health services in Catalonia. To support this endeavour, the government secured substantial funds from the European Investment Bank (Constante Beitia, 2015). In addition, the Ministry of Health of the Government of Catalonia developed the new strategy with the support of the Pharmaceutical Industry of Catalonia and the Centre for Mutual Studies of the University of Barcelona (CESBA). These cooperatives may have specific common characteristics that distinguish them from the usual type of cooperative (Lopez & Villanueva, 2017).

In addition, the Spanish government has encouraged the growth of this sector and promoted several initiatives to encourage the creation of new cooperatives (Lopez & Moreno, 2014). For example, the National Commission for the Protection of Competition (CNE) created a special regime for the promotion of cooperatives, which is a fast track to the creation of civil cooperatives, and the Ministry of Labour introduced a series of measures to facilitate the employment relationship to join cooperatives. Also, the government provided various incentives for creating new cooperative societies, including training, legal advice, and consultations.

Health cooperatives development in Spain

In Spain and some other European countries, there were associations such as guilds (or similar models of organisations), which represented the task of cooperative life in Spain. Although such medieval associations were based on primitive principles, their significance was important for later development. Also, the influence of the Catholic Church was significant, especially in solving the existing social problems of the population. The cooperative movement began to spread in Spain in the late 19th century and early 20th century. Some supporters of cooperation believed in the principle of solidarity and that encouraging cooperation among individuals would help create an atmosphere of mutual aid and social harmony. The emergence of cooperatives and mutual insurance societies in Spain's health system can be traced back to the *igualatorio* (equal) system, known as igualas, which originated in the 19th century. Those systems gave rise to mutual insurance societies, cooperatives, and "sickness funds" at that time. Initial Spanish cooperatives were formed in Catalonia, in Girona, and one of the examples is a cooperative formed in 1865 under the name Economica Palafrugellense. The early cooperative had a small foothold through mutual aid societies and other Western European countries that had developed in that form. Those were primarily small organisations aiming to provide life or accident insurance. However, agricultural cooperatives formed in a significant number during the second half of the 19th century traces their proliferation back to the

Law of Agricultural Unions enacted in 1906. However, the earliest legislation pertaining to that matter can be traced back to 1869, which focused on the freedom to establish anonymous and credit companies. The first comprehensive law specifically addressing cooperatives was introduced in 1931 (Coopératives Act), allowing for the formation of cooperatives across various sectors and signalling the gradual decline of cooperatives with more traditional business characteristics. The legal origins of Spanish cooperatives were developing within the framework of commercial legislation, considering its interconnection with broader themes such as freedom of association, the establishment of public limited companies, and the legal responsibilities assumed by investors in both cooperatives and non-cooperative business entities (Guinnane & Martínez-Rodríguez, 2011).

From a historical point of view, Dr Josep Espriu provided a significant contribution in the area of further development of health cooperatives. The largest health cooperative in Spain – Fundación Espriu – is named after him. Dr Espriu was born in 1914 in Santa Coloma de Farners, and as a doctor, he had the opportunity to see the shortcomings of the public health system of Spain both from the side of patients and doctors. In Bilbao in the 1950s, he introduced the fee-per-service model and the free choice of doctors. In addition, Dr Espriu showed a great interest in cooperatives, which he proved through the formation of the Asisa model, as well as his dedicated work on the formation and ideological concepts of the life of health cooperatives in general. Also, those models later strongly influenced the development of health cooperatives worldwide, especially in Latin America (Zarko, 2006).

Where advantageous for their members, cooperative enterprises and groups have preferred to supplement or replace national coverage for members, employees, and dependents. That was the choice of the Mondragon Cooperative Corporation in the Basque Autonomous Region in Spain. In response to the exclusion of cooperative members from the public social security system in 1958 due to their classification as self-employed, the Corporation established a special insurance branch called Lagun-Aro within its financial component, Caja Laboral Popular. Lagun-Aro provided members with health, unemployment, and pension insurance. In 1973, Lagun-Aro became a separate component of the Corporation. Members of individual industrial, agricultural, housing, and school cooperatives and the three other secondary cooperatives automatically become members of Lagun-Aro and benefit from its social security and welfare services, including health insurance, which the secondary cooperative administers (UN, 1997, p. 65). The Board of Directors of Lagun-Aro is appointed by the Association of Cooperatives, which serves as the directorate of the group and includes representatives from all primary cooperatives. Through their participation in the political process of Lagun-Aro, these representatives contribute to decision-making. The Mondragon Cooperative, including Lagun-Aro, does not operate its own health services. Therefore, the health insurance provided to members is used to obtain services when needed from external providers outside the Cooperative Group. Members are free to choose between public or private for-profit providers, and their expenses are reimbursed by the cooperative based on the terms of their insurance coverage.

The 1980s was a turning point in developing cooperative life in Spain. Namely, in the 1980s, attempts were made to structure cooperatives under the auspices of trade union organisations, and it seems that the idea was to place cooperatives under the control of the state. In 1987, the First Cooperatives General Act was adopted, modernising cooperatives in Spanish society ((EU) 2021/522 of the European Parliament and of the Council of March 24, 2021).

Currently, health cooperatives in Spain are represented by organisations such as the Cooperativa Sanitaria de Galicia (COSAGA), CES Clínicas in Madrid, and the entities forming the Fundación Espriu. COSAGA, established in 1985, provides comprehensive accident, emergency, outpatient. and hospital care. CES Clínicas, founded in 1980 as a dental worker cooperative, has expanded to offer a wide range of dental and women's health services. The Fundación Espriu, created in 1989, promotes social cooperatives and the concept of comprehensive health cooperativism.

Pharmaceutical cooperatives in Spain primarily operate as distribution companies and hold a significant market share. These cooperatives, owned by pharmacies, ensure equal access to pharmaceutical references nationwide, regardless of size or geographical location. Mutual insurance societies in Spain are divided into mutual provident societies and mutual insurance societies collaborating with social security. Mutual provident societies offer voluntary insurance that

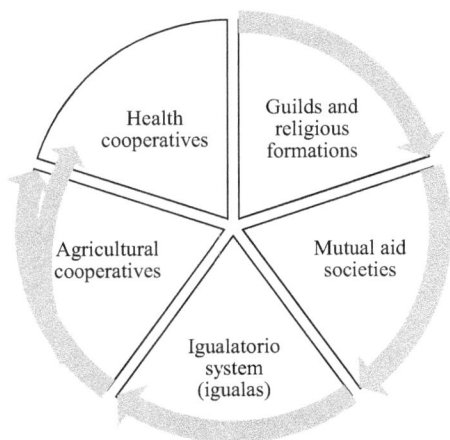

Figure 2.2 Historical development of health cooperatives in Spain through the organisational prism, created by the author.

complements the mandatory social security system, while mutual insurance societies collaborating with social security focus on protection against occupational accidents and diseases.

In Spain, health cooperatives are considered complementary organisations to the public social security system, offering services not provided by the national health system. They operate as private entities and generate income by selling specialised health services. These cooperatives contribute to reducing waiting lists and lowering costs for a specific population group, as they provide services to individuals who contribute to the public system through taxes but require fewer services, thereby freeing up resources for the benefit of all.

Case study – Foundation Espriu

The Fundacion Espriu, also known as the Espriu Foundation, is a non-profit organisation founded in 1989 in Spain by Dr Josep Espriu. The foundation is focused on promoting the principles of social economy and cooperative healthcare, and it is based on the idea that healthcare should be a universal right for all individuals. The foundation is committed to advancing the social and health well-being of society, and it provides affordable and high-quality healthcare services through a network of healthcare cooperatives that the patients themselves own. The Fundacion Espriu is a significant player in Spain's healthcare system, providing quality healthcare services to its members and improving the overall health of Spanish communities. Its cooperative structure allows it to focus on the interests of its members, and its profits are reinvested in improving its healthcare services. The cooperative model is based on mutual aid, with members contributing financially to the cooperative and receiving healthcare services in return. Members of the Espriu Foundation are not shareholders, but rather stakeholders in the cooperative, which means they have a say in how the cooperative is run. As of 2021, the Espriu Foundation has more than 1.5 million members across Spain (Espriu Foundation, n.d.). The Espriu Foundation has a decentralised organisational structure. It consists of 22 autonomous cooperatives, each of which is responsible for the provision of healthcare services in its particular region. The cooperatives are grouped into four different federations, which provide support and assistance to the individual cooperatives. The federations are also responsible for coordinating the activities of the different cooperatives and representing their interests to external stakeholders (Espriu Foundation, 2021).

The Espriu Foundation is financed by its members. Members pay an annual fee to the cooperative, which gives them access to healthcare services. The cooperative also generates revenue by providing healthcare services to non-members, although the majority of its revenue comes from its members. In addition, the Espriu Foundation has established partnerships with several insurance companies and healthcare providers, allowing it to offer its members a wider range of services (Espriu Foundation, 2021).

The Espriu Foundation provides its members with a range of healthcare services, including primary care, specialist care, hospital care, and dental care. It also offers a number of other services, such as home care, medical transport, and health promotion and education programs. The cooperative employs more than 8,000 healthcare professionals across Spain, including doctors, nurses, and support staff (Espriu Foundation, 2021). The Espriu Foundation is a not-for-profit organisation, which means it does not distribute profits to its members. Instead, any surplus the cooperative generates is reinvested in the organisation to improve its services and infrastructure. The cooperative has also established a social fund, which is used to finance social projects and provide assistance to members in need (Espriu Foundation, 2021).

The Espriu Foundation is an example of a successful healthcare cooperative operating in Spain for over 30 years. By providing quality healthcare services to its members, the cooperative has built a loyal and dedicated membership base while reinvesting any surplus into the organisation to improve its services and infrastructure.

The foundation is a pioneer in cooperative healthcare and has been recognised globally for its innovative and successful model. The foundation's model is based on the social and solidarity economy principles, which means that are based on self-management, democratic governance, and shared ownership. The foundation's vision is to create a healthcare system that is patient-centred, socially responsible, and sustainable. Also, the foundation model that has been successful in Spain is replicated in other countries, such as Italy, Portugal, and Chile.

Italy

Healthcare system development in Italy

Italy has a long and complex history of health insurance, which can be traced back to the Middle Ages. Monks and other religious orders were responsible for providing medical care. Over time, this system evolved into the modern health insurance industry. In 15th-century Italy, medical care was only available to the wealthy. Those who could not afford treatment often resorted to self-harm to cure their illnesses (France et al., 2005). People experiencing poverty used to suffer from different epidemics including malaria and smallpox. However, things began to change in the 16th century. During the Renaissance (1300–1600), Italy experienced a period of economic and military expansion, which, in turn, led to the flourishing of art and science. One effect of the growth was that numerous private hospitals and medical colleges were established to meet the growing demand for health services. One such hospital was the Ospedale degli Innocenti in Florence, built in 1419 by a Dominican order of priests. At first, the hospital treated only children, but its practice expanded to treat adults over time.

One of Italy's first comprehensive health insurance schemes was implemented in Florence in 1589. It was called *Ordine dei Cavalieri di San Giovanni e dei Francescani* (Order of the Knights of Saint John and the Franciscans). Under the new scheme, each member of the order had to contribute every month to the upkeep of the hospital. In addition, members had access to free medical care at the hospital. The development of health insurance in Italy was further enhanced by introducing the social insurance system in Florence in 1797. Under that system, employers were required to contribute to an employee's monthly salary towards their pension. The later health insurance model included a plan established in the late 1800s. At the time, most Italians relied on charities to provide medical care. As the country industrialised, health insurance programs expanded to cover more workers. The first national health insurance program in Italy was launched in 1938. At the time, it was one of Europe's most advanced health insurance programs. The program was initially designed to cover workers in the agricultural and industrial sectors. The Italian national health system was established in 1978 to provide universal healthcare coverage to the population (Ferre et al., 2014). The system was initially entirely public, which helped provide universal coverage but posed sustainability and organisational difficulties. Over time, market elements were introduced, and a devolution process was implemented to delegate autonomy in healthcare provision to the regions. However, there were differences in implementing the healthcare system across the country, with poorer communities experiencing limitations in dealing with new healthcare needs, such as new forms of social exclusion (Ferre et al., 2014). Reforms were enacted to remedy the limitations of the health system, with regional administrations becoming responsible for the planning, financing, and delivery of healthcare services, as well as the organisation and delivery of services related to nutrition, food safety, and medical research.

The constitutional reform law of 2001 made further changes to the roles of the central and regional administrations within the health system, with the government issuing a National Health Plan and stipulating a set of essential healthcare services that all regions must supply to guarantee a universal standard of healthcare (Grijpstra et al., 2011). Despite regional differences in waiting times, coverage by the National Health system is generally of high quality and accessible to all Italian citizens. However, complementary health insurance schemes offer the possibility of avoiding waiting lists and covering out-of-pocket costs for private and semi-private assistance (France et al., 2005). Health expenditure in Italy in 2021 was 9.45% of the total GDP (World Bank, n.d.-b).

Government-sponsored programs, known as *Servizio Sanitario Nazionale* (National Health Service) or SSN, provide coverage to citizens who their employers do not cover. Taxes or workers usually fund these plans through payroll deductions. SSN plans are also available to employees of private companies that do not have health insurance programs. Coverage includes essential medical services, hospitalisation expenses, outpatient visits, and dental care.

Private companies also offer health plans, which are often more comprehensive and cover a broader range of services than SSN plans. The Italian government has pledged to improve access to care and increase insurance in the coming years. However, the nation must provide affordable healthcare for all its citizens (OECD, 2019). SSN plans are also available to employees of private companies that do not have health insurance programs. Coverage includes essential medical services, hospitalisation expenses, outpatient visits, and dental care. Private companies also offer health plans, which are often more comprehensive and cover a broader range of services than SSN plans (Saltman et al., 2007).

The Italian national health system has undergone significant reforms to address sustainability challenges and regional differences in healthcare provision. Despite the challenges, the system provides universal coverage to the population and is generally of high quality. However, complementary health insurance schemes and out-of-pocket payments are still necessary to cover certain costs and avoid waiting in some regions.

Health cooperatives development in Italy

The cooperative sector in Italy is well-developed and encompasses various types of cooperatives, including mixed, production, service, housing, and agricultural-oriented cooperatives. Three national organisations, namely the *Lega Nazionale delle Cooperative e Mutue* (National League of Cooperatives and Mutuals), *Confederazione delle Cooperative Italiane* (Confederation of Italian Cooperatives), and *Associazione Generale delle Cooperative Italiane* (General Association of Italian Cooperatives), represent this cooperative movement (Donati et al., 1990). Throughout its history, it has contributed to the country's development, and more recently, it has made notable interventions in the agricultural and tourism sectors. These organisations bring together different types of cooperatives, such as consumer, agricultural, and producer cooperatives, facilitating trade and cooperation among them. Individual cooperatives are organised into unions, known as *consorzi*, which have local, regional, national, or international responsibilities. These consorzi play a crucial role in developing the Italian cooperative movement by providing a wide range of services to cooperatives or raising funds that individual cooperatives may not be able to obtain independently. The promotion of the cooperative movement in Italy was mainly supported by socialists and Catholics, each with their own perspective. Socialists focused on labour cooperatives for farm workers, aligning with the demands of resistant leagues (Hollis & Sweetman, 1998). On the other hand, Catholics worked in the credit sector, establishing associations to organise the rural middle classes that the socialists did not reach. *Casse Rurali* (rural banks) in Italy were modelled after the German Raiffeisen credit cooperatives and found success in the northern part of the country. The performance differences between northern and southern Italy can be attributed to various factors, including social capital levels, local environments, and institutions. It is interesting to mention an example of a long history of health-related organisations in the 19th century showing the historical significance of developing such organisations. *l'Ente Cooperativo di Mutuo Soccorso di Auronzo* (The Cooperative Mutual Aid Organization of Auronzo) was one of the early cooperatives, with over 800 members to date, originated in 1872 as an insurance company focused on providing mutual welfare and social security to working members. In 1876, it expanded its activities by establishing a drawing school for crafts in collaboration with other local entities. In 1906, it further diversified its ventures by acquiring a pharmacy.

In Italy, health cooperatives can be classified as a specialised subset of social cooperatives that primarily focus on healthcare services rather than social care. The national apex cooperative organisations have actively promoted the development of these provider-owned cooperatives. According to statistics reported in June 1993 by the major national apex organisations, Lega Cooperative and Confcooperative, there were approximately 1,826 social cooperatives associated with them. It was estimated that the total number of social cooperatives in the country was at least 2,000. The growth of social cooperatives was significant, with around 500 in 1986, 1,242 by the end of 1988, and 2,125 in 1990. A survey conducted in December 1992 by the Centro Studi of the National Consortium of Social Solidarity Cooperation Gino Mattarelli provided insights into the activities of these cooperatives. Out of the 1,826 social cooperatives surveyed, 422 were engaged in social, educational, or health services, 110 focused on integrating disadvantaged individuals into their communities through employment, and 128 were involved in both types of activities (UN, 1997, pp. 40–41). Only 13% (71 cooperatives) among the 549 social cooperatives providing health services were primarily dedicated to healthcare, often in conjunction with social care. Establishing these cooperatives was relatively recent, with only 12 of the 660 surveyed social cooperatives existing before 1976. The majority were established between 1981 and 1992. Also, disabled, elderly, and young individuals were commonly the target population of social cooperatives as a whole. The total number of users across the 660 cooperatives surveyed was 42,000, but the exact number of users accessing health services from health and mixed-activity social cooperatives alone was not specified. Those cooperatives were complex entities owned by both users and providers. Membership comprised ordinary worker members, paid collaborator members (professionals, administrators, or consultants), voluntary members, subsidiser members (providing financial capital), legal-person members (institutions and public agencies), and user members. Inactive members who were founders or sympathisers of the cooperative were also present but did not actively participate or use its services. However, most of the active members were workers, collaborators, volunteers, subsidisers, and legal persons, totalling 21,300, compared to 1,638 user members and 1,523 disadvantaged worker members. Functionally, these health cooperatives can be considered a specific type of provider cooperative. This classification is particularly applicable to social cooperatives that exclusively provide health services, given the professional qualifications required of provider members. From the perspective of the survey's classification system, health cooperatives within the group of Italian social cooperatives are considered provider cooperatives, while the remaining social cooperatives are more likely to have joint ownership structures.

In the 1990s, Italy was home to approximately 2,000 social cooperatives in the health and social care sector. These cooperatives are primarily owned by producers at the primary level and are collectively called social cooperatives. Most of their members comprise professional personnel and members, employing around 40,000 individuals. Most of these cooperatives are affiliated with either the Confederazione Cooperative Italiane or the Lega Nazionale della Cooperative e Mutue, the two major national apex organisations. The establishment of these cooperatives started in the late 1970s. Among these social cooperatives, only a small percentage, possibly 13% to 15%, are specifically health cooperatives. The remaining cooperatives provide various social care services, focusing on young people, individuals with disabilities, and older adults. The membership primarily comprises providers, including professionals, paraprofessionals, salaried staff, and volunteers. In some cases, users, such as individuals with disabilities employed in sheltered workshops, are also members. The cooperatives collaborate closely with individuals and institutions providing financial support, including local government authorities (UN, 1997, pp. 40–41). In 1993, approximately 13% of public spending on social welfare was allocated to financing those cooperatives. While they can be found throughout the country, there is a certain concentration in the Emilia-Romagna and Tuscany regions. Italy has a national apex organisation, *Consorzio Nazionale della Cooperazione di Solidarietà Gino Mattarelli*, which also oversees a research centre. Additionally, research initiatives are underway in the Department of Economics at the University of Trento. *Unipol Assicurazioni*, a cooperative insurance enterprise, has recently launched a health insurance venture named Unisalute. This initiative aims to develop health and social security programs for cooperative and trade union members and provide health plans for the workforce of various enterprises, complementing existing public programs.

In Italy, mutual societies and cooperatives have been integral to the healthcare system for over a century. Initially, mutual societies were the most common form of protection before forming the national health system. Cooperative enterprises in Italy are legally recognised as mutual associations under Article 45 of the Italian constitution. The cooperative law was reformed in 1992 to increase flexibility in cooperative financing. Each cooperative must comply with certain mandatory principles or rules when established, such as a minimum number of members ranging from 50 for consumption cooperatives to 15 for production and worker cooperatives and nine for other types, including agricultural cooperatives. Cooperatives enjoy tax exemptions on legal persons and local taxes if total members' remuneration exceeds 60% of other costs comprising the added value of the undertaking. The tax rate is halved for remuneration between 40% and 60%. Institutional accreditation recognises healthcare assistance providers to private structures, including cooperatives specialised in healthcare, physician cooperatives, pharmaceutical cooperatives, and mutuals. The two mentioned cooperative federations in Italy have launched different projects to put together social cooperatives, medical cooperatives, and mutuals to promote a shared vision and organise an integrated response system whose objectives are stated in terms of health instead of services (Grijpstra et al., 2011). The rise of mutual societies and cooperatives in the Italian healthcare system is partly due to their ability to address social, health, and care needs that the healthcare system and families can no longer meet. These organisations have been historically significant healthcare institutions, even during the Fascist era.

Today, social cooperatives, in particular, play a vital role in the Italian healthcare system, with the law distinguishing between two types of social cooperatives. Type-A cooperatives deal with the management of social health services, training, and lifelong education. In contrast, type-B cooperatives foster the employment of disadvantaged people in industry, commerce, services, and agriculture. Type-A cooperatives can work with the public sector to complement some of the services furnished by the health system, improving its functioning.

Since its establishment, the Italian NHS has often needed help increasing its health services. This is mainly due to a need for more economic resources. For example, the NHS has yet to be able to respond to the increasing needs that have characterised the Italian context since the 1980s. The search for greater efficiency led to the evolution of the Italian NHS, in which regional governments are responsible for local health facilities. Social cooperatives are essential in providing social and healthcare services in Italy, and they are based on both public social security regulations and community-based principles. SPES Trento – *Servizi pastorali educativi sociali* (pastoral, educational, and social services), a social cooperative that provides social health services to the population of Trento, Italy – is one of many health cooperatives operating in Italy. The work of the cooperatives for health provision in Italy is also seen in the numbers showing that in 2014, a total of 6,756 health cooperatives in Italy employed 233,000 people (IHCO, 2018a).

Case study – Cadiai Social Cooperative

Cadiai Social Cooperative is a cooperative based in Italy that provides social and healthcare services to the elderly and disabled. The Cooperative was founded in 1999 by a group of healthcare professionals and has grown to employ over 400 workers across Italy. The cooperative operates on the principle of self-management and democratic decision-making, with all members having an equal say in the organisation's running. The Cooperative also strongly emphasises the well-being of its workers, providing them with a range of benefits and opportunities for professional development. Cadiai Social Cooperative is an example of how the cooperative model can provide quality social and healthcare services while prioritising workers' well-being and promoting democratic decision-making (Cadiai Social Cooperative, n.d.). As a non-profit organisation based in Bologna, Italy, it was founded in 1984 when a group of healthcare workers and activists in Bologna came together to create a new healthcare model based on the principles of social solidarity and democratic participation. The Cooperative is owned and controlled by its members, who use and provide healthcare services. Membership in the Cadai Social Cooperative is open to anyone who agrees with the organisation's values and principles and is willing to pay a membership fee.

Members have the right to participate in the decision-making process of the cooperative, including electing the board of directors and approving the budget and financial statements. The governance of the Cadai Social Cooperative is based on the principles of democratic participation and transparency. The organisation is managed by a board of directors elected by the members for three years. The board is responsible for setting the organisation's strategic direction, approving the budget and financial statements, and ensuring that the organisation operates following its values and principles. Regarding financial information, the Cadai Social Cooperative reported a total revenue of €1.8 million in 2020. Most of the revenue (80%) came from public funding, while the rest came from membership fees and other sources. The Cooperative reported a net surplus of €16,000 in 2020 (Cadiai Social Cooperative, n.d.).

The health-related services provided by the Cadai Social Cooperative include home care, daycare, and residential care for elderly and disabled people. It also provides services for people with mental health issues and children and young people with disabilities. As of 2021, the Cadai Social Cooperative operates ten residential care facilities, eight daycare centres, and two home care services, serving 150 members. The Cooperative employs nearly 400 staff members, including nurses, social workers, and administrative personnel.

The Cadai Social Cooperative represents a health cooperative owned and controlled by its members, providing high-quality, community-based healthcare services. The Cooperative's commitment to democratic participation, transparency, and social solidarity has helped it to build a solid and loyal membership base and to achieve financial stability and sustainability. Over the years, the Cooperative has grown and expanded its services, becoming a leading provider of health-related services in the region (Legacoop, n.d.).

France

Healthcare system development in France

The Republic of France is in Western Europe and includes several over-seas regions and territories. As of 2016, France is divided into 18 adminis-trative regions and 101 departments. The French population is approximately 68 million. The French healthcare system is based on social insurance and has historically had a more centralised character with a stronger role of the state than in other social insurance systems. The system displays the typical traits of Bismarckian systems, such as employment-based access to health protection, financing based on cost sharing between employees and employers, and admin-istration entrusted to para-public sickness funds. However, it also has distinctive features, such as the increasing importance of tax-based revenue for financing healthcare, which has made it more oriented towards the Beveridgean model. Statutory health insurance (SHI; *assurance maladie*) covers the resident popu-lation through various employment schemes. Care provision includes private doctors, private pay hospitals (FFS; fee-for-service), public hospitals, private non-profit hospitals, and private (for-profit) hospitals. Successive policies and reforms since the 1990s have aimed at regional devolution, establishing several regional institutions to represent stakeholders. In 2009, the Hospital, Patients, Health and Territories (HPST) Act was enacted to improve the system's efficiency (legifrance.gouv.fr, LAW No. 2009–879, 2009). The new law concentrated on the multiple institutions handling healthcare at the local level into a single regional health agency (*agency régionale de santé*; ARS), whose responsibility is to ensure the effectiveness of healthcare provision by promoting coordin-ation between ambulatories and hospitals, as well as health and social care providers while keeping expenditure within the national budget allocation. The ARSs plan health and social care for older adults and people with disabilities through a regional strategic health plan (*Plan Stratégique Régional de Santé*; PSRS) involves the ambulatory care sector for service provision. In 2016, the French government reformed healthcare for foreigners, replacing the Coverage Maladie Universelle system with Protection Universelle Maladie, which guar-antees access to French healthcare and reimbursements for everyone who works or lives permanently in France longer than three months. Moreover, the reform eliminates up-front payments for most medical services, which are now paid for directly by the government or the health insurer. The French healthcare system assures coverage to all residents regardless of age, income, or status through a network of public and private hospitals, doctors, and other medical specialists (Akrong, 2021). The state covers costs mostly via public healthcare insurance scheme, which mandates that residents register with a French health insurer and a doctor to seek access to most treatments. The determination of insurance premia is centrally calibrated based on the insured's income. In

France, healthcare provision is a national responsibility, and the Ministry of Social Affairs, Health, and Women's Rights defines the national strategy. Health administration is entrusted to the Regional Health Agencies responsible for the population's health, including prevention, care provision, public health, and social assistance. In 2013, total French expenditure on health was estimated at 235 billion EUR (10.9% of GDP) above the average for EU countries (World Bank, n.d.-a). Total expenditure on health as a share of GDP has also risen slightly faster than in European partners except for the United Kingdom, from 10.4% in 1995 to 11.6% in 2013 (World Bank, n.d.-a). These organisations have been growing, especially in collective care, such as health centres targeting low-income patients, nursing homes, hospitals, and residential facilities for dependent or disabled people. Associations, foundations, and mutuals run a significant percentage of these institutions. However, cooperatives have been almost absent, despite the potential for cooperative efforts among patients, physicians, and healthcare personnel to overcome issues like "medical deserts" (Girard, 2014). Mutual societies primarily engage in supplementary health insurance, with two types present in France: mutual assurance companies and mutual societies. The former carries out risk selection, while the latter operates on a non-profit basis, owned by policyholders without share capital (Girard, 2014). Further promoting the development of cooperatives and innovative solutions to address health needs could improve the situation as studies have shown that cooperatives can be valuable in health systems, especially in areas with limited resources and underserved populations.

Cooperatives development in France

France has a long history of cooperative development, traced back to the time after the French Revolution. The first consumer cooperative was founded in Lyon in 1835 at 95 Montée de la Grande-Côte initiated by Michel Derrion and Joseph Reynier; since then, France has seen a proliferation of cooperative societies and associations, many of which are focused on specific sectors or sectors of the economy. During the cooperative movement of the 18th century, the French government played an essential role in supporting and encouraging the development of cooperatives. Throughout the 19th century, the cooperative movement continued to grow in popularity. The first cooperative bank in France was founded in 1871, while the first cooperative insurance company was founded in 1882. The beginning of the 20th century was a time of great transformation of the cooperative movement in France. The first labour cooperative was founded in 1907, while the first agricultural cooperative opened in 1913 (Nieddu, 2017).

The 1930s were a time of great economic crisis in France. In response, the government encouraged the use of cooperatives as an alternative to commercial capitalism. Many new cooperatives were created during the 1930s to support the development of the modern French economy. The WWII caused a significant decline in the development of cooperatives in France. However, the cooperative movement regained momentum in the post-war period. Many new cooperatives were formed in response to the growth of the post-war European economic community. Those efforts helped establish broader support for the cooperative movement in France.

Today, there are over 1,500 cooperative societies and associations in France. These organisations provide services in various areas, including agriculture, food distribution, renewable energy, finance, and healthcare. About one-third of these organisations are consumer cooperatives. The French cooperative sector is highly diversified and plays a substantial role in the country's economy. According to data from 2016, cooperative societies and associations in France generated a significant income of €31.1 billion, equivalent to 34.6% of the nation's GDP. This highlights the economic significance of cooperatives in France. Additionally, the sector has been thriving in attracting foreign investment, with foreign investment in cooperatives reaching €8.9 billion in 2016 (Babinet, 2017). Also, this demonstrates the appeal and international interest in the French cooperative model. The strong presence and economic impact of cooperatives in France underline their contribution to the overall economic landscape and their ability to attract investment abroad.

Health cooperatives and mutuals development in France

In France, mutual assistance groups have been prevalent since the Middle Ages, helping individuals within the same profession and their dependents in times of unemployment or illness. Those groups gained legal recognition in 1852 as mutual societies, known as *sociétés de secours mutuels*. Over the course of the century, their numbers grew from 2,000 (with approximately 100,000 members) in 1850 to around 13,000 (with about 2.1 million members) by the end of the century (UN, 1997, pp. 108–110). The first legal code dedicated explicitly to those societies was the Municipal Code of 1898. It defined them as associations that aimed to fulfil one or more of the following objectives: assisting members and their families in case of illness, injury, or disability; establishing funds for the welfare of their members; offering private or collective life or accident insurance for the benefit of members; and covering funeral expenses and providing assistance to the descendants, widows, or orphans of deceased participating members. Additionally, those mutual societies had the authority to create professional courses or offer job placement services to their members and allocate funds accordingly.

Later, in the years following WWII, many additional changes were made to the system in an attempt to improve access to high-quality healthcare and lower costs for consumers (De Jongh & Bester, 2011). One of the most significant changes then was the global health cooperatives development (or re-development in many cases). Health cooperatives have been relevant in the

French health system since the late 1980s. This is especially true in light of the changing demographics of the French population. For example, health cooperatives have successfully served the needs of patients who are not covered by insurance or have insurance that does not cover all of their medical expenses. In addition, health cooperatives have successfully reached populations traditionally underrepresented in the French health network, including women and older individuals. As the French health system has undergone significant changes in the last few decades, consequently, mutuals and health cooperatives in France have become a source of care for many individuals. For example, parents of children with severe mental disabilities have initiated social care cooperatives offering support and services. The *Syndicat National des Associations des Parents d'Enfants Inadaptés* (National Union of Associations of Parents of Disabled Children), a national apex organisation, has been established to coordinate their efforts. In addition to the national social security system, mutual assistance organisations play a complementary role through formal agreements. They provide health insurance and offer specific health and social care services. These organisations come together at the national level under the *Fédération Nationale de la Mutualité Française* (National Federation of French Mutual Insurance). While they may not be classified as cooperatives, they share many characteristics with health service and insurance cooperatives. They serve as a model for demonstrating how various types of mutual assistance associations can effectively collaborate with the public sector (UN, 1997, pp. 108–110).

In 2012, Social Security, France's public health insurance system, accounted for 90.7% of health expenditures. However, complementary organisations such as health mutuals and private insurers have increasingly played a role in collaborative care settings. This includes health centres catering to low-income patients; nursing homes where 63% are managed by associations, foundations, and mutuals; hospitals where 700 out of 2,700 are association-based; and residential facilities for dependent or disabled individuals, 30% of which operate under non-profit management. Despite the active presence of the non-profit sector, cooperatives have yet to be predominantly present in this landscape Encouraging local governments to foster the development of cooperatives and other innovative responses to health needs may be a potential solution. Mutual societies primarily engage in supplementary health insurance in France. There are two types of mutual societies: mutual assurance companies, which can select risks and mutual societies. Policyholders own mutual insurance undertakings, operate on a non-profit basis, and do not have share capital (Girard, 2014). In the following, we are listing some cases of health-related cooperatives and mutuals in France:

- Les Opticiens Atol – a cooperative of opticians with over 800 stores in France;
- Harmonie Mutuelle – a health insurance cooperative with over four million members;

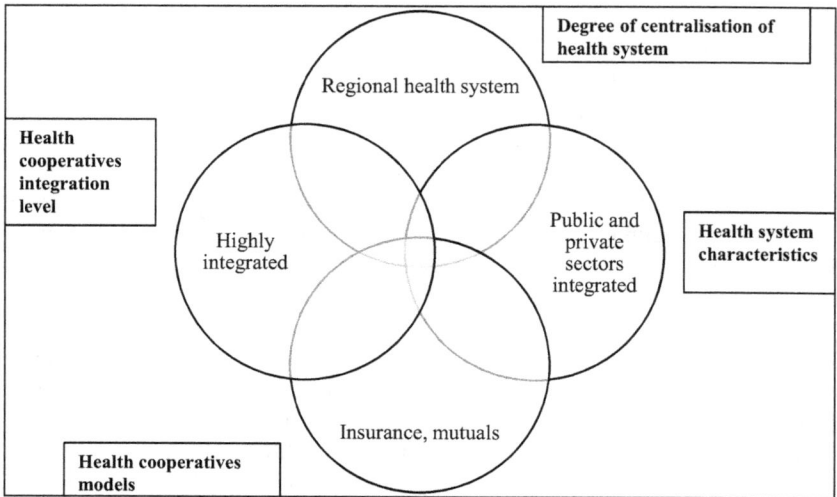

Figure 2.3 Overview of health cooperative types in the healthcare system set up in France, created by the author.

- La Vie Claire – a cooperative of organic food stores focusing on natural health and wellness;
- Coopaname – a cooperative of independent workers in various sectors, including healthcare;
- Center de Santé Dentaire Mutualiste de Paris – a cooperative dental health centre in Paris;
- Biocoop – a cooperative of organic food stores offering natural health and wellness products;
- Mutuelle Générale de l'Education Nationale (MGEN) – a health insurance cooperative for French education professionals with over 3.5 million members;
- Optic 2000 – a cooperative of opticians with over 1,200 stores in France.

Health cooperatives in France provide a wide range of affordable services. Cooperatives allow customers to buy essential items in bulk without worrying about the price being too high. Cooperatives are also great for people who want to purchase organic products offering food delivery and personal care services, including beauty services and cosmetical treatments. The government regulates French health cooperatives, providing a wide range of services, including dental care, hospitals, home care services, ambulatory care, midwifery, and more. While some of the services offered by health cooperatives are free or low-cost to their members, others may cost a fee. All fees collected are used to finance the work of the cooperatives themselves, also meaning reinvestment in the business depending on the type and organisation model of the cooperative.

Case study France – The Cancer Cooperative groups

The Cancer Cooperative Groups (GCO) is a French network of ten GCOs that conduct clinical and translational research on cancer in France, Europe, and other countries and regions. The groups are primarily organ-specific and have a strong record of designing and completing trials that have reduced the impact of cancer in many ways. GCO is a not-for-profit organisation accredited as a "French cooperative intergroup of international dimension in the field of cancer" by the French National Cancer Institute (INCa). They are committed to respecting principles relating to statutory operating procedures, not-for-profit management, scholarly communication of all research project results, and financial transparency. GCO collaborates with the pharmaceutical or biotechnological industries, and the Charter of Collaboration between the Cancer Cooperative Groups and the industry outlines the principles that must be respected to establish a partnership convention. GCO plays a vital science dissemination role through numerous publications in leading medical journals and presentations at the main oncology congresses (GCO (Grupos Cooperativos en Oncologie), n.d.) The GCO network includes the following cooperative groups: ARCAGY GINECO, FFCD, CIGAL, GERCOR, GORTEC, IFCT, LYSA, LYSARC, IFM, ANOCEF-IGCNO, and SFCE. CIGAL is an intergroup comprising five cooperative groups: ALFA, FILO, FIM, GFM, and GRAALL. The physicians of the GCO are not paid and work as volunteers within the research association (GCO (Groupes Cooperateurs en Oncologie), n.d.).

Charter of collaboration between GCO and industry

"Charter of Collaboration between Cancer Cooperative Groups (GCO) and Industry" recognises that collaboration between academic research groups and the pharmaceutical and biotechnological industries is necessary for producing high-quality scientific results and effective treatments. However, cooperative groups and industries must consider the potential differences in their approaches when creating an effective and transparent partnership. In addition, the sector must respect principles essential to the success of cooperative groups, including their independence and industrial confidence.

All clinical trials and biological studies or ancillary statistical analyses conducted by the GCO with their industry collaborators are designed to find answers to scientific issues under analysis. These trials could involve the use of marketed drugs or not, or research on biomarkers, diagnostics or prognostic tools, or concepts of epidemiology, pharmacoeconomics, and quality of life.

The conception, analysis, and coordination of these trials should be conducted transparently and independently, with the GCO acting as study promoters and benefiting from their operational resources (GCO (Groupes Cooperateurs en Oncologie), n.d.).

When collaborating with industry partners, the GCO ensures that all clinical trials, biological studies, and statistical analyses are designed and written by an editorial committee of GCO representatives. The committee follows the standard formats and recommendations from regulatory bodies that may provide funding. Although the industry partner(s) may provide input, the editorial committee has the final say on implementing the protocol. The statistical phase of the protocol is the responsibility of the GCO, who may involve statisticians from industry partners to establish the methodology and statistical analysis plan. However, the editorial committee, which must have at least one statistician, is responsible for producing the final version of the statistical section. In addition, the GCO designates the Principal Investigator and members of the study's steering committee, and they are responsible for selecting the participating centres. The study is conducted according to written operating procedures and a partnership convention that outlines the responsibilities of both the sponsor and industry partner regarding access to and management of study data, pharmacovigilance, monitoring severe adverse events (SAEs), confidentiality, data ownership, and publication.

Ideally, the GCO serves as the official study sponsor and conducts the trial in compliance with existing regulations. However, they may delegate this responsibility to a healthcare institution if necessary. In either case, the sponsor (GCO or healthcare institution) is responsible for conducting the trial and owns all resulting data. If an industry partner is a sponsor, a cooperation agreement must be established between the GCO and their representative(s) to cover issues of pharmacovigilance, monitoring and interpreting SAEs, potential interruption of the study, co-ownership, freedom of analysis, and publication of the data by the GCO.

The Cancer Cooperative Groups (Groupes Coacteurs en Oncologie – GCO) is a group of research organisations operating as not-for-profit entities regulated by the French law of 1901. The GCO is committed to following certain principles to ensure the integrity and transparency of its operations. These principles include statutory operating procedures, academic communication of all research project results, and financial transparency.

The GCO requires that its member groups comply with specific operating procedures outlined in their statutes. These procedures include creating a collegiate body and a scientific council that oversees the association's medical research projects. Members must also contribute and participate in designing and implementing research protocols. The GCO also ensures that the scientific council members are independent and have established procedures to manage conflicts of interest. The GCO has also established a Charter for collaboration that formalises the industry's acceptance of the essential cooperative group principles (Sung et al., 2021).

The GCO operates on a not-for-profit basis, and they pledge to follow specific principles to ensure their financial integrity. These principles include not paying for any executive operations, not distributing any form of profit directly or indirectly, and not allowing group members to receive any assets. Physicians who are part of the GCO are volunteers who work without payment within the research association.

The GCO's commitment to these principles ensures that the research organisation operates with integrity and transparency. By adhering to the principles of statutory operating procedures, academic communication of research project results, and financial transparency, the GCO can maintain the trust of its members, industry collaborators, and the wider public.

Although having variation of the non-profit model, this organisation shows how the social economy could be adjusted to another networking application in medical research increasing scientific knowledge and managerial implications in clinical trials.

Case study: Biocoop

Biocoop is a cooperative based in France that specialises in organic food products. It was founded in 1986 and has since become one of France's leading distributors of organic products. This case study shall provide an introductory overview of the organisation, members, governance, services and products, and relevant financial information. Biocoop's mission is to promote organic farming and to provide consumers with healthy and sustainable food products. Its vision is to create a fair and responsible food system that benefits everyone, including farmers, consumers, and the environment. Biocoop is based in Vannes, France, and has over 700 stores throughout France. Over 1,200 members, including farmers, producers, and consumers, are committed to promoting organic agriculture and sustainable food production. Biocoop is a cooperative that is governed democratically by its members. It has a board of directors elected by its members, and its decisions are made through a consensus-based process. The cooperative also has a social and environmental responsibility committee that ensures its operations align with its mission and vision. In the early years, the cooperative faced significant challenges, including a need for more access to financing and a limited supply of organic products. However, it persisted and gradually grew to become one of France's leading distributors of organic products. Biocoop provides a wide range of organic food products, including fresh produce, dairy products, meat, bread, and packaged goods. It also offers various services, including cooking workshops, educational programs, and community events. Biocoop is committed to providing high-quality organic products that are locally sourced and produced in an environmentally sustainable manner

(Land Crops, n.d.). According to its 2020 financial report, Biocoop had a turnover of €1.87 billion, an increase of 13.2% from the previous year. The cooperative's net income was €18.2 million, an increase of 22.9% compared to the previous year. Biocoop's financial performance is a testament to its success in promoting organic farming and sustainable food production (Biocoop, 2021).

By promoting healthy food and providing supportive education and social-related activities, Biocoop, although not a health cooperative in narrow terms, still presents an important model contributing to the health of the population using those services.

Belgium

Healthcare system development in Belgium

During the earlier period of the 19th century, the French influenced Belgium's healthcare services development. An illustrative instance of this influence can be seen in 1813 when, under the French regime, a miners' fund was established following a mine pit disaster in Ourthe. Financed by employers and workers, this fund provided allowances to miners in the event of permanent disability or medical incapacitation, exemplifying the early organisations focused on mutual aid. In 1844, the first welfare fund was introduced, offering insurance coverage to sailors for various contingencies such as illness, disability, old age pensions, work-related accidents, and unemployment. Subsequently, in 1849, the government began providing subsidies to these societies, establishing a national bank that supported pensions. Towards the end of the 19th century, Belgium witnessed the enactment of the first national law pertaining to health insurance. This development set the foundation for social insurance, officially introduced in 1945.

Today, Belgium is a federal constitutional monarchy governed by a parliamentary system, divided into three regions and three communities. The Belgian health system operates on the principle of social insurance, emphasising solidarity and universal coverage. The system is structured with responsibilities at both federal and regional levels. The federal government overlooks compulsory insurance, accreditation criteria, hospital financing, and professional regulations. Regional governments are responsible for maternity and child health services, elderly care, and hospital management. Insurance is mandatory, and individuals must participate in one of the existing health insurance funds. The system combines public and private healthcare, allowing patients to choose their service providers freely (Grijpstra et al., 2011). Health expenditure in Belgium has been consistently high, accounting for over 10% of the country's GDP since 2009 (Kavita, 2017). In 2017, current health expenditure as a percentage of GDP was 10.3%, with a per capita expenditure of US$PPP 5119. Most health financing is public, representing 77.2% of current health expenditure, while private financing primarily comes from out-of-pocket payments, co-payments, and extra-billings. The Belgian population generally enjoys good health and has access to high-quality health services, contributing to their long life expectancy. However, challenges persist in areas such as pharmaceutical care appropriateness, accessibility to mental health and dental care services, socio-economic inequalities in health, and the need to strengthen prevention policies. The health system also adapts to accommodate an ageing population, increased chronic diseases, and technological advances. Ongoing efforts focus on improving the quality and efficiency of the health system in Belgium. Reforms since 2014 have included the transfer of additional health competencies to federated entities, redesigning the hospital care landscape and modernising health professional regulations. Policymakers aim to enhance access to high-quality services while ensuring financial sustainability and efficiency. Those measures are promoting multi-disciplinary and integrated care, the concentration of medical expertise, patient care trajectories, patient empowerment, evidence-based medicine, and outcome-based care (Gerkens & Merkur, 2020).

The Belgian health system operates on the principle of social insurance, which emphasises solidarity between rich and poor, healthy and sick individuals organised to decrease discrimination risk. This system allows for therapeutic freedom for physicians, patient choice, and remuneration based on fee-for-service payments. Nearly the entire population, over 99%, is entitled to a comprehensive benefits package covering more than 8,000 services listed in the nationally established fee schedule. Financing of the system is based on direct progressive taxation, proportional social security contributions, and alternative financing, such as value-added tax. Patient co-payments, supplements, and non-reimbursed medical acts, drugs, and devices account for approximately 20% of healthcare expenditures. Co-payments are uniform for all but those with preferential reimbursement status. Decision-making in the Belgian health system involves negotiations among various stakeholders, including government representatives, mutual health funds, employers, salaried employees, self-employed workers, healthcare providers, and sickness funds. National conventions and agreements between healthcare providers and sickness funds regulate an essential part of the health system. Health policy responsibilities are shared between the federal and federated entities (regions and communities). The federal level regulates and finances compulsory health insurance, determines accreditation criteria, finances hospital budgets, and heavy medical equipment legislates professional qualifications, and controls the registration and price of pharmaceuticals. The federated entities are responsible for health promotion and prevention, maternity and child health services, elderly care, home care, coordination and collaboration in primary healthcare and palliative care, implementation of accreditation standards, and financing (Bilsen et al., 2018). Inter-ministerial conferences are regularly held to promote collaboration between the federal government and regional governments in Belgium. Compulsory health insurance is managed by six private, non-profit national associations of mutual health funds and one public national association sickness fund. The INAMI-RIZIV, overseen by the Federal Public Service for Social Security, coordinates healthcare and disability insurance, allocates funding, defines care provision schedules and refund rates, approves care providers and facilities, and manages financial accountability for mutual health funds. Belgium's healthcare system includes public health services, independent ambulatory care professionals, independent pharmacists, hospitals, and specialised facilities for the elderly. Most medical specialists work independently in hospitals or private practices on an ambulatory basis. General practitioners, dentists, and pharmacists also work independently. Belgian patients participate in healthcare financing through co-payments and co-insurance, covered by third-party payers.

Health cooperatives and mutuals development in Belgium

In Belgium, mutual societies play a central role in the national health system, providing compulsory health insurance coverage to the population. The development of mutual societies in Belgium dates back to the 19th century when workers voluntarily formed those societies to enhance risk protection from illness, unemployment, and other social needs. Over time, mutual societies were integrated into public agencies, and government benefits and subsidies facilitated access to health services. The concept of pooling risks through free membership and collective decision-making gained popularity over time. By the early 20th century, the mutual movement experienced significant expansion, with local societies joining national federations and unions.

One of the oldest cooperative insurance group – P&V, established in 1907 in Belgium – originated from the efforts of the Belgian Worker's Party. It aimed to address the challenges faced by lower-income families, who often fell victim to unethical practices of unregulated private for-profit insurance companies. P&V experienced significant growth by emphasising the importance of mutual assistance and solidarity (UN, 1997, p. 63). Since 1934, P&V has allocated a significant portion of its surplus to support social welfare and humanitarian programs. The organisation remains committed to providing social security and services specifically tailored to independent workers. The Belgian health model operates at both regional and federal levels. Regional governments are responsible for hospital management, health promotion, services for older adults, and support for pregnant women and children. They also manage and oversee the funds for compulsory health insurance. What sets mutual societies in Belgium apart is their ability to carry out independent prevention activities and services, benefiting the general population beyond their members. They also cater to specific population groups, such as young and older women, and offer services in marginalised areas. Belgium's mutual societies are typically large organisations grouped into five national associations based on ideological and political preferences. These include the National Alliance of Christian Mutualities, the National Union of Neutral Mutualities, the National Union of Socialist Mutualities, the National Union of Liberal Mutualities, and the Union of Free and Professional Mutualities. In 1994, there were approximately 2,500 primary-level cooperative pharmacies operating in Europe. These pharmacies served around 30 million members and held a market share of approximately 10%. Such cooperatives in the health sector were primarily found in a few countries, particularly those that were members of the European Union. The European Union of Social Pharmacies includes cooperatives and other types of organisations within the social economy, such as mutual associations. Those cooperatives and organisations were active in countries such as Belgium, France, Italy, the Netherlands, Switzerland, Finland, Ireland, and the United Kingdom. Also, cooperative or social pharmacies operate within a comprehensive health service approach, providing drugs and equipment, advice, follow-up care, background information, and preventive measures. Their goal was to ensure the efficient and rational use of medicines, emphasising a holistic approach to healthcare. With the support of the Belgian tertiary organisation, efforts were made to establish prototype primary cooperative pharmacies in the Czech Republic. By January 1996, ten cooperative pharmacies had already been established, equipped to a high standard and offering their members a wide range of drugs. Additionally, preparations were underway to establish two more cooperative pharmacies (UN, 1997, p. 34). As of 2009, there were 57 mutual societies in Belgium, with the majority having more than 15,000 members. The law mandates that individuals join or register with a mutual benefit society for compulsory health insurance, allowing individuals to choose their preferred mutual society (Corens, 2007).

Belgian mutual health funds distinguish themselves from other social economy enterprises due to their size, long history, and unique relationship with public authorities. However, they face similar challenges as other organisations, including resistance to competition, commercialisation of goods and services, and maintaining internal democracy. Nevertheless, mutuals in Belgium have a special status, as their role in implementing compulsory sickness-disability insurance has led to their perception as semi-public institutions. Additionally, the National Bank of Belgium includes a portion of their activities within the public administration sector, highlighting the high degree of integration of mutuals within the Belgian system.

Today, health mutual aid societies play an important role in Belgian society. They provide access to medical care and support for members when they are sick. Many such organizations provide supplemental health insurance to their members; for example, the mutual aid society offers supplemental health insurance and a prescription drug discount program.

Pharmacy cooperatives also play a significant role in the Belgian health sector. These cooperatives, known as professional unions, bring together

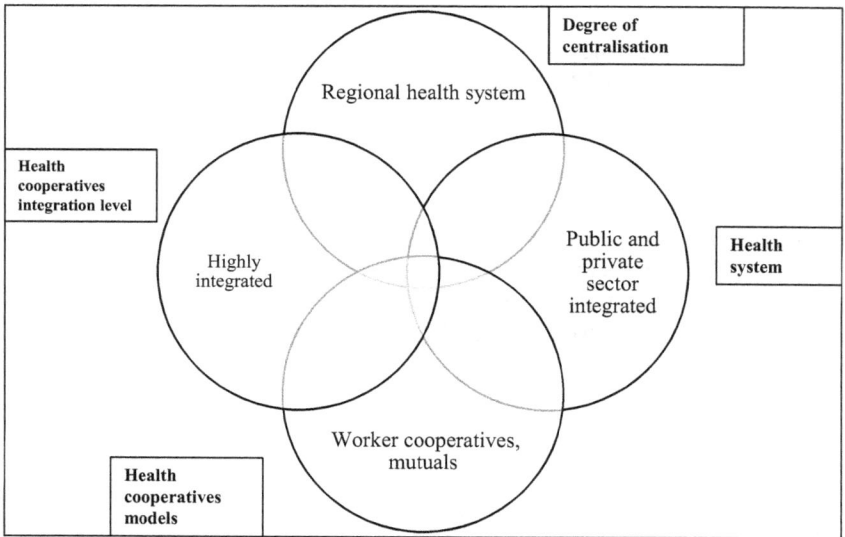

Figure 2.4 Overview of health cooperative types in the healthcare system set up in Belgium, created by the author.

cooperative pharmacies and wholesale dispatchers, representing a significant portion of the market. They adhere to the principles and values of the social economy and operate following the Charter and commitments of the European Union of Social Pharmacies. The establishment of cooperative pharmacies dates back to the 1880s, coinciding with the rapid expansion of the cooperative movement. It is worth noting that private pharmacist associations have increased alongside the growth of cooperative pharmacies (Grijpstra et al., 2011). OPHACO (Office Des Pharmacies Cooperatives De Belgique) is the recognised professional Union representing 600 cooperative pharmacies in Belgium, accounting for approximately 20% of the ambulatory pharmacy market. OPHACO is present at the institutional level and is a member of the International Cooperative Alliance and the International Health Cooperative Organisation, among others. The cooperative dividends paid to each cooperator based on purchases and profits have been a point of contention, with private pharmacist associations considering them as a form of unfair competition. Despite opposition, cooperative pharmacies have grown and now have an annual turnover of around 600 million EUR, meeting the needs of approximately 2.2 million people and employing nearly 3,500 people, including nearly 1,000 pharmacists (EPHEU, 2013).

Sweden

Healthcare system development in Sweden

The country of Sweden has a parliamentary government and a monarchy. It is the third largest member of the European Union, with a population of 10.3 million as of 2022 (World Bank, n.d.-d). The country is divided into 290 municipalities and 20 county councils or regions. The Swedish healthcare system has a long history of public funding and ownership, focusing on expanding hospital services and improving equal access to care. Sweden's first public hospital, the Serafim Hospital, was established in Stockholm in 1752. Initially, it had eight beds intended to cater to the healthcare needs of Sweden and Finland, which was under Swedish rule at the time. Having recognised the limited availability of hospital services outside the capital, an agreement was reached in 1765 among the four estates, enabling local authorities to use locally collected resources to construct hospitals. By the end of the 19th century, Sweden claimed to have approximately 50 hospitals and 3,000 beds (Agnell, 1950). The development of the present structure can be traced back to the establishment of county councils in 1862, which marked a significant milestone in healthcare governance. National government-owned hospitals were transferred to the county councils, while mental health services and provincial general physicians remained under national government ownership. Over the years, more hospitals were established by the county councils, supported by industrialisation and economic growth. In 1928, the Hospitals Act made the county councils legally responsible for inpatient hospital care (Engel, 1972).

The post-war era witnessed substantial growth in the healthcare sector, particularly in hospitals, with most physicians employed by hospitals. However, outpatient services remained relatively weak, prompting the "seven-crown reform" in 1970, which transferred responsibility for outpatient services to county councils and introduced fixed co-payments for outpatient care. Additionally, the national parliament decided to socialise private pharmacies, establishing the National Corporation of Swedish Pharmacies in 1971 (Anell, 1996). Public healthcare provision in Sweden has undergone significant changes, and initially the Collegium Medicum was responsible for administering public healthcare. In 1813, that responsibility was transferred to the Sundhetscollegium, which later became the Royal Medical Board in 1878. In 1968, the Royal Medical Board merged with the Royal Board of Welfare to form the National Board of Health and Welfare. This authority played a crucial role in shaping the modern healthcare structure implemented during the 1970s and continues to supervise healthcare and provide health and social services statistics (Anell & Claesson, 1995). During the late 1970s, the county councils took on most healthcare services, with a few exceptions. Ownership of the Karolinska Hospital in

Stockholm and the Academic Hospital in Uppsala was transferred to the county councils in the early 1980s. Additionally, in 1985, county councils became responsible for payments to private practitioners, and in 1998, they took on the expenditure related to prescription drugs. Those reforms aimed to clarify the division of responsibilities between the national government and local authorities, enhance cost control, and align economic incentives (Harrison & Calltorp, 2000). In the 1990s, there was a shift in transferring responsibilities from county councils to municipalities. The ÄDEL reform in 1992 transferred the responsibility for long-term inpatient healthcare and care for older people from county councils to municipalities. Subsequently, the municipalities cared for the physically disabled and individuals with long-term mental illnesses. Those reforms sought to improve services by integrating care and social services within municipalities. However, that shift also transferred about one-fifth of county council healthcare expenditure to municipalities.

In recent decades, there has been a growing emphasis on cost control, efficiency, value, and quality in the governance of healthcare services. The criticism of county councils and municipalities regarding cost control and efficiency led to the implementation of New Public Management (NPM) reforms in the early 1990s. Those reforms included a purchaser–provider split, new provider contracts, and increased choice for inhabitants. Although short-term improvements in efficiency were observed in county councils that implemented those reforms, the long-term sustainability of the purchaser–provider split has been questioned. Sweden's merger of county councils was a significant development in the late 1990s. The establishment of the Region Skåne and the Västra Götaland Region in 1999 resulted from the merger of two and three county councils, respectively. Those new regions took on the responsibility of providing healthcare services and assumed increased accountability for regional development, previously managed by county administrative boards under the national government. The discussion regarding further mergers and the formation of additional regions has continued in recent years (Palme et al., 2002). The implementation of NPM and similar reforms primarily occurred at the individual county council and regional levels rather than at the national level. That decentralised approach aligned with the nature of Swedish healthcare, which developed during the 1970s and 1980s. However, certain reforms, such as the choice of providers for residents and privatisation of services, received explicit support from centre-right-wing national governments in the early 1990s and mid-1990s, as well as since 2006. Since January 1, 2010, the Health and Medical Services Act has made it mandatory for the population to have the freedom to choose their primary care provider and for private care providers accredited by local county councils to establish their services. This shift also signifies the formal abandonment of the previous focus on primary care providers' responsibility for a specific geographic population. Several county councils and regions already implemented similar reforms between 2007 and 2009 (Swedish Competition Authority, 2010).

Another significant national decision was re-regulating the Swedish pharmacy market, allowing new owners to operate pharmacies starting in 2009. That re-regulation involved the sale of approximately half of the state-owned pharmacies operated by the National Corporation of Swedish Pharmacies. As a result, the number of pharmacies in Sweden has increased by about 20% since the reform (Swedish Competition Authority, 2010). Those government decisions concerning the organisation of primary care and pharmacy services can be seen as a partial return to the conditions before the "seven-crown reform" and the socialisation of pharmacies in the early 1970s. Also, collaborative initiatives have been implemented between the county and national councils, including transparent comparison systems for clinical indicators across county councils, increased transparency in priority setting, and the development of evidence-based medicine, including cost-effectiveness to determine the value of services. The Swedish healthcare system is founded on the principles of social responsibility and ensuring the health of all citizens. The Swedish welfare state places significant importance on providing quality healthcare to everyone. The Health and Medical Services Act of 1982 guarantees equal access to services based on need and emphasises the vision of equal health for all. Three fundamental principles guide healthcare in Sweden. The principle of human dignity asserts that everyone, regardless of their status in the community, is entitled to equal dignity and rights.

Sweden's national public health policy aims to create social conditions that equally promote good health for the entire population. It is based on 11 domains of public health objectives, which guide all public authorities at various levels (Swedish National Institute of Public Health, 2023). These objectives encompass crucial determinants of public health in Sweden, such as participation and influence in society, economic, and social prerequisites; conditions during childhood and adolescence; health in working life, environments, and products; health-promoting health services; protection against communicable diseases, sexuality, and reproductive health; physical activity, eating habits, and food; and tobacco, alcohol, illicit drugs, doping, and gambling. Sweden boasts one of the highest life expectancies in the world. Life expectancy has increased over the past three decades, making Sweden one of the world's oldest populations. Mortality rates in Sweden have dropped significantly, particularly in circulatory system diseases. Preventive measures, such as reduced smoking rates and improved treatment methods, have contributed to declining mortality and morbidity associated with circulatory diseases. Despite those improvements, circulatory system diseases remain the most common cause of death for both women and men.

The Swedish health system operates at three levels of government: national, regional, and county councils. The Ministry of Health and Social Affairs is responsible for health policy, while the regional level ensures the quality of health services and finances them for citizens. Municipalities provide care for the elderly and disabled, while primary care centres and hospitals are run mainly by county councils. Additionally, there are eight government agencies dedicated to health and public health. The health system has covered all legal residents since 1982, with emergency coverage provided to patients from European Union and European Economic Area countries and other countries with bilateral agreements with Sweden.

Historically, local and self-government have played an essential role in the evolution of the Swedish health system. County councils and municipalities have primarily introduced reforms in healthcare. Concerns related to distributive justice, cost control, efficiency, value, and quality have become more prominent in the governance of healthcare services, leading to a critical attitude towards councils and municipalities as providers of healthcare services with the NPM, including the purchaser–provider split, has been gradually introduced. The decentralisation of healthcare in the 1970s and 1980s increased the importance of county councils and regions in service management. The conservative and centre-right national governments from the 1990s to 2006 favoured policies of privatisation of services, leading to competition between public and private primary care providers.

Later reforms have focused on improving primary care and coordinated care for the elderly. Private companies act as primary care providers, but public ownership of health centres is prevalent. Reforms in the hospital sector have aimed at the specialisation and concentration of services. Additionally, reforms have been carried out to reduce service waiting times and improve primary care, psychiatric care, and care coordination for the elderly. National-level reforms have focused on defining the competencies of county councils and municipalities, guaranteeing direct benefits for patient groups, and achieving regional equality of services.

Various ways have been used to incorporate non-public service providers into the public system, such as public procurement, citizen choice, management, and employee buy-out. The political goal was to ensure fair competition among all providers, including cooperatives, public, and for-profit entities. Price regulations have been implemented to allow citizens to choose services regardless of their financial capacity. Strong public regulation is also implemented regarding accreditation, and private healthcare providers must agree with the county council to receive public reimbursement. Patients must pay the entire charge to the provider if no agreement exists. Some private providers, such as physicians and physiotherapists, are funded by county councils based on earlier state regulations, which operate in parallel and sometimes in conflict with more recently adopted principles of payment to private providers (Thomson et al., 2011).

Like other European countries, Swedish mutuals have become an integral part of the health system, and they are now public law entities and regional bodies responsible for managing the compulsory health insurance system. The Swedish health system is supported by local and national taxes, guaranteeing access to highly subsidised health services for the entire resident population. Social insurance, including sickness insurance, parental insurance (leave), a basic retirement pension, a supplementary pension, child allowance income support, and housing allowance, is administered by the Swedish Social Insurance Agency (Försäkringskassan). The Agency operates throughout the country and is also involved in preventing and reducing ill health through programs that restore individuals to a productive life whenever possible. In addition, the system allows voluntary supplemental health insurance, which can be administered by promising mutual enterprises. However, the extent of public coverage leaves little room for the private sector, which only supplied coverage to less than 3% of the population in the early 2000s. For this reason, insurance mutuals are much more active in the non-life insurance market (Anell et al., 2012; Grijpstra et al., 2011; European Observatory on Health Systems and Policies, 2009; Jonsson & Ekman, 2002).

Since the turn of the century, for-profit companies have increased their share in private health production, leading to a more concentrated sector with larger companies. There is an ongoing political debate on the issue of distributing profit to owners in health sector enterprises. Some Swedish municipalities and regions are experimenting with agreements with civil society organisations, including cooperatives, to test alternative business models in the welfare system. A government initiatives has also proposed reforming public procurement legislation favouring not-for-profit providers.

Health cooperatives development in Sweden

In the 1970s and 1980s, the Swedish state started to run different kinds of social care institutions for children and older adults. That created opportunities for health cooperatives to enter the market and provide services that were not available before. In Sweden, health cooperatives are not only a provider of services, but they also have a public-related role. This means that they can influence the way the state runs healthcare. Furthermore, these organisations have an essential role in the governance of healthcare services, as they have different funding sources than public hospitals. From the 1980s until the 1990s, the healthcare sector saw significant changes in organisation and financing. That created opportunities for health cooperatives to enter the market and provide services that were not available before. The main challenges for health cooperatives in Sweden are the same as for other non-profit providers. They have to compete with for-profit companies, which can be difficult because they have more financial resources. In addition, cooperatives face the same challenges as other providers regarding attracting patients and retaining staff. This means that they need help offering attractive working conditions for the employees. In this context, groups of users, such as the elderly, formed associations and applied for public financial support. They then hired professional and paraprofessional workers to deliver the necessary services to themselves or individuals for whom they had responsibility as family members or guardians. As of September 1995, an estimated number of these user-led social care cooperatives existed. By the end of the 20th century, there were estimated 1,600 user-owned cooperatives in Sweden, with around 1,400 of them being child-care cooperatives (UN, 1997, pp. 48–57). These cooperatives derived approximately 64% of their income from local or national government authorities, which served as payment for the care provided to beneficiaries of the national health and social security insurance system. Citizens view user-owned social care cooperatives as a means to influence their living conditions and ensure high-quality services directly. They actively participate in the development and operation of these cooperatives. In psychiatric care, cooperatives primarily owned by patients, and in some cases including professional staff as members, have seen significant growth. Examples of such cooperatives can be found at Husomtarna and in the Enskede-Skarpnack psychiatric section of Stockholm County. Residential service cooperatives have also been established by individuals with disabilities in cities like Gothenburg, Jonkoping, and Stockholm. These cooperatives employ staff members to provide necessary personal services, such as home help and personal assistance, while owned and managed by the individuals. Additionally, cooperatives formed by elderly individuals have emerged. One notable example is the Stockholm Association for Independent Living, founded in 1987 by individuals with significant disabilities requiring regular care. By assuming the role of employers rather than clients, association members have the autonomy to choose their own caregivers and avoid dependency on a rigid public service system. The association serves as a recruitment and organisational entity, representing its members' interests. As of November 1992, it had 85 members, and by 1994, its membership had exceeded 100 in the Stockholm metropolitan region. The association manages around 400 caregivers, each employed temporarily (UN, 1997, pp. 49–57).

In several countries, parents have joined various daycare cooperatives established by service providers. The cooperatives actively support individuals with disabilities, including those with physical or mental impairments and those facing social challenges, such as former prisoners, individuals struggling with drug or alcohol addiction, single parents, victims of domestic violence, homeless individuals, and long-term unemployed individuals. Those with disabilities who are employed by these cooperatives have full participation in management. The cooperative's policy fosters their self-confidence by providing unrestricted opportunities to engage in all aspects of cooperative life. The selection of individuals is primarily based on their ability to perform tasks on par with any other employee. Furthermore, these worker-owned cooperatives strive to create a flexible operational environment to enable individuals with disabilities to carry out their work effectively. While the number of such cooperatives

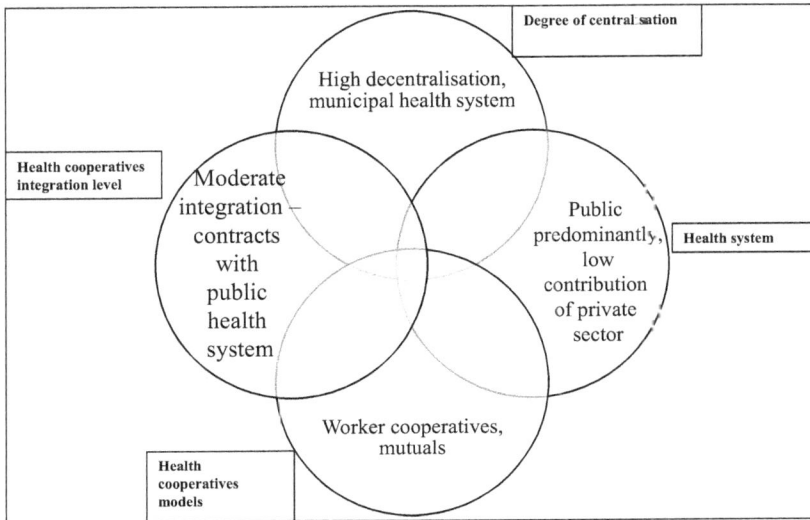

Figure 2.5 Overview of health cooperative types in the healthcare system set up in Sweden, created by the author.

remains relatively small, they have successfully integrated individuals with disabilities into the labour force.

The Medikoop model, a collaborative effort between housing cooperatives, insurance cooperatives, and local government authorities, emerged in the early 1990s as a community-based and cooperatively organised healthcare model. It aimed to integrate preventive healthcare services with care for the elderly. Elderly members of housing cooperatives actively participated in establishing cooperative primary healthcare initiatives, including home nursing and home help services. One example is the Snopptorp housing area in Eskilstuna, where a cooperative has been providing home help and home nursing services since 1991.

From the late 1980s to 1994, the Swedish national and local governments, including municipalities and county councils, established a favourable legal and economic framework for entrepreneurial activities in the social care sector. That environment supported various types of organisations, including cooperatives, in providing social care services. User-owned, provider-owned, and multi-stakeholder social care cooperatives emerged as a result. However, a policy shift occurred after 1994, with local governments reversing their earlier support for those initiatives. Some provider-owned social care cooperatives faced pressure to return to the public sector.

Non-public service providers have been integrated into the Swedish public healthcare system through various means, such as public procurement, citizen choice, management and employee buy-outs. The objective was to ensure equal competition among all providers, including cooperatives, public entities, and for-profit organisations. Price regulations are in place to allow citizen users to choose healthcare services regardless of their financial capacity. The system also enforces strong public regulation regarding accreditation, requiring private healthcare providers to have agreements with county councils to receive public reimbursement. Providers without agreements are not reimbursed while patients must pay the full charge themselves. However, some private providers, such as physicians and physiotherapists, are reimbursed based on earlier state regulations, sometimes conflicting with more recently adopted payment principles (Anell et al., 2012).

Similar to other European countries like Germany, Swedish mutuals have become integral to the healthcare system. They are now public law entities and regional bodies responsible for managing the compulsory health insurance system. The Swedish health system is primarily funded through local and national taxes, ensuring highly subsidised health services for all residents. The Swedish Social Insurance Agency administers social insurance, including sickness insurance, parental insurance, retirement pensions, child allowance, income support, and housing allowance. The Agency also works on preventing and reducing ill health through programs to restore individuals to productive life. While voluntary supplementary health insurance administered by proper mutual enterprises is allowed, the extensive public coverage limits the role of the private sector, which served less than 3% of the population in the early 2000s. Since the early 2000s, there has been an increase in the share of for-profit companies in private healthcare production in Sweden (Grijpstra et al., 2011). According to the IHCO report on health cooperatives in 2018, there were 298 health cooperatives employing nearly 20,000 people (IHCO, 2018a). Additionally, the sector has witnessed consolidation, with larger companies growing. The distribution of profit to owners in healthcare enterprises has been a topic of ongoing political debate. Some Swedish municipalities and regions are exploring agreements with civil society organisations, including cooperatives, to test alternative business models and leverage the qualities of third-sector organisations.

3 Historical and modern aspects of health cooperatives development in Eastern Europe (Serbia, Croatia, Bosnia and Herzegovina, Slovenia, Poland, and Romania)

Serbia

Healthcare system development in Serbia

The history of health support in Serbia can be traced back to the Middle Ages with the development of monastery medicine. Particularly interesting are early medical writings notes in the monastery Hilandar on Mount Athos in today's Greece. Namely, the Hilandar medical codex, discovered in 1952 at the Hilandar monastery, is a medieval manuscript containing the knowledge of European medical science holding immense significance as the only known copy of the extensive collection of medical records from the Salerno-Montpellier school, written in the Old Serbian vernacular (Serbian redaction of Old Slavic). Although the exact date of its creation remains uncertain, the Hilandar medical codex is believed to have been produced in the 15th or early 16th century, with some of its writings dating back even further. The contents of this manuscript encompass various subjects, including diagnostics, writings on infectious diseases, pharmacological records, writings on complex medicines, pharmacotherapy, a comprehensive essay on phlebotomy, a file dedicated to paediatrics, and a file focused on toxicology. During the later period when Serbia was under the Ottoman Empire, there were Oriental knowledge impacts on medicine and treatment.

In the more recent period of the 19th and 20th centuries, the evolution of healthcare and health insurance in Serbia can be divided into three periods: pre-WWI, between the two World Wars, and post-WWII. The development of health insurance in Serbia, from its inception until the mid-1950s, took place within the framework of legislation and social insurance institutions. Serbia experienced significant constitutional developments, profoundly impacting the healthcare system and health insurance (Stamenović et al., 2017).

Understanding the constitutions developed is relevant for both regulatory framework understanding and historical state development, considering that in this section, we are also presenting the other states that were united with Serbia

DOI: 10.4324/9781003183068-3

at some point. Notably, after the Berlin Congress in 1878, Serbia adopted several constitutions, including the Radical Constitution (1888), the October or April Constitution (1901), and the Constitution for the Kingdom of Serbia from 1903 (an amended version of the Radical Constitution from 1888). Following the unification into the Kingdom of Serbs, Croats, and Slovenes in 1918, two constitutions were adopted: the Constitution of the Kingdom of Serbs, Croats, and Slovenes (June 28, 1921 – Vidovdan Constitution) and the September or October Constitution (1931). After WWII, other constitutions were adopted, including the Constitution of the Federal Republic of Yugoslavia (1946), Constitutional Law (1953), Constitution of the Socialist Federal Republic of Yugoslavia (1963) until the Constitution of the Republic of Serbia (2006). The current constitution, in effect since 2006, was adopted by the Republic of Serbia after the Republic of Montenegro became independent. The development of health insurance and social insurance in Serbia, as in other countries, was closely linked to the growth of the labour movement. During the late 19th and early 20th centuries, the first workers' organisations emerged in Serbia, marking a significant milestone in the labour movement. Those organisations included the Opančar Workers' Union in Belgrade (January 1896), the Workers' Union in Negotin (late 1896), the Workers' Union in Belgrade (early 1897), the Belgrade Workers' Union (March 1901), the Union of Construction Workers, Association of Bookbinding Workers, and Association of Trade Assistants (1901), among others. In May 1903, a primary labour union was established, bringing together most existing labour organisations. That consolidation played a pivotal role in advancing the labour movement in Serbia, creating the groundwork for the development of later social insurance (Cuzovic et al., 2019, pp. 182–192).

Initially, voluntary insurance programs based on guaranteed assistance for workers were introduced. The first societies, later evolving into societies and cooperatives, aimed to provide mutual aid in illness and death and were established as early as 1875. The Mining Law, enacted in Serbia, mandated the establishment of brotherhoods to support miners and their families. Subsequently, a revised mining law in 1900 made it compulsory for each mine to have fraternal mining funds that would offer assistance in cases of illness and death. Furthermore, a collective mining fraternal fund was created to provide disability benefits and pensions. The 1910 Act on Activities introduced compulsory social insurance for illness and workplace accidents in Serbia. However, implementing that insurance scheme was disrupted by the outbreak of wars shortly afterwards, including the Balkan wars and WWI. The Act also introduced the concept of lockouts, temporary work exclusions imposed by employers. The origins of health insurance in Serbia can be traced back to the 1879 Law on establishing the National Health Fund. This Law governed the development of health institutions and the funding of public health services. The National Health Fund was financed through interest on essential capital, general hospital taxes, and fixed grants from the state budget (Kosanović & Anđelski, 2015).

Additionally, voluntary independent funds existed for mutual assistance among specific worker groups, such as graphic artists, craftsmen, and military-technical institute workers. During the interwar period, the Kingdom of Serbs, Croats, and Slovenes (later known as the Kingdom of Yugoslavia) laid the foundations for health and social insurance. Those principles were established in the Vidovdan Constitution of 1921. Article 130 of the constitution mandated the approval of all existing regulations and temporary measures by the National Assembly, including the Decree on the Arrangement of Workers' Insurance for Cases of Illness and Accident at Work, which was issued in 1921. That Decree, which later expanded to encompass insurance for disability, old age, and death, was published in 1922.

The Workers' Insurance Law embodied modern insurance principles such as compulsory insurance, comprehensive coverage of risks, involvement of workers and employers in insurance matters, state assistance and supervision, and other fundamental principles. It encompassed all insurance risks except for unemployment. It applied the principles of compulsory insurance, nationwide coverage, funding through contributions from employees and employers (with employers solely responsible for financing workplace accident insurance), and inclusivity for various employment categories. Inspired by Germany's progressive social insurance system introduced during Bismarck's chancellorship in the late 19th century, that Law was considered one of the most advanced regulations of its kind in Europe. The Workers' Insurance Law included following types of compulsory insurance: illness, exhaustion, old age, and death; workplace accidents; and unemployment. However, the implementation of those provisions was only partially realised. Health insurance coverage was implemented nationwide in 1922, followed by accident insurance (disability). Insurance for disability, old age, and death (pensions) was only partially implemented starting September 1, 1937. The introduction of unemployment insurance, except for miners and smelters covered by specific regulations, did not materialise. Compulsory insurance applied to all employed individuals throughout the territory of the Kingdom. However, the number of displaced individuals remained relatively low, representing 4.2 per 1,000 inhabitants. Contributions for illness, disability, old age, and the breadwinner's death were shared equally between workers and employers, while employers alone were responsible for contributions related to workplace accidents. The implementation of insurance was overseen by the Central Office for Workers' Insurance, headquartered in Zagreb, in conjunction with district offices for workers' insurance. Alongside those institutions were pension institutes for furniture insurance, fraternal funds for miners and smelters, commercial sickness insurance providers, and other companies.

In the post-WWII era, social insurance in Serbia progressed further, marked by expanded population coverage under national insurance and the broadening of entitlements. The development of social insurance, influenced by economic and political factors, unfolded through several stages. Understanding that evolution is best achieved by examining the legislative measures enacted during that period. Countries worldwide exhibit diverse healthcare financing systems, ownership structures for healthcare facilities and equipment, coverage of public health insurance, as well as the content and scope of health insurance rights. These factors categorise healthcare systems into three fundamental models based on the primary source of financing, ownership, and population coverage. These models include the national health service system (e.g. Great Britain, Ireland, Scandinavian countries, Greece, Italy, Portugal, Spain, among others), mandatory social insurance system (e.g. Germany, France, Austria, Belgium, Switzerland, among others), and private insurance system (e.g. the United States). However, determining the optimal healthcare system model is not straightforward, as it depends on historical, economic, social, cultural, and other contextual factors. Furthermore, national healthcare systems may transition from one model to another in response to changing circumstances. For instance, former socialist countries in Central and Eastern Europe had healthcare systems resembling the national health service model during the socialist era. Following the collapse of socialism and the transition process, those countries generally shifted towards a mandatory social and health insurance system. The Constitution of Serbia recognises the concept of mandatory social and health insurance. Constitutional changes on social security matters would be necessary to move towards a national health service model, which involves financing healthcare and other rights through the budget.

At present, the healthcare system requires appropriate reforms and adjustments in its organisational structure, professional practices, legal framework, and financial standing to ensure it meets the needs of patients and upholds the right to adequate treatment. Reforms can improve the efficiency and effectiveness of the healthcare system, both within and across primary, secondary, and tertiary-level healthcare institutions. This necessitates embracing a fresh management approach throughout the healthcare system incorporating modern management methods and models. There is also scope for entrepreneurial initiatives and approaches within the healthcare system, not limited to the private sector but also within the state or public sector, including health cooperatives initiatives. Implementing these changes does not necessarily require substantial investments or place an additional burden on the Serbian budget but instead entails a shift in mindset and learning from the examples set by developed countries with extensive experience in this domain. However, it is unrealistic to expect that internal reforms alone will significantly enhance the entire healthcare system, considering that healthcare will continue to constitute a substantial portion of the Serbian budget and public expenditure. It is crucial to highlight the introduction of efficient and effective management in healthcare, treating it on par with management practices in business entities, both in the private and public sectors. The existing healthcare system in Serbia was formulated and regulated during a period of general economic crisis, resulting in the current financial resources only partially meeting the needs of the healthcare system.

Therefore, change is imperative as the first step towards initiating and reorganising the healthcare system in Serbia. To ensure the efficient functioning of healthcare institutions, it is essential to adopt modern management models implemented by well-educated and trained experts with the necessary healthcare management skills and knowledge. These professionals should apply proven methods and techniques that have demonstrated positive outcomes world-wide. The involvement of such experts is crucial in addressing organisational challenges and understanding the processes within healthcare institutions. Due to changing circumstances, including reduced financial resources, healthcare institutions' management needs help in identifying new opportunities for acquiring funds to sustain high-quality operations. Implementing a healthcare management system can solve these issues by serving as a tool for enhancing the performance of healthcare institutions and promoting the application of tech-nology, knowledge, and skills.

Healthcare management encompasses a range of skills and competencies, including efficient resource management, the development of human capital and information management capabilities, the evaluation of organisational per-formance (particularly healthcare quality), and the advancement of healthcare services and the sustainability of the healthcare system. Although the healthcare system is partially driven by market forces, with a significant portion relying on budget funding, healthcare managers strive to bridge the gap between the needs of healthcare institutions and the resources available to them. However, it is essential to acknowledge that modern management principles have limited influence on the overall organisation of the healthcare system, as it is primarily defined by legislation as a non-profit entity. In contrast, market-based models offer greater flexibility in applying modern management principles. "Health for All by the Year 2000" which outlines regulations for international action, urging member countries to review the foundations of health policy and establish a three-tiered healthcare system: primary, intermediate or secondary, and central or tertiary levels. These levels are interconnected, with higher levels supporting lower levels and ensuring seamless coordination.

The Republic of Serbia, in particular, is proud of a vibrant history of health cooperatives from 1921 to 1941, holding significant importance. During that time, the health cooperative movement showcased exceptional achievements and relevance. Its impact was evident in preventive and curative measures, increased equality in healthcare access, improved socio-economic conditions, health edu-cation, and the integration of medicine with agriculture to enhance the quality of life for cooperative members. The historical successes garnered recognition from other nations, disseminating the health cooperative model to countries such as the United States, Poland, Bulgaria, Romania, India, and more. The coopera-tive health system was abolished in 1949 when it was integrated into the health system of the former Yugoslavia. King Aleksandar I Karađorđević, who strongly supported the health cooperative associations, was hailed as the first advocate of health cooperatives. Esteemed figures in the field of medical sciences, including Dr Gavrilo Kojić, professor Milan Jovanović Batut, and Croatian expert Prof. Andrija Štampar, played instrumental roles in initiating and advancing this form of association in the country during that era. They recognised the significance of such a movement, considering the challenging post-war legacy. Today, a century after the visionary initiatives of those remarkable individuals, which led to the establishment of numerous health cooperatives starting in 1921 (although some cooperatives existed before the Balkan wars, they were limited in number, while the massification of cooperatives at the state level began in 1921) – the modern context calls for a renewed initiative to establish health cooperatives (Stamenovic & Sevarlic, 2020).

Cooperatives development in Serbia

When considering the historical development of cooperatives *en général*, we must add particular views on early historical development to readers' perspectives. Namely, there are different theories about the early development of cooperatives, their organisational forms, ownership of the assets, division of labour, and so on. For example, theories about the "family cooperative" as an institution created during the transition from clan to class society have been supported by different authors, such as, Friedrich Engels, Emil Sicard (in later works), and others. This theory should be connected with civilisation progress, shifting the matrilineal or patrilineal family models among early family cooperatives (Mandić, 1974). However, some other authors initially thought that the early development of family cooperatives and the specificities of such development were connected with Slovene people's characteristics (Sicard, 1944). It is important to mention that the same author later acknowledged the early existence of family cooperatives in North Africa and Latin America, which changed the international perspective of understanding the early cooperatives' development (Sicard, 1944). Looking into the regional development of early cooperatives, some of the evidence of family cooperatives were noted within documents from 1272 (i.e. the city of Dubrovnik Statute), where the cooperative was mentioned as "a community of brothers" (Mandić, 1974). Dubrovnik was then part of the Republic of Venice. Today it is located on the territory of the Republic of Croatia, while in the 20th century, it was part of Yugoslavia. Looking into the historical development of cooperatives in Serbia, it was noted that Serbia has a long history of family cooperatives, which also existed for centuries during the Turkish invasion (approx. 15th to 18th century). Modern concepts of cooperatives first appeared in England in Rochdale in 1844, and then they were founded in different countries based on that model. The second global modern agricultural cooperative was created in Sloboviste, Slovakia, and shortly after the Slovaks began to establish them in Bački Petrovac in Vojvodina (1846), Austro-Hungarian Empire (since 1918 territory of the Republic of Serbia, although particular territory claims were noticed earlier in the 19th century). At the time when the first modern cooperative on the territory of today's Serbia was founded in Bački Petrovac, it was clear that was an innovation of great importance for the whole region, which was later confirmed also by the fast development of the Serbian Cooperative Union initiated as early as 1895 (Zadružni savez Srbije, 2023). Also, Serbia was one of the member states contributing to the founding of the International Cooperative Alliance in 1895, with Mihajlo Avramović, a representative attending the London conference.

Health cooperatives development in Serbia

When considering the historical analysis of health cooperatives as an organisational form, we consider the territory of the Republic of Serbia today. We are particularly interested in the period from 1885 to 1949 when the health cooperative movement was established and progressed until its integration into the public health system of Yugoslavia (Stamenović, 2019b). Our research shows that the first health cooperatives were developed in two-folded directions. First was connected to the organisational form of health cooperatives considered by opening health funds among agricultural cooperatives. That decision was re-iterated at the time of the First Agricultural Cooperative Congress held by the Serbian Cooperative Union in 1895. Another approach was developed by creating separate organisational forms from existing agricultural cooperatives by creating health cooperatives involved in healthcare provision in then Serbia and a preferable model for further development until 1949. For this research, we have defined three time frames for historical analysis, each containing certain specificities and deductive reasoning for the historical framework.

The first observed period was from 1844 (the creation of the modern concept of cooperatives in Rochdale) to 1912 (the beginning of the First Balkan War). Within that period, the development of health cooperatives was intercepted by Serbian-Turkish War (1876–1878), during which all potential cooperative development activities were stopped. We acknowledged the first health cooperative development in the Kingdom of Serbia during the first observation period. During that period, health cooperatives, in general, were not widespread (Stamenović,

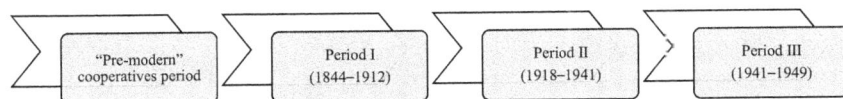

Figure 3.1 Longitudinal framework of significant periods of health cooperatives development in Serbia, created by the author.

2019c). Also, historical data show us that the first health cooperatives were operational even before the First Agricultural Cooperative Congress in 1895. At the Fourth Congress of the Main Union of Serbian Agricultural Cooperatives, held in 1901, it was concluded that the then work of district doctors was changed from a passive to a more active role in healthcare provision (i.e. instead of the patient coming to the doctor, the doctor should provide healthcare throughout the year by visiting patients at their homes; Stamenović, 2018). That had a significant impact, especially in rural areas of Serbia, affecting better access to healthcare and increasing health promotion.

One of the most influential proponents of the health cooperative idea was Dr Gavrilo Kojić, who contributed to establishing the health cooperative movement with tireless efforts. Dr Gavrilo Kojić, born in 1890 in Stari Sivac, located in the present-day municipality of Kula in Serbia, played a significant role in the history of the region. Dr Kojić's collaboration primarily involved experts from the West, with whom he shared universal and progressive goals. However, he also drew inspiration from the experiences of former Serbia and social thinkers like Svetozar Marković, who believed in the possibility of bypassing specific steps in capitalist society to achieve greater equality. Reviewing Kojić's documents reveals his prioritisation of frameworks over steadfast determination, focusing on realising ambitious ideas connected with international health. Through his collaboration with the Cooperative Union of Serbia, Dr Kojić reached a broad cross-section of the population, recognising the cooperative model's ability to inspire trust based on the patriarchal structure of Serbian families. To support his cause, Kojić established an effective information network. The agricultural cooperative members were directly connected to the state, fostering cooperation with ministries and international connections to stay aligned with global trends. That transfer of knowledge, facilitated through state institutions, cooperatives, and their leaders, yielded significant achievements. Moreover, funds provided by the state and international organisations directly reached those in need.

In honour of Gavrilo Kojić's contributions, a health cooperative was established in Stari Sivac after his passing in 1934. That cooperative aimed to provide the village with improved healthcare services of better quality and, most importantly, at more affordable rates. However, with the onset of WWII, the cooperative was forced to close its operations. Beginning in 1921, Gavrilo Kojić assumed the role of office manager at the Association of Health Cooperatives. With the support of the Serbian Child Welfare Association of America (in further text: American Mission), he established the association's initial office in Belgrade. On September 5, 1925, Kojić was elected the Secretary General of the Red Cross. He concurrently held that position alongside his responsibilities at the American Mission until his untimely demise. Kojić's dedication to both organisations aimed to elevate the status of health cooperatives. Although his financial situation did not experience significant improvement through those endeavours, his unwavering commitment to the cause remained at the forefront.

In order to understand the significance of Dr Kojić's work in establishing the first health cooperatives and advancing the health cooperative movement on an international scale, it is crucial to delve into the context that necessitated innovative solutions in healthcare provision. The initial discussions regarding the formation of health cooperatives emerged during the First Congress of the Association of Agricultural Cooperatives in 1895. During that time, hospital funds were first introduced within agricultural cooperatives to provide healthcare services. Mass health cooperatives were introduced at the same Congress, proposing that healthcare and social protection issues of rural populations could be addressed through cooperatives based on agricultural cooperative principles. The primary objective was establishing cooperatives to facilitate mutual assistance during illness.

During the Fourth Congress of Serbian Agricultural Cooperatives in 1901, a decision was reached to re-evaluate the work of county doctors. Rather than patients travelling to doctors for medical care, doctors would travel to designated areas throughout the year to provide healthcare services. That shift in the approach aimed to improve healthcare access in rural regions. Historical documents also highlight the discussions preceding the establishment of the first health cooperatives, particularly concerning the inclusion of medical professionals in those cooperatives and defining their relationship with the cooperatives and their new status. While acknowledging the need for cooperatives to address the interests of those professionals fully, it was advocated for their acceptance as members since the law allowed them to join agricultural cooperatives. It was also emphasised that rejecting their participation could result in a hostile attitude towards the cooperative, suggesting acceptance and collaboration instead. Thus, the concept of mass health cooperatives began to take shape in the late 19th century. Those proposed cooperatives aim to address the rural population's healthcare and social care needs by adopting a cooperative model. Additionally, the suggested change in the role of district doctors, providing healthcare services in specific areas, aimed to enhance healthcare access for rural communities. Regrettably, Dr Kojić's premature death at 37 left his work unfinished, depriving us and many other people of further elaboration and development of his ideas. The significance and universality of the themes raised by Dr Kojić in his 1923 address to the League of Nations (Kojić, 1923) were ahead of time, and his progressive plan encompassed several crucial steps. Firstly, the global implementation of health cooperatives tailored to individual needs and programs, including creating a "health army" in the United States to revitalise world health. Secondly, they mentioned establishing an international Association of Health Cooperatives to undertake the essential responsibilities of national associations, fostering close collaboration with other global organisations. Before that, a professional minimum health standard would be established, outlining health subjects, educational institutions, and health services. That standard would ensure cooperative distribution, tax and customs exemptions, and compensation for owner grievances (Kojić, 1922).

The production of healthcare materials and equipment would adhere to a single international minimum standard based on hygienic and necessary regulations, ideally utilising cooperative principles or alternative non-profit methods. Implementing this plan would require substantial financial resources, which could be obtained through international charitable and humanitarian efforts. The capital invested in this "most important business of any nation," as Dr Kojić called it then, would likely attract generous investment from progressive sources, allowing for a broad consumer-oriented organisation. Governments would play a pivotal role in determining their level of participation and citizens' capital investment to ensure significant international implications of the plan.

The second historical observation period in the development of health cooperatives is from 1918 (end of WWI) to 1941 (beginning of WWII). The Kingdom of Serbia was transformed into the Kingdom of Serbs, Croats, and Slovens from 1918 until 1929, when it became the Kingdom of Yugoslavia. During that period, there was a growth trend in the development of health cooperatives. Before WWII, approximately 100 health cooperatives were developed, with around 70 health stations on the territory of Serbia. The first healthcare cooperatives after WWI were established in 1921, and until WWII began, their number progressively increased. Health cooperatives in Serbia are considered the first modern health cooperatives developed globally (Stamenović, 2020).

According to foreign sources such as UN research (1997) and the work of Johnston Birchall (among others), health cooperatives in Serbia (later Yugoslavia) were instrumental in providing affordable healthcare in many rural areas worldwide. The health cooperative in Požega, founded in 1921, was the first recorded health cooperative in the world that operated according to the principles of modern cooperatives (Johnston, 2011). The success in the work of that association and those that followed that example contributed to the development of the health cooperative movement, which spread its influence to other countries of the world (UN, 1997).

The health cooperative in Požega became a model for other health cooperatives on a global level, thanks to its efficiency in providing affordable healthcare to the local population. That cooperative approach to healthcare delivery contributes to increased community involvement in decision-making and patient empowerment. In addition, health cooperatives successfully overcame challenges such as lack of funding and access to healthcare in rural areas, making healthcare accessible and effective for the wider community. Also, with the number of cooperatives, the number of health services provided by healthcare cooperatives increased. Structural and accelerated development of healthcare cooperatives can be noticed since 1922, and their number continuously grew until the beginning of WWII.

By 1929, the healthcare cooperatives covered 420 villages and about 300,000 inhabitants, and the area of one cooperative numbered about 6,000 inhabitants. The situation improved over time in the context of the number of cooperatives and the financial situation of healthcare cooperatives, and in 1923 there were 55.4% of patients per 100 cooperative family members, while by 1928, that percentage dropped to 22.5%. Cooperatives increased their assets with minor contributions from the cooperative members and the savings they made yearly.

In 1935, 108 healthcare cooperatives and 69 health stations were established; in 1936, there were 112 healthcare cooperatives and 74 health stations. Thus, the number of healthcare cooperatives and health stations (as well as the number of cooperative doctors) increased steadily between the two wars. The development of health cooperatives was followed by adequate financial management and savings of healthcare cooperatives for future investments, which will be discussed later (in the later text, we will show a tabular display of data with its characteristics).

Specific legal solutions from the 19th century onwards always regulated the cooperative movement in Serbia. Initially, the regulations were related to the work of active agricultural cooperatives because there were most of them. They were the first to experience a severe level of development. Health cooperatives came later, and the regulation dedicated exclusively to health cooperative activity was adopted only in the 1930s of the 20th century. The basic principles of the work of health cooperatives were based on the Law from 1889, passed by Serbian King Aleksandar I Karađorđević. Until 1930, health cooperatives on the territory of Yugoslavia functioned following the principles of the Law on Agricultural Cooperatives, and on December 19, 1930, the Law on Health Cooperatives was finally approved. A year later, additional clarification was issued regarding implementing the Law on Health Cooperatives. In 1949, the Basic Law on Cooperatives was amended, and health cooperatives were abolished and integrated into the public health system of the Federal Republic of Yugoslavia.

The third period of historical analysis is the period from the beginning of WWII (1941) up to 1949 when health cooperatives were included in the public health system of the federal National Republic of Yugoslavia. At the beginning of WWII, all activities were interrupted until the end of the war when health cooperatives were re-initiated (1945). Later, as previously stated, in 1949, healthcare cooperatives were incorporated into the public health system and subsequently abolished.

Organisation, characteristics, and financing of health cooperatives in Serbia

Health cooperatives are classified as consumer cooperatives that base their business on buying and selling, such as cooperatives that generate income through their services and goods. Health cooperatives were engaged in the sale of

Table 3.1 Number of health cooperatives and members in the Kingdom of Yugoslavia (1922–1936)

Year	Number of cooperatives	Number of cooperative health stations	Number of health cooperatives members	Number of shares	Membership payments	Number of health cooperative doctors	Number of health cooperative pharmacies
1922	10	10	-	-	110	10	10
1923	13	12	6.432	6.432	146.727	12	12
1924	17	14	8.892	8.892	216.393	14	14
1925	21	16	10.476	10.476	293.102	16	16
1926	28	20	13.139	13.139	411.029	20	20
1927	30	22	14.527	14.527	479.059	22	22
1928	43	32	17.518	17.518	573.431	32	32
1929	53	38	18.119	18.119	678.733	38	38
1930	59	41	19.862	19.862	792.136	42	41
1931	67	48	31.954	31.954	981.892	49	46
1932	70	50	35.417	35.417	1.042.411	52	48
1933	90	59	48.375	48.375	1.021.534	62	54
1934	100	64	56.645	56.645	1.141.122	67	59
1935	108	69	61.064	61.064	1.232.663	75	61
1936	112	74	-	-	-	80	63

Source: Created by the author.

Table 3.2 Development of health cooperatives with an increasing number of cooperatives and number of medical doctors

Year	Number of health stations	Number of health cooperative doctors	Health cooperative pharmacies
1934	64	67	59
1935	69	75	61
1936	74	80	65
1937	81	91	69

Source: Created by the author.

medical and hygiene equipment. In addition, they also sold medicines, vaccines, and veterinary goods, considering that healthy food is one of the foundations of health in rural areas. Furthermore, services are provided in healthcare, prevention and curative, professional engineering, and other assistance for growing adequate varieties of plants and animals. Those goods were available to members of the cooperative and those who were not, although the prices were slightly higher in that case. As the prices of those products were significantly lower than the market prices, it is clear that the health cooperatives received a large number of those who did not support them, primarily from the ranks of private doctors' offices and traders who formed their prices on the more or less free market of that time. Healthcare cooperatives were non-profit organisations of that time, organised exclusively to achieve the interests of their cooperative members following international cooperative principles.

For example, in 1936, the average price of a medical examination in private practice was 20 dinars, while the average price in a health cooperative was seven dinars. From this, there is apparent economic benefit leading to the success of the health cooperatives at that time and a large number of members. At the same time, private practice views on health cooperatives were noted moving towards the direction of anti-dumping (Zdravstveni pokret – Zdravlje, 1936). Also, health cooperatives provided about 30% discount on medicines, and a significant number of services were entirely free for cooperative members.

We can define health cooperatives as those with limited liability according to the type of liability and degree of risk. These health cooperatives consisted of the following organisational and management bodies: Assembly, board of directors, and board for supervision. Following the planned organisational structure, each health cooperative had a doctor, a secretary, a treasurer, and a nurse as a minimum. Patients were treated within the health stations with their own outpatient clinic, pharmacy, and hospital with hospital beds. In addition to health stations, there were organised cooperative health centres, which began to be established in 1929 to provide adequate curative and preventative services (US Government Printing Office, 1943). Diagnostic devices were provided

Table 3.3 Number of health cooperatives and members in the Kingdom of Yugoslavia (1936–1938)

Year	Number of health cooperatives	Number of members	Number and amount of payments for cooperative share	
			In cooperative	*in Union*
1936	112	56,442	605 62.814 257.873 dinars	1.374.038 dinars
1937	127	61,249	621 61.455 277.777 dinars	1.494.189 dinars
1938	134	65,586	653 70.007 276,277 dinars	1,612,576 dinars

Source: Created by the author.

following modern medicine of the time and included an X-ray machine and a microscope (Dragić, 1975).

Interestingly, showing a significant level of understanding of the requirement for diversification in society, the Cooperative Movement founded the Cooperative Youth, as well as the Cooperative Women as sections that contained not only educational content related to the professional aspects of agriculture and health but also represented the "spirit of the village" where young people gathered and reached a higher degree of emancipation through association (Zdravstveni pokret – Zdravlje, 1936).

To a certain degree, this research also shows the transmission of the health cooperatives (or certain elements of that organisational form) model from Serbia to other countries. Also, in the archival documents of other countries, we came to certain conclusions regarding the transfer of the health cooperative movement in the world or some of its elements. For example, the development of Japanese Koseiren cooperatives had a similar approach and was developed much later in the 1930s, although initial health cooperatives were developed in the time of 1920s. Another example connected to Japan is related to the forming of Japan Heath Cooperative Alliance after the visit to the Kingdom of Yugoslavia in 1936, where a similar alliance on a national level already existed. Considering that Japan has a long history of cooperatives (please refer to the section: Japan), there were also significant other influences affecting forming and further development of health cooperatives in Japan.

Another example is India, with the documentation archived about the opening of a pilot project in many thousands of villages in India that should contain health cooperatives based on the model developed in the Kingdom of Serbia (i.e. the Serbian model of health cooperatives). In addition, Poland is another country where we discovered a similar approach and data in both countries (Serbia and Poland), which mention the historical influence of the health cooperative movement from Serbia (please refer to the section: Poland).

For the development of health cooperatives in Serbia, the American Mission from the United States had great importance after WWI on several occasions. It helped the health cooperative movement in Serbia financially in the past. In addition, there are numerous examples of archival texts about visits to the cooperative union of Yugoslavia by delegations from Great Britain, Germany, the United States, India, China, Japan, Romania, Bulgaria, and other countries to determine the ways of functioning of these organisations not only to help them in further development but also to transfer knowledge to those countries.

The health cooperative movement is not developed in the Republic of Serbia today. Namely, since its closure in 1949, health cooperatives have not massed, nor have there been significant initiatives to make this happen until recently. Although the Law on Cooperatives from 2015 defines the possibility of establishing health cooperatives, an important practical question is which health cooperatives could function and how (Official Gazette of the RS, 2015). Therefore, on January 27, 2020, the Initiative for the establishment of health cooperatives was submitted to the National Assembly of the Republic of Serbia, which showed that in today's Serbia, there is both the need and the desire for health workers, scientists, but also necessary – local, national, and international organisations to address the issue of health cooperatives. The Initiative had the support of international apex organisations and was submitted for the public hearing, expecting further support in adopting an adequate legal framework (Stamenović & Sevarlić, 2020). The objectives include highlighting the legal framework that governs the operations of cooperatives and health institutions to facilitate the creation and functioning of diverse business models for modern health cooperatives. These models would be governed by existing laws such as the Law on Cooperatives (Official Gazette of RS, 112/2015), the Law on Health Care (Official Gazette of the RS, No. 25/2019), the Law on Health Insurance (Official Gazette of the RS, No. 25/2019), the Rulebook on Detailed Provisions for Performing Health Activities in Health Care Institutions and Other Forms of Health Care (Official Gazette of the RS, No. 25/2019), and other relevant laws and regulations (Official Gazette of the RS 16/2018).

Furthermore, the Initiative aims to provide recommendations to the Government of the Republic of Serbia on the importance of developing this form of association. It proposes considering forms of public-cooperative partnership and seeking governmental support in establishing a health cooperative movement in the Republic of Serbia. The primary objective of this movement would be to enhance the quality and accessibility of healthcare at the national level. Additionally, the Initiative identifies desired changes in the healthcare system of the Republic of Serbia, which, like many other systems, faces challenges related to sustainability and further development. Numerous media outlets in the Republic of Serbia, but also globally, have reported on this

Initiative, and they say that the further unfolding of events will be seen with the hope that after the Covid-19 pandemic, the necessary conditions will be met for the continuation of work on the formation of these organisations.

Croatia

Healthcare system development in Croatia

The establishment of modern healthcare principles in Croatia can be traced back to 1874 when the Law on the Organization of Health Services in Croatia and Slavonia was enacted. During that time, Croatia and Slavonia boasted 186 mid-wives, 105 doctors, and 88 paramedics, with approximately 50% residing in urban areas. This resulted in a doctor-to-population ratio of one doctor per 6,111 inhabitants. Although the Law did not address the health needs of rural areas or the provision of municipal doctors, it played a pivotal role in shaping the future development of healthcare and the composition of healthcare professionals. Moreover, in Dalmatia and Istria, healthcare was regulated by provincial laws, which remained in effect until 1918. By 1905, Dalmatia reached 142 doctors and 229 midwives, while at the end of the 19th century, Istria had 70 doctors, 3 paramedics, and 230 midwives. In 1906, healthcare in Croatia and Slavonia underwent a reorganisation with the implementation of the Law on Health Care, emphasising the importance of preventive measures in preserving public health. A prominent figure in this transformative period was Andrija Štampar, who assumed the position of head of the Ministry of Public Health in 1919 (The Miroslav Krleza Institute of Lexicography, n.d.). Štampar spearheaded a comprehensive health reform based on social-medical principles to organise the health service. Notably, Štampar pioneered the concept of primary healthcare as an institutional form, blazing a trail globally.

Under Štampar's guidance, various healthcare facilities were established, including hygiene institutes, public health centres, school polyclinics, infant dispensaries, anti-malarial and bacteriological stations, anti-tuberculosis facilities, and clinics dedicated to preventing and treating venereal diseases and trachoma. Those far-reaching reforms left an enduring impact on the healthcare landscape of Croatia.

The roots of organised health insurance in Croatia can be traced back to the 1920s. Throughout the years, numerous reforms and changes have taken place, affecting the name and organisational structure of health insurance institutions. Yet, the underlying objective has remained constant: to ensure the well-being of insured workers.

During the Kingdom of Serbs, Croats, and Slovenes, the National Treasury was established in Zagreb to support sick workers and provide insurance against accidents. Operating from 1922 to 1941, it was known as the Central Office for Workers' Insurance and covered social insurance for workers across

Table 3.4 Demographic characteristics in the Kingdom of Serbs, Croats, and Slovenes (1918–1929), later the Kingdom of Yugoslavia (1929–1941)

1926	12.986.796	35.3	18.8	16.5
1927	13.180.709	34.2	20.9	13.3
1928	13.377.523	32.7	20 3	12.3
1929	13.577.272	33.3	21 8	12.2
1930	13.780.006	35.5	18.9	16.5
1931	13.985.765	33.6	19.7	13.8
1932	14.197.598	32.8	19.1	13.6
1933	14.406.546	31.3	16.9	14.4
1934	14.621.663	31.4	17	14.4

Source: Created by the author.

the country. At that time, medical care in Croatia primarily relied on private means. However, in the 1920s, the government recognised the need to establish a public healthcare system, especially in rural areas where more than 80% of the population resided. Notably, Professor Andrija Štampar, who later became the inaugural president of the World Health Assembly in 1946, played a crucial role in introducing various public health services during the 1920s and 1930s, including establishing primary healthcare centres.

In 1922, health insurance was introduced through three separate private organisations, making Croatia's schemes. These insurance programs also included healthcare providers. Later, Croatia managed its healthcare services through the Ministry of Health as a federal state within the Socialist Federal Republic of Yugoslavia. In 1945, mandatory health insurance was implemented, covering a majority of the population and financed through income-related contributions and state funding. Private medical practices were significantly reduced, except for dental practices, in line with socialist ideology.

Following WWII, all existing social insurance institutions were merged, regardless of the insurance branch or the individuals covered. The Central Institute for Social Insurance and Land Institutes for Social Insurance were established and operated until January 1, 1947, when the State Institute for Social Insurance took over their operations. In the early 1950s, another reorganisation of social insurance providers occurred (Croatian Health Insurance Fund, 2023). The Social Insurance Institute of the People's Republic of Croatia and the City Social Insurance Institutes were established and managed by insured individuals through their representatives. Social insurance funds were created to fulfil the purpose of insurance. Within the Social Insurance Institute of the Republic of Croatia, the Pension Insurance Fund, Children's Allowance Republic Fund, and Health Insurance Fund at the district and city levels were established.

From January 1, 1963, the Republic Institute for Social Insurance and communal social insurance institutes provided health and pension insurance. In 1971, pension and disability insurance were separated from social insurance. The Workers' Health Insurance Association and the Farmers' Health Insurance Association were established as health insurance carriers, which replaced the previous communal associations for social insurance for workers and farmers. Temporary health insurance associations for workers and temporary associations for health insurance for farmers were also established in 1972. From 1974, health insurance operated through a self-governing community of interest called the Self-governing Community of Interest in Health Insurance and Health Care, covering the entire area of Croatia. This structure remained in place until September 1, 1990, when the Croatian Institute for Health Insurance was established. It aims to fulfil the needs of workers, citizens, and society in terms of health and healthcare rights guaranteed by the constitution and the Law. The 1990s brought significant normative reforms and the impact of war events, leading to further healthcare and insurance reforms.

Since August 21, 1993, the Croatian Institute for Health Insurance has been responsible for health insurance, taking over the responsibilities of the previous Republic Health Insurance and Health Care Fund of Croatia. It continues to operate under its current name, ensuring the rights and obligations of compulsory health insurance for all insured persons based on principles of reciprocity, solidarity, and equality (Croatian Health Insurance Fund, 2014).

Croatia's accession to the European Union (EU) in 2013 necessitated alignment with EU legislation. In 2017, the government adopted the National Reform Program to create a financially sustainable health system. The program encompasses a hospital restructuring plan to improve quality, health outcomes, patient satisfaction, and long-term rationalisation of the hospital sector. Subsequently, in 2018, the Parliament approved a new Health Care Act that primarily regulates services offered by community health centres and expands the provision of palliative care (Croatian Health Insurance Fund, 2013).

The 2018 Health Care Act is the primary legal framework governing the Croatian health system. The Ministry of Health serves as the overseer of the health system, with responsibilities including health policy development, planning and evaluation, public health programs, and regulation of capital investments for publicly owned healthcare providers. Publicly funded health services adhere to the principles of comprehensiveness, continuity, accessibility, and universality.

Comprehensiveness entails covering all aspects of healthcare, ranging from health promotion to palliative care. Accessibility is regulated to ensure equitable access to health services, including the appropriate distribution of healthcare institutions and professionals. Primary healthcare addresses the principle of comprehensiveness through measures focused on enhancing health, disease prevention, and providing treatment, rehabilitation, and palliative care (Džakula, 2005).

As regional authorities, counties organise, coordinate, and manage primary healthcare services such as health centres, public health services, and public pharmacies (Croatian Health Insurance Fund, 2020). Both general and specialised hospitals fall under their jurisdiction for secondary healthcare. While most primary care practices have been privatised, some continue to operate as publicly owned health centres. Tertiary care services are the responsibility of national authorities, including the Ministry of Health and the Government.

Cooperatives development in Croatia

The historical development of cooperatives, in general, follows a trajectory similar to that outlined in the previous segment concerning the country profile of Serbia. Specifically, it pertains to the records of Dubrovnik in the 12th century and the establishment of family cooperatives within the Venetian Republic, present-day Croatia. In contrast, the period of significant growth for health cooperatives in these regions (1921–1949) occurred during Yugoslavia's existence and possesses supranational characteristics in today's context.

During the 19th century, the first modern cooperatives emerged, encompassing various sectors such as agriculture, savings and credit, and trade. Serving as a precursor to these modern cooperatives, the Croatian Slavonian Economic Society was established in 1841 to foster economic development and education. Notably, in 1862, the first savings and credit cooperative was founded in Pitomača (Croatian Cooperative Union, 2023).

With the decline of feudalism in the late 19th century, Croatia underwent rapid industrial, commercial, and banking development. This era saw the consolidation of capital and the rise of major industrial, banking, and trading enterprises. Unfortunately, this progress came at the expense of workers, peasants, and artisans, as their interests became increasingly marginalised. In particular, the food industry and trade posed challenges for peasants, who received low product prices while urban consumers paid inflated prices. Moreover, peasants and craftsmen encountered obstacles when trying to access loans, and if they could obtain them, the interest rates charged were exorbitant.

In response to their deteriorating economic circumstances, peasants, workers, and craftsmen established cooperatives to enhance their position and safeguard their interests. Peasants, trade cooperatives by artisans, and consumer and purchasing-sales cooperatives by workers formed agricultural cooperatives. As stated before, the modern cooperative movement originated in England with the Rochdale pioneers and this cooperative model subsequently spread to other European countries, including Croatia.

On Croatian soil, the first cooperative, known as "Pitomačka zanatnička zadružnica," was founded in 1862 in Pitomača as a craft cooperative. It continues to operate under the name "The First Trade Savings and Credit Cooperative."

The oldest savings and credit cooperative in Dalmatia was established in 1864 in Korčula (Croatian Cooperative Union, 2023). Cooperatives in Croatia were influenced by cooperative practices imported from Europe and began flourishing in the early 20th century. During this period, cooperatives evolved into a robust economic system that also impacted political movements. Croatia had over 1,500 cooperatives, with approximately 250,000 cooperative members then. The cooperatives continued to thrive between the two World Wars. Peasant cooperatives in Croatia operated under the Central Union of Croatian Peasant Cooperatives in Zagreb, while economic cooperatives were affiliated with the Croatian-Slavonic Economic Society.

Following WWII, cooperatives faced two challenging periods. In the late 1940s, collectivisation was implemented, following the model of the Soviet Union, resulting in the loss of their original characteristics. In the early 1950s, collectivisation was abandoned, which resulted in a resurgence of cooperatives in Croatia. Various cooperatives, including cooperative savings and banking, were established and strengthened. In the 1960s, the cooperative economic system faced marginalisation due to political and legal measures. Cooperative unions, the cooperative banking system, and land, food, and other plants were transferred to state-run agricultural and food industry combines, which became the driving force in agriculture. This situation persisted until the 1990s when around 200 agricultural cooperatives operated in Croatia. Following the establishment of an independent Croatian state in 1990, the new government did not give adequate attention to cooperatives, perceiving them as remnants of the former socialist system. However, the Croatian Parliament passed the Law on Cooperatives in 1995, primarily due to the efforts of the Croatian Agricultural Cooperative Union. Although flawed, the Law provided a foundation for the survival and development of cooperatives in Croatia. However, the Law on Cooperatives in Croatia had significant limitations as it did not provide clear regulations regarding the democratic structure of cooperatives, membership requirements, cooperative ownership, and cooperative audits. Moreover, the Law allowed all employees to become cooperative members and assume management functions contrary to cooperative principles. Given these shortcomings, the Law on Cooperatives failed to facilitate the transformation of cooperatives from companies with social ownership and a dominant role of employees into cooperative societies with cooperative ownership and democratic member influence to the significant degree.

Health cooperatives development in Croatia

In the history of dental practice development in Croatia in 1903, the founding assembly of the Cooperative of Croatian Dentists was held in Varaždin, Croatia. That event signifies the early establishment of health cooperatives within the present-day Republic of Croatia territory.

Later, after WWI, a cooperative health centre was formed in Northern Dalmatia, Croatia, in the town of Zemunik near Zadar. Such centres were established as sub-centres of cooperative unions operational on a more extensive territory (e.g. republic level). These centres were very effective and, in a short period, led to the formation of many new health cooperatives in the territory where they were established.

For example, from 1932 to 1934, the number of health cooperatives for the northern part of the Danube Banovina doubled, while the number of boats in these cooperatives increased from 16,229 to 39,136. Such cooperative sub-unions provided medical services in prevention and curative and dealt with other aspects of social medicine and education. The health cooperative movement implemented medical visits to peasants' homes as an effective form of preventive action, and such examinations could be ordered for ten dinars. In comparison, a visit to the cooperative itself costs six dinars. Additionally, they organised classes for housewives and various educational projects.

Consultation centres for pregnant women, dispensaries for children, and kindergartens were established. In addition, a service related to death insurance was introduced, and in 1934 there were 42 cashiers accepting payments for this type of insurance. Interestingly, the former Yugoslavia cooperative sub-unions published a German cooperative news (Zdravstveni pokret – Zdravlje, 1934).

The public health situation in the Kingdom of Serbs, Croats, and Slovenes was complex, mainly because WWI had just ended, and Serbia had fought all the Serbo-Bulgarian wars even before that (1913/1914). Health institutions were almost non-existent, and the health culture was at a superficial level, as a result of which the death of infants under the age of five was pronounced. That all led to a situation in which the demographic picture was threatened because of the death of soldiers and various epidemics that occurred during that period (e.g. diphtheria and typhus).

Prof. Dr Andrija Štampar was one of the pioneers of health cooperatives of Croatian origin in Yugoslavia. This world-renowned expert, among other things, was elected president of the WHO in 1946. His importance in developing health cooperatives was significant on the national and regional levels in the Balkan countries and internationally. He dedicated his life to the development of health systems around the world and, among other things, worked as a consultant for establishing health cooperatives in the United States and China.

Štampar regularly wrote about his experiences in the world, so he mentioned a case in Oklahoma in the United States that caused a great revolt of the medical chambers. Namely, it is about forming a health cooperative in a farming area of Oklahoma that one farmer founded, and others joined him to have adequate access to healthcare. Therefore, a newly opened health cooperative was formed in the small town of Elk, which provided low prices for medical services (Štampar, 1939a, p. 101). However, private practice doctors did not like it, so continuous pressure was exerted through the chamber, and Štampar states that

Table 3.5 Number of doctors per region in area of Croatia in 1938

Region	Per one medical doctor	
	Population	km²
Zeta	No. of medical doctors	Not applicable
Vardar	65.715	1.135
Primorje	92.947	2.046
Moravian	48.614	968
Drina	62.162	1.008
Danube	4.8	1.232
Sava	5.716	68
Drava	16.054	205

Source: Created by the author.

it was only thanks to the mayor of that city that the cooperative could continue its work. Also interesting is the description of Štampar, in which he mentions the work on the development of health cooperatives in China in Tingghsein near Beijing. Seeing that in rural areas, no more than 30 cents per capita is spent on medical services per year, and in an average village of 100 families, the total annual cost of healthcare does not exceed US$ 50, a new approach to healthcare was formed, taking into account these socio-economic categories and other exogenous factors (Štampar, 1939b, p. 132). More on the development of health cooperatives in the United States and China can be seen in the separate sub-chapters related to these countries.

Štampar also played a significant role in shaping public health perspectives within the institutions of the Kingdom of Serbs, Croats, Slovenes, and the subsequent Kingdom of Yugoslavia. This influence was greatly supported by the Rockefeller Foundation, the American Mission, and the Milbank Memorial Fund (Dugac, 2011, p. 230). Also, Andrija Štampar played a significant role in increasing and exchanging knowledge with the League of Nations Health Organization, with which he closely cooperated. His role in the work of health cooperatives had both conceptual and practical repercussions for developing this segment of the country's public health system at that time. Specific conflicts were known in the relations with the Agricultural Cooperative Union and during the formation of the School of Public Health in Zagreb. However, the positive aspirations of all stakeholders involved, who were dedicated to developing health cooperatives and the overall public health conditions of the population, ultimately prevailed.

During the early 20th century, the cooperative movement gained significant traction in rural areas of Serbia and later in Croatia in establishing health cooperatives. Pavle Zelić and Jovan Miodragović pioneered this field, founding cooperatives in Žegar and Mokro Polje, respectively (area of Knin). These cooperatives aimed to provide affordable health services to the local population, and their success inspired others to follow suit (Stamenović, 2020).

Health cooperatives emerged in various locations from Serbia, dispersing to the wider area of the Kingdom of Serbs, Croats, and Slovenes, including Radapović, Barajevo, Brusnik, Banjani, Ivanča, and on the Croatian island of Hvar. Founders such as Miloš Milenković and Mitar Ljepavić initiated the cooperative in Radanović, Milan Matejić, and Dragoljub Matejić in Barajevo, Dušan Jeremić in Brusnica, Dobrosav Tomašević in Rajković, Aleksandar Paunović and Tihomir Jevtić in Banjani, and Ante Beritić in Vrbosna on Hvar. Milisav Sordović established the cooperative in Velika Ivarča, while Alimpije Bogdanović, a teacher from Klenovac, generously provided his house to the cooperative in Brusnik. Lazar Marić was the founder of the Smokovic cooperative. Thanks to these pioneering initiatives, health cooperatives have become integral to rural life in Serbia and Croatia, vital in providing healthcare services to local communities.

Today, health cooperatives worldwide are growing in popularity as they allow individuals to pool their resources for purchasing health insurance, accessing medical care, and receiving discounts on products and services. In Croatia, the development of regulations concerning health cooperatives is currently underway. In contemporary Croatian society, there is no dedicated legislation governing health cooperatives. However, Article 117 of the Insurance Act acknowledges the cooperative principle for insurance companies and associations that organise themselves following their by-laws to obtain insurance business authorisation from the Croatian Financial Services Supervisory Agency (HANFA). The legal status of a cooperative is generally determined by the applicable laws of the respective country or state and the cooperative entity is registered as such in the appropriate registry. Registration as a cooperative is typically granted upon the correct submission of an application to the competent authority, providing all necessary information regarding the cooperative's structure. Additionally, various general regulations apply to cooperative activities. For instance, the Commercial Code safeguards the assets of a cooperative, including intellectual property such as patents or copyrights. Other provisions ensure the confidentiality of member lists. Moreover, the Cooperatives Act facilitates the registration of both active and dissolved cooperatives. It is anticipated that specific regulations pertaining to health cooperatives will be developed in the future.

Bosnia and Herzegovina

Healthcare system development in Bosnia and Herzegovina

Bosnia and Herzegovina (B&H) faced various challenges and lacked significant healthcare facilities before the Austro-Hungarian military occupation in 1878. Its mountainous location and proximity to countries with different religions and conflicting interests significantly impacted its progress and stability (Karahasanović, 1977, pp. 19–21). At that time, the literacy rate was low, and education primarily took place in madrasas, mosques, and *maktab* schools, primarily among the Muslim population. Epidemics were frequent, and medical treatments and medications were scarce (Mašić, 2004, p. 228). People relied on various healers, fortune tellers, and priests for assistance, while the wealthy sought treatment in Dubrovnik or brought doctors from the city. There were no formal healthcare facilities and hospitals until the latter half of the 19th century, and most of the population received treatment at home (Mašić, 2010, p. 296).

The arrival of the Turks in 1463 brought significant changes to the social and personal lives of the people in B&H. The Turks introduced new state structures and adopted advanced medical knowledge and literature from the Arabs (Hadžović, 1997, pp. 47–50). They emphasised personal hygiene and introduced public baths, with each Muslim household having a private bathroom. Water supply systems were implemented, improving sanitary facilities throughout B&H. By the mid-17th century, there were 56 public baths in 92 towns in B&H, including four in Sarajevo. Public fountains were built for washing before religious observances, and affluent citizens had water brought to their yards. Modern water supply systems were introduced in various cities, including Mostar, Sarajevo, Banja Luka, and Tuzla, providing access to water in significant locations. However, sewage systems developed at a slower pace, with the first sewage system established in Sarajevo in 1896. The Turkish period brought advancements in personal hygiene and sanitation but did not fully prevent the outbreak of diseases that affected the lives of many Bosnians.

Before the Ottoman Era, the health situation in B&H was closely tied to the country's economic and political conditions, primarily influenced by neighbouring countries. Limited documentation exists regarding the predominantly noble and clerical population, but the region was frequently devastated by epidemics, leading to a high patient mortality rate due to a lack of medication. The Franciscans and Jews from Spain played significant roles in educating the population on health matters. Skilled physicians and pharmacists, trained in medical schools from both the East and the West, practised medicine throughout B&H. Unfortunately, there is limited data available on the prevalence and treatment of mental illnesses during the Turkish period.

Upon the annexation of B&H in 1878 by the Austro-Hungarian Monarchy, educated personnel from various fields, including healthcare, were provided to build, manage, and improve all aspects of life in the region. Inherited healthcare professionals and staff from Vienna, Budapest, Bern, Paris, Prague, and other cities in the Monarchy played a vital role in treating the population, providing healthcare services, and addressing prevalent diseases. This necessitated the establishment of a robust healthcare system in both towns and villages, the implementation of adequate legislation, the construction of hospitals and health facilities, and the employment of well-educated staff.

The first healthcare institutions and medical professionals emerged during the 16th to the 19th centuries, preceding the establishment of Vakuf hospitals in five Bosnian-Herzegovinian cities: Sarajevo, Tuzla, Mostar. Travnik, and Banja Luka. During this period, the population in B&H primarily relied on medicines and herbs for treatment. Some of the documents found were translations of medical manuscripts from other languages, including Arabic manuscripts on Avicennian medicine. Among the practitioners were barbers who also served as surgeons and healers who diagnosed and prescribed alternative medicine. Pharmacy practice in the region began as early as the 11th century when monks in Monte Cassino, Italy, started engaging in medicine. This coincided with the emergence of one of Europe's oldest medical schools in Salerno, Italy, which greatly influenced the development of medicine, pharmacy, and overall health in the 12th century. Numerous works from that period were translated into the local languages, incorporating medicinal herbs and the superstitious beliefs prevalent among the population of B&H. These medical texts also encompassed various perspectives on the world, such as astrology, alchemy, and magic. Towards the end of 1910, the State Hospital in Sarajevo was established, and by the beginning of 1918, it was fully functional and operational under the guidance of Ivan Knotz as the National Advisor.

Following WWI, the territory of today B&H became a part of Yugoslavia, and the development of the healthcare system became intertwined with the Serbian and Croatian healthcare systems. After B&H gained independence in 1990, the healthcare system continued to evolve and adapt to meet the changing needs and demands of the population.

Following the war in B&H, the Dayton Peace Agreement in 1995 established the current political system, which designated B&H as a state consisting of two highly autonomous entities: the Federation of Bosnia and Herzegovina (with a population of approximately 2.2 million) and the Republika Srpska (with a population of approximately 1.2 million). Additionally, the self-governing Brčko District of Bosnia and Herzegovina was created in 2000, encompassing around 90,000 inhabitants.

Within the Federation of Bosnia and Herzegovina, there are further divisions into ten cantons, each with its own government. This complex institutional structure involves multiple administrative units, including the state of B&H, the two entities, the cantons, and the Brčko District. Consequently, there are 14 ministries/departments responsible for health and 13 health insurance funds (two at the entity level, one at the district level, and ten at the cantonal level in the Federation of Bosnia and Herzegovina).

This intricate arrangement of governance and administrative bodies reflects the decentralised nature of the healthcare system in B&H. The distribution of responsibilities among these entities presents unique challenges and complexities in coordinating and implementing healthcare policies and services across the country.

Health policy decisions are decentralised to the entity/district level, with each entity and the district having their Laws on Health Care and Health Insurance. The Republika Srpska operates a centralised health system, with the Ministry of Health and Social Welfare of the Government of the Republika Srpska holding critical authority. In the Federation of Bosnia and Herzegovina, the Ministry of Health has more limited responsibilities and primarily coordinates the setting and implementation of health policies across the cantons. The ten cantonal governments are responsible for planning and delivering health insurance and services.

The decentralised and fragmented nature of the health governance structures and the involvement of multiple decision-makers present significant challenges for health policy-making. Cooperation and coordination between different levels of government are limited, thereby hindering the effective reform and implementation of policies. The repeated attempts to adopt a unified strategy for health system reform have failed due to a lack of consensus. Consequently, the fragmented structure and inadequate planning of services have resulted in a lack of person-centredness within the healthcare systems. Furthermore, patients often have limited options for choosing healthcare providers, thus lacking the ability to exercise freedom of choice in their healthcare decisions. The country's healthcare systems are complex, involving 13 health insurance funds and 14 ministries responsible for health matters. The primary source of public funding for healthcare in B&H comes from mandatory health insurance contributions, which are collected and pooled at the entity, district, or canton level.

While the benefits packages are relatively comprehensive, healthcare coverage is not universally accessible, and entitlements differ across the various health systems. As a percentage of GDP, public expenditure on healthcare surpasses the South-Eastern European average and even exceeds that of the EU. Although there has been a consistent decline in recent decades, approximately 30% of health spending in 2019 was funded privately. These private expenditures mainly consist of out-of-pocket payments, primarily used for purchasing medications and therapeutic devices.

Bosnia and Herzegovina face a significant burden of noncommunicable diseases, including high mortality rates from stroke, ischemic heart disease, and an increased cancer incidence in recent years. Tobacco consumption poses a significant public health challenge, and there is still substantial room for implementing stricter tobacco control measures.

The impact of the Covid-19 pandemic also affected the country significantly, challenging the healthcare system and affecting the average life expectancy.

Health cooperatives development in Bosnia and Herzegovina

When examining the historical development of cooperatives in B&H, it is important to note that part of this early development is connected to the regions of Serbia and Croatia. The inception of cooperatives in B&H can be traced back to family or household cooperatives, with agricultural cooperatives gaining momentum towards the end of the 19th and the beginning of the 20th century during the formation of the Kingdom of Serbs, Croats, and Slovenes, of which today B&H was a territory. Similar trends were observed in the initial progress of cooperatives in Serbia and later in Croatia.

Patriarchal lifestyle in rural areas facilitated networking, contributing to the survival of both individuals and communities. Consequently, family or home cooperatives emerged as suitable solutions. Initially, these cooperatives operated within the confines of the family, either on a smaller or broader scale. However, with the advent of capitalism in these regions, these associations became stratified (Stojisavljevic, 1973). Historical evidence suggests that early cooperatives existed during the Middle Ages before transforming into more modern forms during the 19th century. In most instances, these cooperatives focused on producing goods primarily for internal consumption by the cooperative members themselves. Limited engagement with the market occasionally occurred through barter or exchanging goods for money (Puljiz, 1977).

In the 20th century, a modern agricultural cooperative was formed in 1904 in Tolisa under the Seljačka cooperative (with limited liability). However, it is debatable whether these initial cooperatives operated according to the modern cooperative principles established by the Rochdale Pioneers. Another well-known example is the savings and credit cooperative in Sarajevo, founded in 1912 (Patton, 1928, pp. 129–131).

During the development of the Kingdom of Serbs, Croats, and Slovenes, and later the Kingdom of Yugoslavia until WWII, agricultural and health cooperatives played an important role in B&H, holding social significance. In B&H, health cooperatives relied on the work of the so-called Sokol cooperatives. Sokol societies also existed in Serbia and have a long-standing tradition. A notable Sokol cooperative reaffirmed as a health cooperative in 1933 and located in Pale near Sarajevo serves as a well-known example. Its establishment aimed to address local health problems, particularly those related to typhus epidemics (Jadovno, 2014). Similar health cooperatives in Bosnia shared the same objectives as the previously mentioned health cooperatives in Serbia and Croatia, encompassing preventive and curative activities, education on healthy living, hygienic and sanitary solutions in households, and the emancipation of the peasant population.

After 1949, health cooperatives ceased operations, and since then, only a few isolated instances of health cooperatives can be found across the entire territory of the successor states of the former Yugoslavia. Furthermore, the cooperative landscape was disrupted by the war in the 1990s, leading to the formation of new cooperative laws. However, unlike the Law in the Republic of Serbia, the current Law on Cooperatives in B&H does not explicitly recognise health cooperatives as a specific form of association.

Slovenia

Healthcare system development in Slovenia

Slovenia is a small, predominantly rural country in Central Europe. It has a population of just over two million people and covers an area of slightly more than 29,000 square kilometres. The country has a rich history and showcases numerous remarkable cultural and historical attributes. However, Slovenia is currently experiencing a growing ageing population, which presents considerable health challenges for the nation.

A high level of cooperation between the public and private sectors characterises the Slovenian healthcare system. The Ministry of Health and Social Care is responsible for providing health and social care services. Additionally, local communities play a role in delivering public healthcare through health centres and local clinics. These local clinics primarily handle outpatient care and conduct minor surgical procedures. Moreover, certain municipalities offer community health services, while private companies are at the forefront of providing home healthcare services commercially. It is worth noting that Slovenia boasts a well-developed private healthcare sector that encompasses both primary and secondary care.

The history of healthcare in Slovenia spans several centuries, with significant transformations occurring over time, often influenced by changes in political regimes. Many aspects of the present healthcare system can be traced back to different periods in Slovenia's past. The foundations of organised healthcare were laid during Slovenia's affiliation with the Habsburg monarchy. In 1784, the first civil hospital in Ljubljana was established, followed by the formation of the Slovenian Medical Association in 1861.

During the Austro-Hungarian Empire from 1867 to 1918, a social health insurance model was implemented, inspired by Bismarck's approach. Initially focusing on work-related injuries, the system expanded in 1889 with the establishment of the first sickness fund in Ljubljana, which later extended its coverage to other cities. Further advancements in Slovenia's healthcare system took place during the Kingdom of Serbs, Croats, and Slovenes (1918–1929) and the subsequent Kingdom of Yugoslavia (1929–1941). In 1919, the Association of Health Insurance Funds was formed, and in 1923, the National Institute for Hygiene was established, along with regional social hygiene institutes, influenced by the ideas of Dr Andrija Štampar.

Additionally, the first Community Primary Healthcare Center (CPHC) was founded in 1926 and has continued its operations (Brown & Fee, 2006, p. 1383). These CPHCs, under the administration of municipalities, were established in Slovenia to ensure equitable access to healthcare without imposing financial hardship on individuals. They represent the earliest manifestations of Universal Health Coverage in the country. Initially, the primary focus of CPHCs was on outreach activities, targeted disease prevention, and maternal and child healthcare. These centres played a crucial role in ensuring access to safe drinking water and food, as well as in investigating and controlling infectious diseases while also promoting health education.

Within a decade of their establishment, the efforts of CPHCs led to a significant reduction in infant mortality rates and the burden of infectious diseases in Slovenia, particularly through childhood vaccinations against diseases like diphtheria and scarlet fever. Presently, 63 CPHCs serve as the primary entry point into the healthcare system, where multidisciplinary teams of professionals address a wide range of healthcare needs.

During the Socialist Federal Republic of Yugoslavia (1945–1991), healthcare facilities in Slovenia were nationalised, resulting in all physicians becoming employees of the state, while private practices were prohibited. Despite these changes, CPHCs continued to offer a range of primary healthcare services, including general practice, paediatrics, care for schoolchildren and adolescents, occupational medicine, pulmonary care, and gynaecology. These centres prioritised maternal and child health as well as dentistry.

In 1955, the state-managed social insurance system was replaced by various health insurance and social insurance schemes linked to different employment types. Since 1972, the Health Insurance Institute of Slovenia (ZZZS), a single state-owned entity, has provided statutory health insurance (SHI) through a unified scheme. With Slovenia's independence in 1991 and the subsequent transition to a free-market economy, the introduction of the Health Care and Health Insurance Act (1992) and the Health Services Act (1992) facilitated the modernisation of the country's healthcare system.

The current framework for SHI in Slovenia is established and regulated by the Health Care and Health Insurance Act (1992), which was updated in 2018, as well as the Health Services Act (1992). These acts ensure universal health insurance coverage, permit the privatisation of services, and delegate certain regulatory and administrative functions to professional associations.

The healthcare system in Slovenia operates at both the national and local (municipal) levels of government. The National Parliament holds primary administrative and regulatory authority and is responsible for determining health policy. It adopts health-related legislation and approves relevant budgets on an annual basis. The Parliamentary Committee on Health plays a role in preparing legislative materials and seeking consensus on health-related matters discussed in Parliament. The Ministry of Health (MoH) governs and leads the healthcare system. It implements legislation, standards, and mechanisms to ensure health and healthcare provision. The MoH formulates health and healthcare policies through the national healthcare plan, oversees procurement for significant investment projects, supervises medicines and medical devices, and implements international agreements. It also defines the master plan for public healthcare providers and regulates the number of students admitted to medicine and health sciences programs. The Ministry of Education, Science and Sport regulates and organises medical and health sciences education and financing (Johansen et al.,2020).

The MoH collaborates on health financing and health insurance matters and owns public healthcare facilities at the secondary and tertiary care levels. Within the MoH, there are two component offices: the Health Inspectorate, which ensures compliance with health and healthcare legislation, and the National Chemicals Office, which assesses and manages chemical-related hazards and risks. The Health Council is the highest professional body, supporting the development of health policy and governance issues, including ethics and medical doctrine. The Agency for Medicinal Products and Medical Devices of the Republic of Slovenia (JAZMP) is affiliated with the MoH. It acts as the official quality control laboratory for medicinal products and devices and serves as the national regulatory body for pharmaceutical products and medical devices. The JAZMP is responsible for pharmacovigilance and maintaining the national database of pharmaceuticals.

At the local level, municipalities have the authority to define the local network of primary care providers and pharmacies. They own CPHCs and local pharmacies, and they grant concessions to private healthcare providers operating within the publicly operated primary healthcare system. Municipalities also make decisions, secure funding for local healthcare infrastructure investments, and provide health insurance contributions for individuals without income, although their capacities are limited.

Other ministries, including the Ministry of Finance, Ministry of Internal Affairs, Ministry of Defense, Ministry of Justice, and Ministry of Public Administration, also play significant roles and have responsibilities that influence health policy, services, and health determinants.

At the local level, municipalities hold the authority to define the local network of primary care providers and pharmacies. They also own CPHCs and local pharmacies. Furthermore, municipalities grant concessions to private healthcare providers who operate within the publicly operated primary healthcare system. In addition to these responsibilities, municipalities make decisions, secure funding for local healthcare infrastructure investments, and provide health insurance contributions for individuals without income, even though their capacities may be limited.

The Health Insurance Institute of Slovenia (ZZZS) is responsible for administering the centralised compulsory health insurance system (SHI). It aligns its work with the National Health Plan and the MoH priorities. ZZZS collects healthcare contributions from employees' payrolls; enters into contracts with healthcare providers, pharmacies, and medical equipment suppliers; monitors health expenditures; and negotiates prices for health services. ZZZS operates through regional branches and local offices. The ZZZS Assembly, which includes representatives from employers, the insured population, retirees, people living with disabilities, and farmers, approves the annual financial plan of ZZZS. This plan, prepared by the MoH and the Ministry of Finance, determines the funding allocated for public healthcare services.

The Slovenian healthcare system is widely acknowledged for its high quality, primarily attributed to the substantial trust patients place in their doctors. Despite Slovenia's small size, the healthcare system consistently delivers according to standards of care while maintaining relatively low costs, positioning the country as an appealing destination for international health tourism.

The main drivers of the growth of health sector activities in the Republic of Slovenia are still related to the expanding coverage of the universal health system. While Slovenia is already a member of the European Health Insurance Card and has ratified the Additional Protocol to the EU Accession Treaty, establishing a comprehensive system of health services, it has also joined the Agreement on the European Economic Area. This decision has formalised a standard health insurance system aligned with the EU. In line with this development, the Slovenian MoH has formulated the National Health Care Strategy 2020–2025.

This strategy outlines four strategic goals for the Slovenian healthcare system: disease prevention and health promotion, ensuring comprehensive care for citizens, enhancing management and operational efficiency, and ensuring equal access to healthcare.

Health cooperatives development in Slovenia

The development of modern cooperatives in Slovenia can be traced back to the 19th century when cooperatives involved in milk and dairy production began to emerge. That was followed by the establishment of cooperatives in the regions of Bohinj and Tolmin, which focused on cheese production. Slovenian farmers gained land ownership after 1848 but still faced high taxes. Slovenian peasants resorted to borrowing funds at high interest rates to address those challenges. A similar situation existed in Croatia. For this reason, the first Slovenian savings and credit cooperative appeared in Lutomer in 1872. In 1883, the First Cooperative Union in Slovenia was established, based on the idea of Michael Vošnjak, which initially included savings and credit cooperatives.

Health cooperatives started their business at the beginning of the 20th century (Avsec & Štromayer, 2015, p. 40–48). After that, they worked to develop health cooperatives in the Kingdom of Yugoslavia and later in the Federative People's Republic of Yugoslavia until the declaration of independence in 1990. The first Law on Cooperatives in today's Slovenia can be considered the Law from 1873, which is still in force in Austria today (Slovenia was part of Austria-Hungary).

Until the 1990s, laws enacted by the Kingdom of Serbs, Croats, and Slovenes, and subsequently the Kingdom of Yugoslavia and Yugoslavia, remained in effect. The first Law after the declaration of Slovenia's independence from Yugoslavia was passed in 1992, and that Law has undergone several changes so far: Cooperatives Act (Official Gazette of the Republic of Slovenia, No. 13/92 of March 20, 1992); Act Amending the Cooperatives Act (Official Gazette of the Republic of Slovenia, No. 7/93 February 4, 1993); Act Amending the Cooperatives Act – ZZad-B (Official Gazette of the Republic of Slovenia, No. 41/07 of May 11, 2007); Cooperatives Act – official consolidated text ZZad-UPB1 (Official Gazette of the Republic of Slovenia, No. 62/07 of July 12, 2007); Act Amending the Cooperatives Act – ZZad-C (Official Gazette of the Republic of Slovenia, No. 87/09 of November 2, 2009); Cooperatives Act – official consolidated text – ZZad-UPB2 (Official Gazette of the Republic of Slovenia, No. 97/09 of November 30, 2009) (Zadružna zveza Slovenije, 2023; PisRS, 2009).

Also, health cooperatives are not explicitly mentioned as one of the solutions to establishing cooperatives. One of the modern examples of organisations contributing to health provision showing cooperative background can be seen through the work of the Health Center Ljubljana, founded in 1967 and connects 25 independent centres in the Ljubljana district. In 1974, this organisation switched to the cooperative system due to advantages in terms of functionality, so cooperatives were founded in every municipality in Ljubljana as well as in the municipality of Grospulje under the name Community Health Center Ljubljana. This organisational model was organised as an institution in 1991 following the new Institutes Act and statutory decision (Zdravstveni dom Ljubljana, n.d.).

In 2016, an initiative was launched in Slovenia aimed at enhancing the social economy. One of the publications that the Government of Slovenia made with CECOP (European Federation of Industrial and Service Cooperatives) is precisely related to strengthening the social sector and health cooperatives. The proposal suggests the formation of workers' cooperatives in sectors where there is a scarcity of certain services or products or where there is a need to bolster a particular industry. Among the examples is the provision of access to primary healthcare, education, and social services, and the expansion of business in healthy food and environmental protection (CECOP – CICOPA Europe, 2016).

Additionally, Slovenia is home to Zadrugator, a cooperative organisation that addresses housing issues and resolves them in line with the cooperative members' interests. This cooperative also provides healthcare services to older individuals who obtain their real estate through the cooperative (Care Cooperative, 2023). Initiatives in Slovenia are showing also that health cooperatives are a type of healthcare provider growing in popularity.

Poland

Healthcare system development in Poland

The first healthcare system in Poland was a traditional rural healthcare system. That system was based on the idea that every individual in the village should be able to receive quality healthcare for free. This traditional system was gradually replaced during the 20th century by Poland's national healthcare system. In 1989, Poland became a republic, and the new government decided to overhaul the country's healthcare system. The result was the introduction of a universal healthcare system that provided all citizens with comprehensive free medical care. More recently, in 2006, the government introduced a partial public/private system to improve the availability and quality of health services for citizens not covered by the mandatory health insurance plan. Although the universal healthcare system has been successful, many structural problems still need to be solved in the country's healthcare system.

Today, the primary healthcare system in Poland is well-developed and provides a wide range of services. The government plays a significant role in providing primary healthcare services. State hospitals provide most primary healthcare services. However, private clinics and hospitals are also available. The government subsidises some medicines and supplies, which, as a result, are affordable. Also, the quality of maternity and paediatric services is efficient.

The fragmented governance of the healthcare system poses challenges to coordination and effectiveness in Poland. The MoH and municipal, county, and regional governments share responsibility for health sector governance. Municipalities oversee primary care, while smaller county hospitals fall under the jurisdiction of counties, and larger regional hospitals are the responsibility of voivodeships. Highly specialised tertiary care providers are supervised by the MoH. The Ministry coordinated also the response to the COVID-19 pandemic. Private facilities primarily offer outpatient care, while public hospitals predominantly provide inpatient care. This fragmentation makes achieving effective coordination across the health system difficult, although recent efforts have been made to improve the situation. The National Health Fund (NHF) acts as the sole purchaser in the social health insurance system, operating through its voivodeship branches to manage to purchase healthcare services. Health expenditure in Poland remains relatively low, accounting for 6.5% of GDP in 2019, compared to the EU average of 9.9%. Additional funding was injected in 2020 to support the health sector during the Covid-19 emergency. Per capita health expenditure in Poland is among the lowest in the EU, amounting to EUR

1,582 (adjusted for purchasing power). Social health insurance contributions from payroll taxes constitute the majority of health funding. Public funding represents 71.8% of total expenditure, below the EU average, while out-of-pocket spending accounts for 20.1% of health spending, primarily outpatient medicines (OECD/European Observatory on Health Systems and Policies, 2021b). Voluntary health insurance (VHI), mainly in group insurance packages provided by employers, covers around 8% of total health expenditure. Interest in purchasing VHI has grown during the pandemic, potentially due to challenges in accessing public health services.

In recent years, efforts have been made to improve allocative efficiency in the Polish health system, including the implementation of health needs maps. However, the contracting process continues to be primarily influenced by existing infrastructure, resulting in an ongoing imbalance between hospital care and outpatient care. Compared to other EU countries, Poland has a relatively high number of hospital beds and low occupancy rates, suggesting a potential overcapacity issue in the hospital sector (Sowada et al., 2022). In order to address this problem, plans are being developed to repurpose some hospital beds for other types of care, such as long-term care beds, which have been in chronic shortage. The generics market in Poland is well-established in the pharmaceutical domain, and generics have a significant market share in Europe. However, cost-effectiveness does not currently play a prominent role in pharmaceutical policy decisions, which may be partly attributed to the relatively low share of public spending on medicines.

Health cooperatives development in Poland

The Polish cooperative movement developed slowly during the 19th century. The cooperative union was founded in 1911 in Warsaw, grew into a national body after the declaration of independence of Poland in 1918, and was the largest union of its kind in Poland until the beginning of WWII. During the communist era of rule in Poland, cooperative capacities were systematically used in targeted areas of importance. After 1989 and the fall of the Berlin Wall, interest in cooperatives almost died out in Poland until recently. The period between the two World Wars (1918–1939) was the most significant for developing health cooperatives.

Today, Poland has five members of the International Cooperative Alliance, but unfortunately, none of the members from Poland deals with health-related activities. The most significant number of cooperatives in Poland are housing cooperatives, and the total number of all cooperatives is 8,917, with about 200,000 employees (coops4dev, 2023d). However, according to the analysis of the structure of social cooperatives, there is an increase in interest in cooperatives with health characteristics. Namely, the healthcare and social assistance category had 8.9% in 2007, before it grew to 9.5% in 2011 and then to 10.6% in 2014, leading to growth until today.

After the formation of agricultural cooperatives and the formation of the Cooperative Union after the end of WWI, there was an increasing interest in various areas of cooperatives. In 1935, the Scientific Institute for Cooperation (founded in 1915) began to consider the possibilities of establishing cooperatives that would have their role in providing healthcare. As a result, the first health cooperative was founded in Markowa in 1936, with 150 member families (Parker, 1943, p. 220). That health cooperative progressed rapidly because of good organisation and the need for adequate healthcare. Therefore, in just six months, it increased its membership to 260 families and provided medical assistance in seven villages with a total of about 12,000 inhabitants. After that success, the health cooperatives expanded, and by 1938, seven more health cooperatives were founded (in Markowa, Gać, Sietesz, Lipnik, Chodakówka, Białoboki, and Husów), which were mainly in charge of about seven villages on average (CKGM, 2023). Polish health cooperatives were not authorised to deal with the sale of medicines, but in some cases, they made certain agreements with pharmacies to provide their members with medicines and other necessities of that type. Those cooperatives dealt with curative, preventive, sanitary, and hygienic aspects of household maintenance and healthy food production. It included a small dispensary, where patients were treated or came for check-ups, a doctor, and a nurse (Parker, 1943, p. 220).

In addition, the very initial development of health cooperatives in Poland was initiated through the work of Ignacy Solarz (founder of the Union of Rural Youth of the Republic of Poland and People's Universities), but the light on the development of Polish health cooperatives, especially the first in Markow, was given by Wyszomirski, Kazimierz who described the development of health cooperatives on a personal example in a book from 1937, that is, at the height of the health cooperative movement in Poland (Kyzomirski, 1927, p. 21). Namely, from his archive, it is concluded that the expert also felt lonely and misunderstood the environment for establishing a health cooperative, just like his predecessors in the territory of Serbia, the United States, and other countries. During numerous courses and conferences, whenever Kazimierc raised the subject of health cooperatives in Yugoslavia with peasants or intellectuals, it ignited enthusiasm among all participants. On the one hand, peasants expressed their reservations, stating that organising such cooperatives in a few years might be possible. Hence, the sense of unity within the village still required improvement. On the other hand, intellectuals, for the most part, were sceptical and doubted whether the Polish countryside could successfully implement such a challenging yet remarkable form of cooperative work. Many believed that finding a doctor willing to serve in rural areas under a cooperative would be highly unlikely. However, those opinions proved to be unfounded. Informed villagers, including peasants, established a health cooperative following the Serbian model later implemented in Yugoslavia. Despite significant challenges, they managed to find a doctor for this pioneering Health Cooperative.

Additionally, Kazimierz expresses his gratitude to Dr Gavrilo Kojić, the initiator and founder of health cooperatives in Serbia. Through the establishment of health and other cooperatives, Kazimierz fulfilled a profound duty and supported many in Poland for whom healthcare was not an option at all, considering the vital necessity of having health cooperatives in every village. According to him, these cooperatives embody both ideological values and the presence of competent doctors. Kazimierz wishes to echo the words of Dr Gavrilo Kojić in Poland, the founder of the health cooperative in Yugoslavia, who emphasised the responsibility of the village to safeguard its health (Kyzomirski, 1927, p. 23).

In 1935, the first health cooperative in Poland was established in Markovo, drawing inspiration from similar cooperatives in the Kingdom of Yugoslavia developed earlier in Serbia. However, while opening the cooperative was relatively easy, the members encountered numerous obstacles. The initiative by peasants and youth from the village of Markova began in 1934 and continued until November 1935, spanning over a year and a half to establish the health cooperative. Eventually, the central committee was formed in Markovo, and regional committees were established in villages associated with the health cooperative. Around 150 cooperative members registered shares, which was crucial in the cooperative's establishment. The shares were valued at ten zlotys, with a registration fee of 50 grosz. During the establishment phase, the cooperative acquired medical equipment, and the members planned to cover the doctor's fees through the cooperative's management, charged from the treatment fees.

Kazimierz Wyszomirski, born in 1902 in Warsaw and passing away in 1965, pioneered the development of health cooperatives in Poland. He was a dedicated Polish activist, educator, and member of the Main Board of the Union of Rural Youth. Wyszomirski played a crucial role as a co-founder, alongside Marian Rapacki, Jan Bonowicz, and Józef Dominka, of the "Gromada" Tourist and Recreation Cooperative. He served as its president from 1937 to 1939. Wyszomirski strongly advocated establishing cooperative health centres in rural regions, recognising their significance in providing accessible healthcare to the community (Tulibacki, 2005, p. 5). He believed that health cooperatives could offer high-quality healthcare to individuals who could not afford it and promote public health through education on the importance of preventive care. His work laid the foundation of the Polish health system, and he is recognised as one of the most influential figures in the history of health cooperatives in Poland.

Another important figure in Poland who wrote about health cooperatives and supported the idea mentioned earlier was Ignacy Solarz (1891–1940). Hailing from a peasant family in Podkarpacie, Solarz pursued studies in agricultural engineering. He volunteered during the Polish-Soviet War and became a Polish People's Party "Piast" member in the early 1920s. However, Solarz's involvement in politics went beyond conventional activities. He served as an agricultural instructor and was pivotal in animating the rural youth movement while initiating numerous educational initiatives. His outlook was greatly influenced by his exposure to Denmark's famous folk universities during a scholarship in 1922.

In 1924, Solarz assumed the director position at the Rural People's University in Szyce near Kraków. He also held positions on the presidium of the Main Board and later became the vice president of the Central Union of Rural Youth. Advocating for the independence of the people's youth from the panacea regime in 1927, he co-organised the Union of Rural Youth of the Republic of Poland. He served as president of the Kielce branch for a year. Solarz actively engaged with the People's Party after the unification of the People's Movement.

When the sanitation authorities closed the institution in Szyce in 1931, he established the Rural Orkney University in Gacia Przeworska, Podkarpacie, together with his wife. Initially operating in rented peasant huts and later in a building constructed through contributions and the efforts of thousands of people, that institution became one of the most famous and dynamic peda-gogical experiments in Polish history.

During the existence of the Second Republic in Poland, there was a thesis about the necessity of a state system to be accessible to the entire population. However, the lack of doctors, especially in rural areas, made it difficult to access healthcare. The reason for this was the lack of doctors and medical staff and insufficient infrastructural development, so the roads did not exist or were in poor condition, making it extremely expensive for doctors to travel to the village. So the prices were formed depending on how far the doctor had to travel (visit within seven km – PLN 15, further – PLN 30 to 100, childbirth – PLN 100 to 150 and more) (Prętki, 2011).

Kazimierz Wyszomirski and Franciszek Ksawery Cieszyński spoke and wrote about those problems and stated that, in addition to the fact that Poland at that time (the 1930s of the 20th century) was one of the countries in the world with a minimal number of doctors and medical personnel per population, there were also legal problems by which laws concerning the health of the popu-lation almost bypass the rural areas (Wyszomirski, 1939, p. 76). The idea of health cooperatives was promoted by K. Wyszomirski, whose stay in Yugoslavia due to health cooperatives was written about by numerous scientific and profes-sional journals in the fields of cooperatives, economics, politics, as well as other media, both at the national and at the local level.

In addition, K. Wyszomirski described his observations regarding the health cooperatives in Yugoslavia, and he was fascinated by the fact that the peasants told him that the health cooperatives were "like their child" for them; "they built everything with their own hands" and "doctors are their guardian angels." There is also ample evidence of such an emotional approach to the construction of health cooperatives in the villages of Yugoslavia in the archives of the *Journal of the Cooperative Movement of Yugoslavia*. Although, in today's sense, such statements might sound like propaganda, the rural population was truly inspired by joint work in achieving their interests.

We will mention another archival text about the arrival of Wyszomirski, who sent his associates to study the health cooperative movement in Yugoslavia in 1934. During their visit, they visited health cooperatives in present-day Serbia (Slovac and Banjani) as well as in present-day Croatia (Northern Dalmatia) (Zdravstveni pokret – Zdravlje, 1934, p. 4). His impression was that Rochdale English or Raiffeisen German organisations only partially advanced the cooperative idea in Yugoslavia. Before Raiffeisen's credit union in Anhausen, a Slovak credit union existed in Sobotisht, showcasing the early roots of the cooperative movement. Furthermore, Wyszomirski explained that while Yugoslav peasants were pioneering health cooperatives, Polish peasants were forging new types of cooperatives, such as timber cooperatives. The profound essence of *zadrugarstwo*, which signified mutual assistance, served as the primary characteristic of the Yugoslav rural nation, the fundamental source of health cooperatives, and the overall development of the cooperative movement in Yugoslavia. Mutual aid during hardship, work, emergencies, or prolonged poverty was an intrinsic part of their daily lives, shaped by the challenging natural and historical conditions they faced. Those intrinsic, unwritten cooperatives that were integral to the lives of Yugoslav peasants had the potential to become a crucial factor in Yugoslavia's progress and serve as a Slavic model for establishing a new world, especially in the aftermath of the inhumane attempts of Hitler in Europe and the Mongol efforts in Bolshevik Russia. As he said, the aftermath of the war (WWI) in Yugoslavia revealed the pressing need for improved healthcare, providing fertile ground for the cultivation of the creative force of Slavic *zadrugarstwo* (Wyszomirski, 1939, p. 77). Despite the charitable endeavours of the American Mission and the provision of accessible "Health Homes," the "Zdravstvena Zadruga," (the Health Cooperative), emerged as the dominant force in the country.

As Wyszomirski, explained, Dr Gavrilo Kojić, a native son of the village and inheritor of the peasant life idea, played a pivotal role in that movement. While working for the American Mission, he felt out of place within the mainstream approaches and returned to his roots, recognising it as the most fitting path. Further, Wyszomirski, mentioned that Kojić embodied the centuries-old Slavic spirit of cooperation in a modern form, establishing health cooperatives as their creator (Solarz, 1938). Through the window of an American institution, Kojić caught sight of a sign across the street in Belgrade that read "Union of Agricultural Cooperatives," rekindling his spirit and giving rise to a remarkable movement not only for his fellow countrymen but also for the world.

In Serbia, the first official Health Cooperative after WWI was established on November 21, 1921. The initial stages of the first cooperative and subsequent ones were fraught with challenges. Doctors, pharmacists, and even some authorities opposed their existence and waged confronted them. However, the deeply rooted nature of the idea within the people made it easier to persevere.

The urgent need to address the dire state of public health in post-war Yugoslavia significantly contributed to the movement's growth.

Cooperatives formed alliances and represented a significant portion of the nation. The value of health cooperatives gradually gained recognition among the sceptical professional intelligentsia. Within a year, there were already ten cooperatives with over 5,000 members. The momentum continued to surge over 38 years, transforming from a weak stream into an unstoppable river. Unfortunately, Kojić did not live to witness this resurgence as he passed away at the age of 37 on the brink of the movement's strong revival, almost as if his sacrifice had laid the groundwork for the idea. Health cooperatives came to the fore in Poland less than 20 years after the end of WWI. In that period, health centres were the only pillars of the Polish rural health system, and the problem with hygiene, education of the population, cultivation of healthy branches, epidemics, and lack of doctors and medical personnel was big one (Wyszomirski, 1939, p. 78). However, health cooperatives found their way after the persistence of K. Wyszomirski, and the primary challenge identified was the insufficient cooperation between the state administration and the administration of that era.

Currently, health cooperatives do exist in Poland, although their expansion has yet to reach the significant extent seen in some other European countries. While Poland has a long history of cooperative movements, including health cooperatives, the development and growth of such cooperatives in the healthcare sector have faced particular challenges. The healthcare system in Poland is primarily based on public funding and operated by the National Health Fund (NFZ), which has limited the opportunities for private health cooperatives to thrive. One of the factors contributing to the relatively slower expansion of health cooperatives in Poland is the dominant role of public healthcare institutions, such as state-owned hospitals and clinics. The well-established public healthcare system has created a strong foundation, making it challenging for private cooperatives to compete and gain a significant market share. Additionally, the regulatory environment and reimbursement policies in Poland may only sometimes be conducive to the growth of health cooperatives, potentially limiting their ability to offer innovative services and attract a larger membership base.

Romania

Healthcare system development in Romania

Public healthcare emerged in 1700 when foreign doctors were brought in to provide medical care for the upper class in Romania. Philanthropists established their charity hospitals, offering free healthcare to the peasants. On July 4, 1876, the National Red Cross Society was founded, with Dimitrie Ghica serving as the first president until 1897. The Romanian Red Cross is the only humanitarian organisation in the country with a functional network consisting of 47 subsidiaries, 1,996 under subsidiaries, and 1,307 commissions. Hospitals in Romania have a rich historical background. Some notable ones include: Colțea Hospital in Bucharest, constructed between 1701 and 1703; Pantelimon Hospital, established in 1733; and St Spiridon Hospital in Iași, founded in 1755 and described in a 1757 document as the largest Hospital in Moldavia and Wallachia. It stands as the second-largest Hospital in Romania today.

Philanthropic Hospital was built during the Russian occupation between 1806 and 1812. It had a capacity of 70 beds and has remained operational to date. Brâncovenesc Hospital was opened in October 1838 as a free clinic providing vaccines and medical tests at no cost. Unfortunately, due to urban development, the hospital building was demolished in 1984, ceasing its activities. Vaccination has been practised in Romania since the 17th century, initially using rudimentary methods such as dipping newborns into cow milk from cows with smallpox. However, more modern vaccination techniques have been introduced with advances in medical knowledge. Since 1800, regular smallpox shots have been administered to children. Since the 19th century, it has been mandatory for all children in Romania to get vaccinated (when vaccines become available throughout the period until today) against hepatitis B, tuberculosis, tetanus, poliomyelitis, rubella, and diphtheria. These vaccines are provided free of charge and can be administered by authorised paediatric healthcare professionals. Additional optional vaccines, including flu shots, are free of charge every two years.

Romania has one of the lowest life expectancies in Europe, and the Covid-19 pandemic has affected the progress made since 2000. That crisis underscored the need to strengthen primary care, preventive services, and public health, as the current health system relies heavily on inpatient care. Barriers to access include shortages in the health workforce and high out-of-pocket spending. However, the pandemic prompted the development of electronic information systems to better manage strained health resources, offering potential avenues for strengthening future healthcare systems (Vlădescu et al., 2016).

The Romanian health system is organised at two primary levels, national and district, mirroring the administrative division of the country, with the national level responsible for setting general objectives and the district level responsible for ensuring service provision according to the rules set at the central level (Framework Law no. 195/2006, 2006). The system remains highly centralised, with the MoH being the central administrative authority in the health sector responsible for the stewardship of the system and its regulatory framework. The MoH also exerts indirect control over some functions that have been recently decentralised to other institutions and that are only just beginning to assert regulatory functions, such as the National Authority for Quality Management in Health Care. District public health authorities represent the MoH at the local level. The other key actor at the central level is the National Health Insurance House, which administrates and regulates the social health insurance system. This organisational structure has been in place since 1999, replacing the Semashko model. The NHIH is also represented at the district level by district health insurance houses. A "Framework Contract" lays down the definition of the statutory benefits package and contains information on the terms under which patients can obtain services, provider payment mechanisms, the relationship between providers and the DHIHs, terms of contracts (e.g. quality criteria for providers), providers' rights and obligations, and transposition of EU regulations with relevance to healthcare provision. It is adopted every two years and forms the basis for individual contracts between the DHIHs and health service providers.

Between 2000 and 2019, life expectancy in Romania increased by over four years but experienced a temporary decline of 1.4 years in 2020 due to the impact of Covid-19. There is a significant gender gap, with women outliving men by almost eight years. Cardiovascular diseases are the leading cause of mortality, while lung cancer is the most common cause of cancer-related deaths. Nearly half of all deaths in Romania can be attributed to risky health behaviours. The population reports higher alcohol consumption and unhealthy diets compared to the EU averages, although adult obesity rates are the lowest in the EU. Smoking rates among adults are slightly lower than the EU average. These risk factors are more prevalent among men than women. Among adolescents, there are high rates of overweight, obesity, and smoking, which have been steadily increasing over the past two decades (OECD/European Observatory on Health Systems and Policies, 2021a). While health spending in Romania has increased over the past decade, it still ranks as the second lowest in the EU in terms of both GDP share and per capita expenditure. In 2019, approximately 44% of health spending was allocated to inpatient care, the highest proportion among EU countries. Although the public share of health spending aligns with the EU average, out-of-pocket payments exceed the EU average, primarily driven by outpatient pharmaceutical costs.

Health cooperatives development in Romania

Cooperative ideas began to develop significantly at the beginning of the second half of the 19th century, thanks to Romanian students and scientists from abroad. First, the banking sector (savings and credit cooperatives) began to develop to support rural areas' development, which was contributed to by the laws of 1873 and 1881 (i.e. Rural Land Credit and Agricultural Housing Credit). That pattern has already been analysed and observed in numerous countries of Eastern Europe, and it mainly refers to the transition from the feudal relationship to the initial capitalist concepts.

Later sets of laws only improved the possibilities for further and faster development of cooperatives in Romania at that time (1887 Commercial Code,

1903 Law on Rural Banks, 1935 Law on the Cooperatives, etc.) (Wolz et al., 2020). The situation with healthcare at the end of the 19th and the beginning of the 20th century was difficult. Namely, the sources of the time state the characteristics of other countries of Eastern Europe at that time, which are reflected in the use of magical medicine, an uneducated population, the absence of a healthcare network, primary healthcare problems, especially in rural areas, endemic diseases such as syphilis, and epidemics characteristic of that time. Constantin Bărbulescu warned that a "demographic apocalypse" was coming (Bărbulescu, 2018). When in 1934, Krum Mihalescu (inspector of the Ministry of the Kingdom of Romania) came to Yugoslavia to study the work of health cooperatives, he was impressed by their success (Zdravstveni pokret – Zdravlje, 1934, p. 4). After that, he visited the health cooperatives of Yugoslavia several times. Before WWII, Romania developed health cooperatives, and although those did not cover a significant population, they were successful in terms of pastoral support. They provided healthcare and managed to achieve this goal through the cooperation of their members and the government. The government provided them with the necessary facilities, which in most cases were existing buildings renovated for the needs of the cooperative. According to the statute of these institutions, "cooperative members who paid a monthly fee of one new crown" could receive the following services for free: prescribing and dispensing medications, medical assistance, X-ray and laboratory services, dental care, and mental health assistance. Health cooperatives also provide education and training to their members. Most of the training was provided by doctors and dentists; however, there were plans to create educational facilities. To become a member of a Romanian health cooperative, a person had to provide proof of residence in a given area. That requirement helped ensure that cooperative members were residents of the area where they operated. Considering the time frames of the beginning of WWII, health cooperatives were not developed significantly. Today, health cooperatives in Romania exist but work in a limited number and in specific health-related areas.

4 Historical and modern aspects of health cooperatives development in North America (USA, Canada)

United States of America (USA)

Healthcare system development in the USA

The US Constitution defines the structure of American federalism. The 10th Amendment, ratified in 1791, designates specific responsibilities to the federal government and the states. It includes a "residual powers clause" stating that powers not delegated to the United States by the Constitution are reserved to the states or the people. However, the interpretation of this clause is subject to legal debate (Weissert & Weissert, 2006, p. 247). Throughout the US history, the balance of power has shifted between the federal and state governments. The healthcare system in the United States has undergone dramatic changes over the past two centuries. In the 19th century, individual practitioners mainly provided healthcare, and no formalised system existed. That changed at the beginning of the 20th century when the first hospitals and clinics were established. Healthcare in the United States today is a complex mix of public and private providers, with the government playing a significant role in funding and regulating the system.

Looking historically, following the American Civil War (1861–1865), centralisation occurred as the federal government gained strength. During the Reconstruction (1865–1877), the federal government aimed to rebuild the Southern Confederate states and initiate cultural transformations. However, a subsequent backlash after 1877 led to governmental decentralisation and increased state power. That decentralisation contributed to the segregation and disenfranchisement of African Americans, primarily in the South, for nearly a century and arguably continues to some extent today. The pendulum of federalism shifted again during President Franklin D. Roosevelt's New Deal (1933–1936), as the federal government centralised power to address the challenges of the Great Depression. The civil rights movement in the 1960s also brought significant changes.

In more recent period, the Trump Administration and previous Republican-led administrations generally advocated for a reduced role for the federal

DOI: 10.4324/9781003183068-4

government. This approach and level of centralisation are under reconsideration by the democrats in the current political settings. In the health sector, states play an important role in governance. They fund and manage various public health functions, contribute to the cost of Medicaid and mental healthcare for the impoverished, support public hospitals and health departments, and oversee environmental protection. States establish regulations for health insurance policies not covered by self-insured employer plans, as self-insured employers are regulated by federal law under the Employee Retirement Income Security Act, which supersedes state law. States also have the option to regulate increases in health insurance rates (Weissert & Weissert, 2006, p. 236). State boards of health and public health advisory boards perform essential functions in approximately half of the states. The roles of these agencies vary, ranging from quasi-legislative organisations to quasi-judicial bodies that enforce rules and regulations through hearings and appeals. Some agencies have oversight functions and the authority to appoint or remove the state health officer or make binding decisions related to personnel, finances, or organisational matters (Hughes et al., 2011). States also contribute to healthcare providers' education, credentialing, and regulation. Under the Constitution's residual powers clause, states license practitioners. National-level, non-governmental professional associations establish practitioner education and certification standards, counterbalancing individual states' power. These education and credentialing functions involve the transfer of power from public to private non-profit entities and voluntary organisations, such as the American Medical Association, which establish their admission standards (Bauchner et al., 2015).

Also, there has been a growing acknowledgement that the healthcare system is not the primary determinant of people's health. Instead, other factors, often called social determinants of health, are significant and can be even more influential. These factors encompass various cultural and environmental elements and hold considerable importance. The list of social determinants of health is extensive. It includes factors such as parents' education, poverty, family upbringing, language barriers, neighbourhood effects, racial segregation, safety, workforce issues, social capital, and environmental factors like clean air and water access. Furthermore, these factors interact with each other, creating complex relationships. For instance, higher income enables individuals to avoid hazardous occupations and live in dangerous neighbourhoods. These social determinants of health serve also as guidance for the development of modern health system in the United States.

In addition, over the past few decades, the United States has witnessed notable increases in life expectancy and reductions in various causes of mortality. However, despite similar trends observed in other high-income countries, the United States still needs to improve its relative position and rank in key indicators such as overall life expectancy, infant mortality, and potential years of life lost.

There are numerous challenges facing the healthcare system in the United States today. These include rising costs, an ageing population, and the increasing prevalence of chronic diseases such as obesity and diabetes. Despite these challenges, the healthcare system in the United States provides quality care to its citizens. Also, significant reforms have been carried out to improve the efficiency and effectiveness of the system, and it is expected that these changes will continue in the years to come. As mentioned, the healthcare system in the United States is a complex mix of public and private providers. The government plays a significant role in funding and regulating the system, but many private insurers and providers exist. Government-sponsored programs such as Medicare and Medicaid provide coverage for a significant population. Patients in the United States have many different health insurance options with dominant private solutions.

Cooperatives development in the USA

In the United States, a cooperative was opened in 1752 thanks to the assistance of Benjamin Franklin, who, together with his friends, opened that organisation whose goal was mutual protection from the consequences of fires through the formation of a monetary fund. That organisation was called "The Philadelphia Contribution for the Insurance of Houses from Loss by Fire" and was later known as "Union Fire Company" (USDA, 2000).

Several decades later, in 1785, there was the first attempt to form an association of farmers for agriculture in Philadelphia (Philadelphia Society for Promoting Agriculture). Later, early agricultural cooperatives such as a dairy cooperative (1810) from Connecticut, a hog marketing cooperative (1820) from Ohio, a cooperative butter manufacturing plant (1820) from New York, and others were formed. Interestingly, in 1867, Dairyman Cooperative already had more than 400 processing plants. Also, in the United States, the first associations appeared early during the second half of the 19th century, so the National Grand was formed in 1869, Farmers Alliance in 1880, American Society of Equity in 1902, National Farmers Union in 1902, National Council of Farmer Cooperatives Association in 1912, and National American Farm Bureau in 1919. After the pioneers from Rochedale opened a cooperative on Toad Lane in the suburbs of Manchester in 1844, a more significant development of modern cooperatives also took place in the United States. Cooperatives and associations were founded for various economic activities (Confecoop, n.d.). Thus, a student cooperative was founded at the University of Tennessee in 1862, and in 1873, tobacco growers formed a cooperative for storage. In 1865, a law was approved in Michigan that recognised cooperatives and their business methods. After the formation of the International Cooperative Alliance in 1895, the first cooperative magazine began to be published in the United States under the name *The American Cooperator* for New England cooperative members.

In 1914, President Wilson approved the formation of the first commission to study European cooperatives and savings and credit associations. In 1917, Aurora, a production cooperative, was formed to supply the institution later known as Fitzsimons Army Hospital, while in 1920, the first gathering of experts was formed in the state of Washington on the foundation of the cooperative law for all states, later known as the Standard Act.

In 1923, James Warbasse founded the Cooperative Leagues of America and played a significant role in publishing Cooperative Democracy, which later became the National Cooperative Business Association (NCBA). The concept of cooperatives received support from US President Truman in 1940, particularly in the telephony industry. However, towards the late 1980s, there was resistance to the cooperative model, which aimed to promote collective contributions towards equality. That resistance was partly influenced by several notable cooperative failures during that period, such as the Grand Forks potato producer cooperative in North Dakota, which was forced to sell its factory, and the limited success of ethanol cooperatives. The Farmers Union also sold its North Dakota property to private entrepreneurs. In 1922, the US Congress passed the Capper-Volstead Act, which had significant implications for farmers and their associations. Throughout the 1920s, Congress established various agencies to support the cooperative movement financially, including the Farm Credit Administration in 1929. As a result of the National Consumer Cooperative Bank Act in 1978, the First National Cooperative Bank was established. As recognised by Congress, the purpose of that act was to address the challenges consumers and self-help cooperatives faced in accessing communal credit facilities and technical assistance. Congress acknowledged the need for a National Consumer Cooperative Bank to provide financial and technical support, ultimately strengthening the nation's economy (USA Public Law 95–351, 1978).

Following its founding in 1981, this bank underwent a rapid privatisation process. However, despite the change in ownership, it remained committed to its mission of fostering development in underserved markets. The bank played a crucial role in assisting cooperative organisations in unlocking their business potential and expanding their operations (Deller et al., 2009). There are currently 29,285 cooperatives operating in the United States, with 856,310 employees and 350,871,790 members (coop4dev, 2023e). Today, the United States has ten members in the International Cooperative Organisation (coops4dev, 2020):

- National Cooperative Business Association (NCBA);
- Nationwide Mutual Insurance Company;
- National Cooperative Bank (NCB);
- National Rural Electric Cooperative Association (NRECA);
- Credit Union National Association, Inc. (CUNA);
- CHS Inc;
- National Co+op Grocers (NCG);

- CoBank, ACB;
- National Society of Accounts for Cooperatives (NSAC);
- Land O'Lakes International Development.

Considering cooperative regulations connected with healthcare, in the United States, 43 statutes have been enacted for general purposes, 38 for agricultural cooperatives, 47 for mutual insurance, and seven specifically addressing healthcare. For instance, Arkansas has implemented the Community Health Care Access Program (Ark. Stat. §§ 20-77-1501 to 20-77-1501). In Colorado, the Health Care Coverage Cooperatives are governed by CRSA §§ 10-16-1004 to 10-16-1016. Conversely, Wisconsin has established cooperative healthcare associations under WI-Gen § 185.981(5), recognised as charitable and benevolent corporations. Additionally, healthcare plans operated by cooperative associations that qualify as health maintenance organisations are subject to § 609.655 under WI-Gen § 185.981 (USDA's Rural Business-Cooperative Service, 2001; NCBA CLUSA, 2003; ICA, 2021).

Health cooperatives development in the USA

In 1929, the first cooperative for the provision of health services in the United States was formed. That cooperative was formed in the town of Elk, Oklahoma. Support was provided by the Farmers Union of Elk City and the Farmers Union Cooperative Health Association. That cooperative faced numerous problems, primarily the influence of the private health sector, which could have looked more favourably on forming cooperatives in its sector. However, that cooperative influenced the spread of cooperatives in the United States of America. It contributed to organising the Group Health Co-op from Puget Sound in Seattle.

In 1936, President Roosevelt formed a commission to study cooperatives in Sweden and other European countries. In 1937, The Farm Credit Act was approved in Congress, and the Cooperative League of the United States formed the Bureau of Cooperative Medicine. In many respects, that institution was the predecessor of later developments in the approach to healthcare through cooperation. It should be noted that the formation of the Health Maintenance Organization as one of the models enabled insurance to provide healthcare, which was used later in 1974 through the formation and promotion by the Farmers Union, especially for rural areas of the United States (USDA & Rural Business/Cooperative Service, 2001).

The first Health cooperative in the United States was founded in Elk by pioneer Dr Shadid Michael Abraham (1882–1966). His contributions to cooperative medicine, especially the Cooperative Hospital he founded in Elk City, Oklahoma, and the first health cooperative in the United States triggered the health cooperatives movement in the United States. Shadid was born in Lebanon, and he immigrated to the United States in 1904 and settled in Elk

City, Oklahoma. He was a Lebanese-American physician and the founder of the Cooperative Health Care Movement in the United States. In the 1920s, Shadid became interested in cooperative healthcare models. In 1929, he co-founded the Farmers Union Cooperative Health Association in Elk City, Oklahoma, the first rural cooperative health insurance plan in the United States. Shadid's cooperative model proved successful, and it inspired the creation of other cooperatives across the country, which helped improve access to affordable healthcare for rural and underserved communities. Shadid's contributions to the development of the Cooperative Health Care Movement have had a lasting impact on the healthcare industry in the United States (Haddad, 2010). In 1909, Shadid founded the Elk City Cooperative Hospital, which served as a model for other cooperative hospitals nationwide. Shadid's hospital was the first in the United States to be owned and operated by a cooperative, and it was one of the first to offer health services on a sliding scale basis. Shadid's hospital was also one of the first to offer health insurance to its members. In addition to his work at the hospital, Shadid founded the Cooperative Health Association, which provided health services to cooperatives nationwide. He was also a director of the National Cooperative Bank and a member of the board of directors of the NCBA. Shadid was an early advocate for the reform of medical practice. In 1912 he published "The Self-Physician" outlining his proposed changes. Despite facing opposition from the Beckham County Medical Society, the Oklahoma Medical Association, and the American Medical Association, the hospital based on the cooperative continued to thrive.

Furthermore, Shadid established the Cooperative Health Federation of America in 1947 and served as its president from 1947 to 1949. In 1960, he constructed Hospital Haramoon in his hometown in Lebanon. Dr Michael Shadid passed away in Kansas on August 13, 1966, and was laid to rest in Fairlawn Cemetery in Oklahoma City. Shadid's contributions were recognised and honoured by various organisations. He received recognition from the Sigma Delta Chi Journalism Society at the University of Oklahoma. He was awarded the Order of Merit in Lebanon and was inducted into the Hall of Fame of the Cooperative League of the United States of America.

Another pioneer in global health cooperatives contributing to the development of those cooperatives in the United States was also Dr Andrija Štampar (later president of WHO). Štampar was serving as a public health consultant at the time of the development of health cooperatives in the United States and was discussing those points with global healthcare leaders, taking into consideration his experience from Yugoslavia initiated in Serbia. In his books from the 1930s, he wrote about the development of health cooperatives in the United States, where Major of Elk had supported cooperative health development. However, the US Medical Chamber stopping activities had a noted impact (Štampar, 1939a, p. 112). By that involvement in developing the initial health cooperative in the United States, it is presumed that those ideas came from Yugoslavia, where health cooperatives were already operational and numerous with the support of US experts and farmers. Initially, the idea of developing health cooperatives in Serbia (before forming Yugoslavia) came from the Welfare Association for Children from the United States, so with those arguments, we can clarify that the pathway of the idea for the development of health cooperatives was a reversal. Namely, the American Mission, initially known as the "Serbian Relief Committee," was established in the United States during WWI. During the war, the organisation's activities were evident through the work of related societies connected to refugee centres and those operating near the Thessaloniki front. In 1915, members of the American Mission arrived in Serbia and played a significant role in providing financial and organisational assistance, donating various materials and equipment for healthcare provision. The Mission engaged experts with prior experience in similar projects in the United States. One notable positive impact of the American Mission was the establishment of the Health Fund in Krupanj, which operated under the authority of the Krupanj agricultural cooperative. The fund received donations from the American Mission and the Ministry of Public Health and material aid such as laundry, washing soaps, towels, and so on. Those items were sold, and the proceeds were used for the fund's needs. Local health funds were established first, followed by county health funds, which took over the management of health centres. The Mission played a significant role in efforts to create accurate statistical yearbooks, aiming to understand the public health situation better. Dr Rudolph Rex Reeder's work and the activities of the American Mission in Serbia are also documented in other sources, such as the cooperative magazine *Zdravstveni pokret – Zdravlje* (Healthcare Movement – Health). Those sources highlight that despite Dr Reeder's passing, the Mission continued its operations, establishing clinics and a representative office. Dr Reeder emphasised to his colleagues that all their efforts would be in vain if the Mission ceased to exist after his departure. The Mission played a crucial role in supporting the establishment of the first cooperatives by providing dispensaries and goods as initial capital. Zdravstveni pokret – Zdravlje (1936) emphasises that cooperatives represent a significant movement in healthcare, embodying the principle "of the people, by the people, and for the people," advocated by American President Lincoln.

As previously mentioned, in the United States, the pioneer of the health cooperatives movement was Dr Shadid. That visionary leader encountered significant challenges, including opposition from the local medical society. Nevertheless, with the support of the Oklahoma Farmers Union, he secured a loan to establish a hospital and develop a prepaid insurance plan. In addition, Dr Shadid believed the government should subsidise tuition fees for the economically disadvantaged. At the same time, consumers would oversee business operations, and physicians would retain control over the professional aspects of care. Dr Shadid's success inspired the formation of regional health cooperatives offering healthcare plans and provider networks.

The success of cooperatives in various economic sectors in the United States has relied on their ability to leverage collective purchasing power to obtain lower rates. Rural electric cooperatives, for instance, emerged during the Great Depression following the establishment of the Tennessee Valley Authority Act (TVA) in May 1933. That act empowered the TVA board to construct transmission lines to serve "farms and small villages not otherwise supplied with electricity at a reasonable rate." Using federal assistance for rural electrification gained momentum when President Roosevelt assumed office in 1933 and initiated his New Deal programs. On May 11, 1935, Roosevelt signed Executive Order No. 7037, which created the Rural Electrification Administration (REA). A year later, the Rural Electrification Act was passed, marking the launch of the lending program that eventually became the REA. Most rural electrification efforts were undertaken by local electric cooperatives that borrowed funds from the REA to build infrastructure and provide services on a non-profit basis. Today, the REA has evolved into the Rural Utilities Service and operates as part of the US Department of Agriculture. A significant development in the history of electric cooperatives was the establishment of energy marketing agencies known as PMAs. The Bonneville Power Administration became the first PMA in 1937, followed by the creation of four additional PMAs responsible for selling electricity generated by 133 federal dams nationwide. The federal law governing PMAs grants priority in selling electricity at cost to public entities and electric cooperatives. The availability of affordable electricity for electric cooperatives has stimulated economic growth and offset the expenses of serving sparsely populated areas.

Later, HealthPartners, based in the Twin Cities of Minnesota, and Group Health Cooperative, based in Seattle, emerged as highly successful examples of cooperative health systems. These consumer-driven healthcare organisations served over 500,000 members across broad geographic areas. In addition to providing insurance, they deliver healthcare services directly through non-profit integrated delivery systems, owning their own hospitals and employing dedicated multispecialty physician groups. Their approach emphasises integrated, coordinated, high-quality care while ensuring prudent resource utilisation. Despite encountering obstacles throughout their 50-year histories, including opposition from organised medicine and internal conflicts, these organisations continue to serve as exemplars of value-based healthcare delivery. However, the cooperative landscape does contain instances of failures. For example, the Group Health Association in Washington, DC, collapsed in the early 1990s due to intense conflicts between consumer-led management and the medical group. Similarly, Group Health Inc. (GHI) in New York has faced challenges but is on the verge of profitability. Operating within a market that rewards for-profit insurance and fee-for-service care, these organisations have had to deviate from their original governance structure and consumer-led Mission. The collective experience of successful and unsuccessful cooperative healthcare ventures underscores the difficulty of reconciling the public's demand for affordable, high-quality care with physicians' desire for professional autonomy and control over healthcare resources. It is also challenging to uphold the principles of consumer-driven healthcare in a market that prioritises volume over value. In the future, if the value-based healthcare approaches would be implemented this might change. Moreover, legal obstacles arise from proponents of existing market incentives. For example, in response to the growth of member/patient-owned cooperatives, several states have enacted laws prohibiting physicians from being employed by non-physicians, effectively impeding the establishment of cooperative health plans.

For cooperative healthcare to effectively curb the rise of healthcare costs and achieve savings, the cooperative insurance organisation should have the authority to negotiate care at favourable terms. This can be accomplished by ensuring the cooperative health plan can secure the lowest price offered to the most favourable customer. Currently, commercial insurers dominate the market in most regions. The two most effective health insurance plans account for 50% or more of all private insurance enrolees in all but three states. These plans leverage their purchasing power to negotiate lower rates with local healthcare providers. However, hospitals and other providers can resist and demand higher rates in markets where certain healthcare providers have significant influence. The outcome of multiple negotiations between numerous insurers and providers incurs substantial administrative costs but fails to establish a competitive market price applicable to all customers. Instead, it results in favourable rates for the most influential negotiators. An alternative approach to increase purchasing power would involve a national cooperative negotiating supplier prices for all customers. This is the model employed by German "hospital funds." These member cooperatives, facilitated by consumer committees, negotiate with regional provider organisations on behalf of all patients for standardised health benefits. In the United States, such a process could be entrusted to a national "Health Value Authority" and applied to all health plans participating in insurance exchanges. In this scenario, a consumer-driven non-profit entity acting in the public interest would oversee the reform of payment and delivery systems rather than leaving such reforms to the market power of insurers or providers in a specific geographical area or a political process influenced by special interests.

Revamping the American healthcare system offers two potential paths, as proposed by members of Congress: a cooperative strategy and a public insurance plan. The cooperative approach involves establishing a national cooperative organisation that would change the insurance provision and facilitate the development of local cooperative healthcare delivery systems. A selected national entity could provide various forms of support, including grants and loans to initiate local cooperative healthcare systems, actuarial technical assistance, and other necessary aid. Additionally, this national organisation could be empowered to negotiate provider payment rates and methods for all public and private insurers, thereby eliminating administrative inefficiencies caused by countless individual price negotiations. Furthermore, it could introduce new payment models that shift the focus from competing for service volume to rewarding better patient outcomes and more efficient resource utilisation. National authority may be required to overturn state laws that hinder the establishment of cooperative healthcare systems or insurance products. This strategy would break new ground and lead to a healthcare system delivering high-quality, high-value care. The role of insurance would involve pooling risks comprehensively and restructuring local competitive markets to align incentives with the provision of high-value care.

The history of successful local cooperative healthcare delivery systems demonstrates the potential for swift change. However, careful consideration, time, and expertise would be necessary to develop and implement a national Health Value Authority's responsibilities, powers, and structure. Alternatively, another option might be to create a new public health insurance plan offered by the US Department of Health and Human Services (HHS). This plan would adopt value-based payment methods, leverage the existing Medicare network of hospitals and doctors, and compete with private insurers in the national health insurance exchange. Despite adhering to the same rules as private insurers regarding benefits and coverage, this public plan could offer lower premiums than current premiums in the individual and small business markets. The exact reduction would depend on whether providers are reimbursed at Medicare levels or between commercial and Medicare rates. HHS could also be granted the authority to modify prices for individual services, including reducing rates for overpriced services that have contributed to the significant increase in service volumes observed in studies like the Dartmouth Atlas. The savings generated from cutting prices for overpriced services could be divided between the federal budget and a bonus fund for high-performing providers. The payment rates of the public health insurance plan could also be made available to private plans, incentivising doctors to participate in the network. By fostering competition between public and private plans on a level playing field regarding provider payment, substantial cost savings could be achieved initially and over time. Under such a reform, most providers would continue to experience revenue growth, albeit slower.

Extending coverage to the uninsured would generate new provider revenue, while improved benefits would reduce bad debt. If the public plan paid providers at a rate between Medicare and commercial rates, physician and hospital incomes would grow as stated by the industry coalition in a letter to President Obama.

Similarly, the healthcare system should adopt a comparative philosophy that genuinely serves the people's needs. Therefore, the fundamental objectives of healthcare reform should be centred around redesigning the system to prioritise people and ensuring that care is focused, easily accessible, and well-coordinated. Ultimately, the public bears the cost of healthcare, whether through

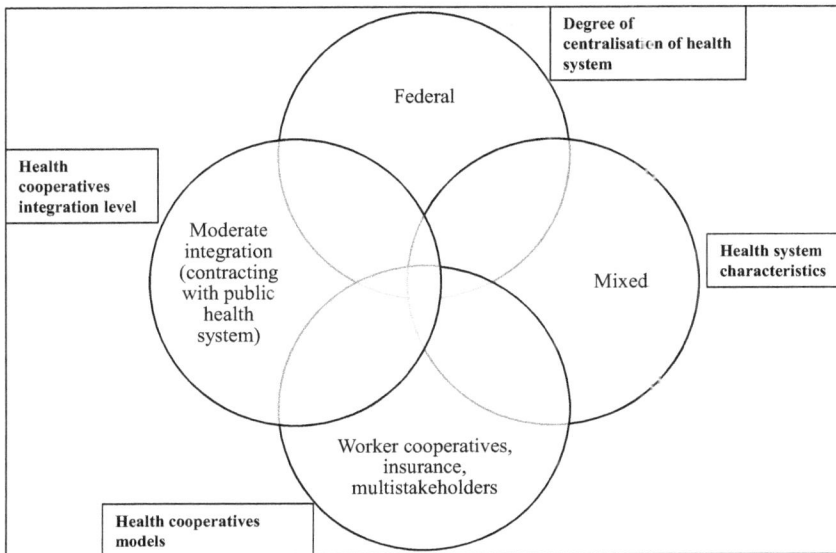

Figure 4.1 Overview of cooperative health types in the healthcare system set up in the United States.

Source: Created by the author.

direct expenses such as premiums and healthcare services, reduced wages due to higher premiums in employer-sponsored plans, or increased taxes to support Medicare, Medicaid, and other public health programs. Therefore, healthcare reform must establish mechanisms to ensure accountability and value in how healthcare organisations and providers utilise the resources entrusted to them (Commonwealth Fund, 2009; Oklahoma Historical Society, 2023). In further text, we are providing the list of some of the significant health cooperatives in the United States today:

- Group Health Cooperative: Founded in 1947 in Seattle, Washington. It is a non-profit healthcare system that provides care and coverage to more than 600,000 members in Washington State and Idaho.
- HealthPartners: Founded in 1957 in Minneapolis, Minnesota. It is a non-profit, consumer-governed healthcare organisation that provides care and coverage to more than 1.8 million members in Minnesota, Wisconsin, Iowa, Illinois, North Dakota, and South Dakota.
- Kaiser Permanente: Founded in 1945 in Oakland, California. It is a non-profit, integrated managed care consortium that provides care and coverage

to more than 12 million members in California, Colorado, Georgia, Hawaii, Oregon, Washington, Maryland, Virginia, and the District of Columbia.
- CareOregon: Founded in 1994 in Portland, Oregon. It is a non-profit health plan that provides care and coverage to more than 375,000 members in Oregon.
- Health Alliance: Founded in 1980 in Urbana, Illinois. It is a health plan that provides care and coverage to more than one million members in Illinois, Iowa, Nebraska, and Washington.

Innovations in healthcare, mainly through cooperative approaches, can help address the significant challenge of meeting the growing demand for health services resulting from Ontario's ageing population. Cooperative innovation involves collaboration between organisations to develop new and better solutions, leveraging the strengths of each party involved. Cooperative innovation in healthcare effectively reduces costs and improves health outcomes by pooling knowledge, data, and skills and incentivising the design and implementation of innovative solutions. Also, cooperatives can enhance access to high-quality health services by bringing together doctors and hospitals to work towards common goals and share the savings from collaborative efforts. Additionally, cooperatives can provide access to suitable suppliers who may otherwise need help to serve a large population. Cooperatives can reduce costs by sharing resources, including facilities, by working together. Finally, collaborative innovation can improve care quality by focusing on patient safety and improving coordination between healthcare providers.

One of the concerns for cooperative solutions is the availability of personal care workers. A similar model has been successful in the United States, where the Cooperative Home Care Associates (CHCA) was founded in 1985 to provide quality home care services by providing quality jobs for direct care workers. CHCA, a nationally recognised worker-owned home care agency in the Bronx, now employs over 2,000 workers and offers free training to over 600 low-income and unemployed women annually through an employer-based workforce development program in collaboration with the non-profit organisation PHI (CHCA, 2023; The Ontario Cooperative Association (OCA, 2018)).

Canada

Healthcare system development in Canada

Provincial governments have a rich history of offering subsidies to hospitals to provide care for all individuals, regardless of their economic abilities. The government of Ontario established the foundation for this approach with the Charity Aid Act of 1874. Subsequently, in 1914, the provincial government introduced worker's compensation legislation to ensure medical care for all eligible workers in case of work-related accidents or injuries. Less than two decades later, Ontario became the first jurisdiction to implement a province-wide medical service plan covering all social assistance recipients. While most provinces followed Ontario's lead by offering targeted public health services and coverage, the provinces in Western Canada paved the way for universal hospital and medical care coverage, which eventually became known as Medicare. Saskatchewan initiated this movement in 1947, followed by British Columbia in 1948 and Alberta in 1950, each implementing their own "hospitalisation" programs. In 1957, the Government of Canada passed the Hospital Insurance and Diagnostic Services Act, which outlined the criteria that provincial governments needed to meet to receive shared-cost financing through federal transfers. A year later, in 1958, Saskatchewan, British Columbia, Alberta, Manitoba, and Newfoundland agreed to operate within the federal framework. By 1959, Ontario, Nova Scotia, New Brunswick, and Prince Edward Island also joined the initiative. Quebec, however, did not participate until 1961, shortly after the election of a government committed to modernising the provincial welfare state. With the implementation of federal cost-sharing for universal hospitalisation, the Saskatchewan government had the financial means to proceed with universal coverage for physician services. However, introducing a prepaid, publicly administered medical care insurance plan sparked a contentious province-wide doctors' strike in 1962 that lasted for 23 days. The strike concluded with a compromise known as the Saskatoon Agreement, which emphasised the contractual autonomy of physicians from the provincial government and maintained fee-for-service as the primary payment method. In 1964, the Hall Commission, the Royal Commission on Health Services, presented its report to the prime minister (Angus & Manga, 1990). This federal commission was established following the polarised debate in Saskatchewan regarding the merits of single-payer, universal medical care insurance compared to the alternative of state-provided subsidies for private insurance, supported by provincial governments in Alberta, Manitoba, Ontario, and organised medicine. The Hall Commission ultimately favoured the Saskatchewan model and recommended that the federal government encourage other provinces to implement universal medical care insurance through conditional grants. In 1966, the federal government passed the Medical Care Act, and federal cost-sharing transfers began in 1968 for provinces that met the four conditions of universality, public administration, comprehensiveness, and portability. By 1971, all provinces had implemented universal medical care coverage alongside their existing hospital care coverage. That led to the deep universal healthcare, commonly known as Medicare. During the 1970s, public coverage and subsidies for health services were rapidly expanded beyond hospitals and medical care in the provinces and territories, referred to as extended benefits. These initiatives included prescription drug plans and subsidies for long-term care. However, due to the lack of national principles or federal funding, these programs varied significantly across the country, depending on individual provinces' fiscal capacity and political ambitions. Simultaneously, the federal government initiated a shift in thinking towards the determinants of health beyond medical care, encompassing biological factors, lifestyle choices, and environmental, social, and economic conditions. In 1974, the Canadian Minister of Health Marc Lalonde summarised this new approach in a report titled "A New Perspective on the Health of Canadians." The Lalonde report emphasised the upstream determinants of health and influenced subsequent studies, providing the intellectual groundwork for "wellness" reforms introduced by provincial governments in the early 1990s. In 1984, the federal government replaced the Hospital Insurance and Diagnostic Services Act and the Medical Care Act with the Canada Health Act. The Canada Health Act established five criteria that initially served as funding conditions but later came to represent the principles and values underlying Canadian Medicare. These national standards were derived from the previous legislation, and the 1984 law aimed to reinforce the existing system. Notably, the Canada Health Act required the federal government to deduct from a provincial government's share of Established Programs, Financing the value of any extra billing and user fees allowed within that province. That provision addressed concerns that some provinces had allowed the imposition of patient user fees, hindering reasonable access to insured services. The Act also added accessibility as a fifth criterion, underscoring the importance of unimpeded access without patient charges. Over time, extra billing and user fees were virtually eliminated for all insured services under the Canada Health Act. While the Act has not always been strictly enforced, federal health ministers' formal letters to provincial counterparts threatening deductions have effectively curtailed violations. In addition to providing financial security, universal Medicare has positively reduced health disparities since its inception.

Today, Canada operates as a constitutional federation, where sovereignty, authorities, and responsibilities are divided between the federal and provincial governments. In the original Constitution, established in the 1860s and delineated powers between the central and provincial governments, the authority over health or medical care was not explicitly addressed, except for jurisdiction over hospitals and psychiatric institutions, which were exclusively assigned to the provinces. Consequently, the authority over healthcare can only be inferred from various provisions in the Constitution.

While the three northern territories have a constitutional status subordinate to the federal government, they were delegated the responsibility of administering public healthcare by the federal government. However, the federal government retains significant "steering" responsibilities related to critical aspects of Medicare through the Canada Health Act. The provinces must adhere to its principles to receive their total share of the Canada Health Transfer.

The public health system is available to all Canadians, regardless of their income or insurance status. A combination of taxes and user fees finances the system. It is based on the principle that all citizens should have access to necessary medical services without the direct financial concern of the patient. A private healthcare system is available to citizens who have access to a sufficient amount of money. The system is financed primarily from private insurance premiums. It is designed to meet the needs of individuals by offering personalised healthcare services. The community healthcare system is mainly designed to help those unable to afford medical services. Non-profit organisations and government grants finance it. It provides many essential services, such as family planning and health education.

The country's leading hospitals and research centres provide state-of-the-art technology and treatments that are not available in other countries. The quality of Canadian healthcare is also highly respected by patients and professionals. For example, in the areas of cancer treatment and chronic diseases such as diabetes, Canada has one of the highest survival rates in the entire world (Girard, 2003).

Canada provides its citizens with high-quality healthcare at a relatively low cost. The universal system is financed primarily through taxation, thus ensuring equal coverage. In addition, a universal system has significantly lower costs than a privatised one because the government can negotiate better prices for services and drugs. Finally, the community healthcare system is a valuable resource for those who cannot afford private insurance. This third system ensures that everyone can receive primary medical treatment regardless of their financial situation. The Canadian healthcare system provides accessible and affordable medical care to all its citizens.

Health cooperatives development

The concept of cooperative delivery of wellness, health, social services, medical, and related services has a long history in Canada, predating the establishment of the Canada Health Act. The inception of the first health cooperative in Canada dates back to 1944 in Québec City. That cooperative, now known as *Services de santé de Québec – SSQ* (Quebec Health Services), operates across the entire province of Québec. In 1946, British Columbia witnessed the establishment of the CU&C Health Services Society, the first health insurance cooperative in the country. That cooperative was created to offer prepaid, affordable medical-hospital plans.

In Saskatchewan, the Cooperative Commonwealth Federation, led by Tommy Douglas, won the provincial election in 1960 with the promise of North America's first publicly funded medical service. This led to the formation of the Community Health Services Association Ltd. in 1962, initiated by a group of pro-medicare citizens, including doctors (Panayotof-Schaan, 2009). In 1962, during the introduction of Canada's first universal healthcare system, 90% of doctors in Saskatchewan closed their offices in protest. As a result, they gained the right to bill patients directly, charging amounts exceeding the provincial health insurance plan's reimbursement (Archer, 1980). Today, Saskatchewan boasts five provincially funded and supported cooperative healthcare associations actively providing community services. Hence, Canadian health cooperatives' history is spanning over 60 years.

In British Columbia, a significant milestone occurred a few years later, establishing the first health insurance cooperative, CU&C Health Services Society, officially incorporated in 1946. It aimed to provide prepaid, affordable medical-hospital plans. Although it no longer operates as a cooperative (having merged with the Medical Services Association in 1997 to form the Pacific Blue Cross), it remains the only health insurance cooperative to have operated in Canada (Cooperatives Secretariat, 1999).

Health cooperatives are not intended to undermine government-provided health services. On the contrary, governments across Canada often fund health cooperatives due to their success in meeting the healthcare needs that the public sector may need help to address effectively. This natural alignment between health cooperatives and the public sector strengthens their collective ability to provide comprehensive healthcare services.

The increasing prevalence of health user cooperatives can be attributed to the need to address healthcare delivery gaps, including developing preventive services and enhancing overall well-being. These cooperatives often ensure access to treatment based on specific pathological categories or provide tailored services for at-risk user groups. In Canada, for instance, consumer model clinics have emerged to offer specialised healthcare services for seniors, indigenous people, individuals with limited financial resources, and those with chronic illnesses. Consumer cooperatives also play a crucial role in filling healthcare gaps in marginalised and sparsely populated areas where access to public health services is challenging (Craddock & Vayid, 2004).

The establishment of a publicly funded healthcare system in Canada resulted in the implementation of the Canada Health Act in 1984, which drew inspiration from the healthcare model in the United Kingdom. However, this universal healthcare system has certain limitations. It places more emphasis on rehabilitation than prevention, excludes vision and dental care from publicly funded plans, and experiences long wait times, particularly for diagnosing and treating mental illnesses and age-related diagnostic procedures and surgeries. In response to these challenges at the community level, health cooperatives have emerged as a solution. These cooperatives are tailored to meet their respective communities' specific needs and priorities, with a primary focus on delivering healthcare services (EURICSE, IHCO, 2018).

Cooperatives in Canada have the flexibility to incorporate at the federal level or in any of the ten provinces or three territories. The process is straightforward, accessible, and affordable, with professionals such as cooperative developers, accountants, and lawyers available nationwide to assist. At the federal level, no specific regulations or incentives regarding the legal structure of organisations providing services funded through the Canada Health Act exist. While Ontario

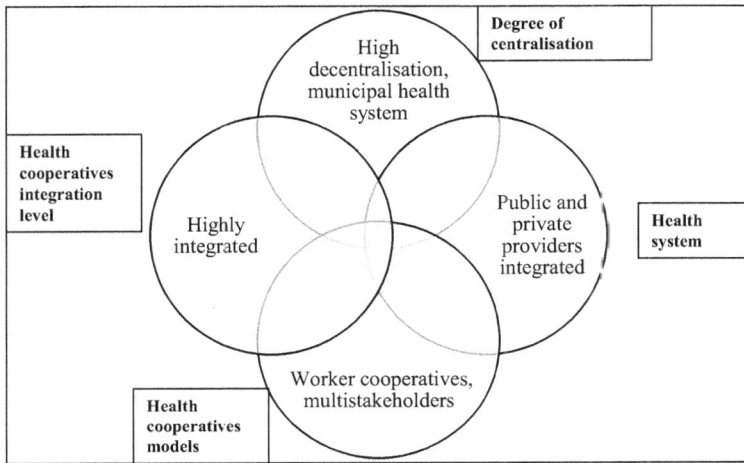

Figure 4.2 Overview of health cooperative types in the healthcare system set up in Canada.

Source: Created by the author.

has some restrictions, other provinces and territories do not prohibit cooperative ownership of health or medical services, whether within or outside the services funded through the Canada Health Act. It is important to note that no organisation can demand payment, such as a membership fee, for accessing services funded under the Canada Health Act.

However, tracking the growth of the cooperative sector in healthcare has been challenging due to the need for consistent tracking systems across Canada and the absence of a widely accepted definition within the cooperative sector. Inconsistent analysis by Cooperative Registrars and variations in internal and external definitions have hindered understanding of the sector's scope and the development of an accurate list of cooperative organisations in the Cooperative Secretariat. Furthermore, the Secretariat's move from Agriculture Canada to Industry Canada in 2013, coupled with understaffing, exacerbated the problem.

Across country, health cooperatives have emerged in response to community-based challenges or opportunities specific to each situation. Even in Saskatchewan, where several cooperatives were formed in response to the physicians' strike, the remaining cooperatives reflect the diverse priorities of their respective communities. In most parts of Canada, health cooperatives primarily focus on service delivery rather than the insurance aspects of medicine and healthcare. Based on the report for 2020, there are 486 registered health cooperatives in Canada showing growth over time (Government of Canada, n.d.).

Established in 2011, Health Co-ops Canada plays a crucial role in coordinating and supporting health cooperatives, despite initially facing limited support from the cooperative sector and no government backing. Health Co-ops Canada has significantly progressed through networking, learning, and sector understanding. While not all health, wellness, social service, and medical cooperatives outside Quebec are members, many are affiliated with Health Co-ops Canada. According to Health Co-ops Canada's definitions, it is estimated that there are over 120 sector cooperatives in Canada, with approximately 20 providing services covered by the Canada Health Act. Additionally, cooperatives in other sectors, not supported by the publicly funded system, significantly impact their community's access to clean water, adequate food, and safe housing – fundamental aspects of community wellness. Members of Health Co-ops Canada offer various services, including ambulance and mobile wellness and health services, home care, employment and life-skills support for individuals with disabilities, housing support, medical services, and complementary and integrative services.

Case study – Saskatoon Community Clinic

For this case study, it is essential to distinguish between a cooperative health centre and a community health centre. At the same time, a health cooperative can also function as a community health centre, while not all are health cooperatives. The key distinction lies in ownership (similar to models from Slovenia). A community health centre is typically owned by a few individuals or managed by a government agency, whereas a health cooperative is owned and operated by its members. In a health cooperative, any profits generated are reinvested in the centre or distributed among its members. This fundamental difference in ownership can lead to distinct motivations. A health cooperative prioritises serving its members, fostering a healthier community, and addressing the social determinants of health on a broader scale. Situated in the heart of the Canadian prairies between Alberta and Manitoba, Saskatchewan borders the United States to the South and the North-West Territories to the north. Saskatoon stands as the third-fastest-growing city in Canada. However, alongside its growth, the city faces an increasing disparity between the rich and the poor. Gentrification in specific core neighbourhood's forces residents to relocate further from essential services. Many smaller communities in Saskatchewan also suffer from isolation, while some First Nations communities lack services in indigenous languages tailored to indigenous culture. As provincial finances come under pressure, income inequality continues to rise. In response to the doctors' strike, the Saskatoon Community Clinic was founded in 1962 and has served the community for 55 years (Gruending, 1974). Initially operating in donated space, the clinic eventually moved to its current location in downtown Saskatoon. The formation of the cooperative was a direct response to the loss of medical services caused by the strike. Given the province's solid cooperative presence, the advantages and process of establishing a cooperative were familiar to the community. Recognising the urgent need for services, many individuals willingly purchased CAD 1,000 debentures, a significant investment during the 1960s. In the early years, support primarily came from the members, including the doctors who had to advocate for hospital privileges. After two years, credit unions offered some assistance (IHCO, 2018b). Later, additional debentures facilitated the construction of a purpose-built building for the cooperative in the late 1960s. Subsequently, the New Democratic Party Ministry of Health provided program funding. In 1972, in line with membership guidance, a new clinic was established in the low-income Westside neighbourhood. This small clinic catered to the local, impoverished, and Aboriginal populations. Recently, the Westside Clinic relocated to a larger space to better serve the growing indigent population, providing services such as HIV/AIDS care, a methadone program, and various other essential healthcare services. As a member-owned cooperative, the Saskatoon Community Clinic currently operates facilities in two locations (Rands, 1994). The leading clinic in downtown Saskatoon serves diverse populations. In contrast, the Westside Clinic, located in an older neighbourhood, primarily caters to Aboriginal and economically disadvantaged communities. The cooperative was initially established in response to the doctors' strike, which occurred when the provincial government decided to implement universal Medicare. The Saskatoon Community Clinic estimates that it serves approximately 10,000 patients in its leading clinic and varying numbers in the Westside facility, where drop-in visits are accommodated. The cooperative offers various services, including but not limited to doctors, nurse practitioners, registered nurses, X-ray and lab services, physiotherapy, pharmacy, nutritionists, occupational therapy, counselling, HIV/AIDS care, methadone treatment, and outreach counselling. To ensure comprehensive care for their clients/members, the Saskatoon Community Clinic collaborates with community organisations such as the University of Saskatchewan and the Saskatoon Health Region. The Saskatoon Community Clinic has continuously evolved to meet changing community needs. It embraces new healthcare programs and innovative service delivery methods and incorporates diverse voices within the community. Rather than remaining stagnant, the clinic represents an ever-evolving primary healthcare model and community outreach in the 21st century.

5 Historical and modern aspects of health cooperatives development in South America (Argentina, Brazil, and Colombia)

Argentina

Healthcare system development in Argentina

The history of medicine in Argentina encompasses several significant milestones and advancements. In 1780, during the administration of Viceroy Juan José de Vértiz, the Tribunal del Protomedicato de Buenos Aires was established as the regulatory body for medical activities and professional training, with Miguel O'Gorman serving as its first physician. However, in 1822, Bernardino Rivadavia, the Minister of Government under Governor Martín Rodríguez, dissolved the institution. In 1796, a smallpox epidemic struck, and Miguel O'Gorman, an Irish-origin physician affiliated with the Protomedicato, pioneered smallpox crust inoculations. Following the method developed by the Englishman Daniel Sutton, O'Gorman employed this technique to combat the epidemic and protect the population.

In 1801, the School of Medicine of the Tribunal del Protomedicato of Buenos Aires was established, replacing the former School of Nursing of the Society of Jesus. The Society of Jesus had been dissolved over 30 years earlier due to their expulsion from the territory. Under the guidance of Cosme Argerich, a professor of medicine, and Agustín Eusebio Fabre, a professor of Surgery, Anatomy, and Childbirth, the School of Medicine commenced its operations. In 1821, the University of Buenos Aires was established, absorbing the assets and activities of the School of Medicine through its Department of Medicine. That development further solidified the educational and academic groundwork of medicine in Argentina. Advancements in medical procedures continued to shape the history of medicine in the country. In 1847, the British physician John W. Mackenna conducted the inaugural surgery with general anaesthesia using ether at the British Hospital of Buenos Aires. This groundbreaking achievement ushered in a new era of pain management during surgical procedures (Alvarez, 2008). The National Academy of Medicine was also established to promote further progress in the field.

DOI: 10.4324/9781003183068-5

In 1914, Dr Luis Agote performed the first blood transfusion using blood preserved with sodium citrate at the Rawson Hospital in Buenos Aires. That marked a significant milestone in transfusion medicine (Parker, 2007). During the mid-20th century, Dr Carlos Galli Mainini made noteworthy contributions to medical diagnosis. Between 1942 and 1947, he developed the early pregnancy diagnostic test, commonly known as the frog test, at the Rivadavia Hospital in Buenos Aires. A pivotal moment in patient protection and regulation occurred in 1964 with the implementation of National Laws 16,462 and 16,463, collectively known as the Oñativia Law. Those laws aimed to safeguard patients by establishing rational regulations for producing and selling medicines in Argentina, laying the groundwork for enhanced healthcare practices (Pasqualini, 1987). The history of medicine in Argentina is characterised by notable accomplishments, encompassing the establishment of regulatory bodies and educational institutions, pioneering medical procedures, and advancements in patient care and regulation. These milestones have profoundly impacted the nation's healthcare landscape and continue to play a pivotal role in advancing medical science and practice (Abeldaño, 2017).

Argentina has made significant strides in improving its healthcare system and achieving universal health coverage (UHC). In 2004, the Argentinean Plan Federal de Salud was introduced, a comprehensive primary healthcare (PHC) program encompassing pharmaceutical policies, maternal and infant health, and public health insurance. The primary objective of this program is to provide coverage to all citizens, particularly those at risk or with low income (Machado, 2018). In 2007, the Plan Nacer was implemented, focusing on pregnant women and children up to five years of age. Subsequently, in 2013, it was renamed Plan Sumar to expand coverage to at-risk and low-income citizens. These initiatives have resulted in a significant reduction in low birth weight mortality rates and neonatal mortality.

In Argentina, the Programa Remediar (Remedy Program) was initiated in 2002, primarily focusing on providing generic prescription medicines for chronic conditions at the primary healthcare (PHC) level. Subsequently, in 2008, it was integrated into the country's health service networks, expanding its coverage to encompass all citizens nationwide. Despite having the highest healthcare expenditures in the region, with 10.2% of its gross domestic product (GDP) allocated to healthcare, only 3% is allocated to public health expenditures. The per-capita health expenditure is approximately £1,390 comparable to public health expenses in Mexico and Brazil (França et al., 2016).

Nevertheless, Argentina has achieved nominal UHC, guaranteeing enrolled individuals the right to access healthcare services. Furthermore, the country is actively working towards implementing a more effective UHC by transferring capitated payments to the provinces, enabling the provision of services included in their UHC health benefits packages. These ongoing efforts are aimed at further enhancing the accessibility and quality of healthcare services for all citizens in Argentina.

The notion of "self-management" in public hospitals was once highly esteemed and significant. However, over time, it has undergone a transformation that has resulted in various challenges. The self-management model in public hospitals has veered away from its original purpose. Presently, hospitals possess the authority to bill social services for the care provided to their members. Additionally, technology-driven companies have been entrusted with outsourcing internal hospital services, charging for the self-management model. Regrettably, this concept distortion has failed to address healthcare issues in Argentina effectively. Technology integration has caused a deformation of the health system, resulting in a notable cost increase. The private medicine sector has also encountered regulatory obstacles. The absence of regulations has allowed anyone to sell medication, leading to numerous complaints from Consumer Defense organisations (Barr, 2004). The need to expand the coverage of prepaid medical services has compelled companies to recognise the necessity of regulating the healthcare system to safeguard certain rights for the people. However, these policies often deviate from what the law prescribes up to the current moment.

Cooperatives development in Argentina

Cooperatives in Argentina have acquired a more contemporary significance since 1889, following the reform of the Commercial Code (Articles 392–294) to incorporate cooperatives and cooperative associations. However, this legislation was perceived as poorly drafted, lacking a clear distinction between cooperatives and other types of organisations and failing to uphold or define the principles of the pioneers from Rochdale. Consequently, cooperative development remained limited until 1926. The history of cooperatives in Argentina can be examined within the legal framework of two distinct periods: pre-1926 and post-1926 when cooperatives operated under Law 11,388 (formerly Law 20,337) (Ley 11.388, 1926). Also, it was noted that European settlers initiated the establishment of cooperatives in Argentina.

The first cooperatives in Argentina were reflected in the formation of the Cooperative Society of Production of Buenos Aires, which was founded in 1875 and followed the teachings of Adolphe Vaillant, a French expert who propagated cooperative ideas in Argentina and other Latin American countries. (e.g. Uruguay). Later, in 1885, the "Consumer Cooperative" was formed, with its organisers migrating to France, underscoring the French influence on Argentina's cooperative movement. This influence was further solidified in 1888 with the opening of the French representative office of the French Cooperative Society (Montes, 1974).

In researching the historical development of health cooperatives, it is essential to note that the Cooperative Society Pharmacy was founded in 1886. Also, in the context of associations to provide healthcare, previously formed mutual aid societies were characteristic of Argentina, initially formed by Spaniards and Italians, and later emigrants from Germany, France, and Portugal joined and became members. The primary objective of these associations was to protect against diseases. As early as 1875, 74 distinct mutual societies had been established, predominantly in the province of Buenos Aires and the Santa Fe region. Italian immigrants founded most of these societies (14), the Spanish established seven, and the French and Swiss formed three. The French Society for Mutual Aids (1854) and the Society of Mutual Aids San Crispin emerged two years later.

Apart from the early influence of French experts, the cooperative formed by the French and the representative office of their cooperative union, the influence of German and Italian emigrants should also be addressed. Therefore, we will mention that in 1887, a cooperative for food services (bakeries) was founded by a German emigrant. Additionally, the Unione Cooperativa Italiana was established in the same year, which focused on savings and credit. However, it is important to note that the subsequent development of cooperatives was guided by the principles introduced by the pioneers from Rochdale.

The often-quoted Raimundo Real in 1900 provided insight into the development of cooperatives in Argentina, highlighting the limited significance of the cooperative movement in society. Real attributed this limited impact to various factors, including a lack of awareness, insufficient economic education, weak unionisation, inadequate organisation, and a lack of discipline. These factors have impeded the progress of cooperation as a viable model. Through time, many authorised and registered cooperatives either require establishment or have faced failure.

Following the legislative change in 1926, the cooperative movement in Argentina witnessed significant growth, leading to the registration of 143 rural and 79 urban cooperative organisations by the Ministry of Agriculture. Those cooperatives were primarily concentrated in the territories of Buenos Aires, Cordoba, and Litoral. The registered organisations encompassed various sectors, including credit, consumer, educational, housing, and insurance cooperatives.

During the initial period spanning the 19th century and the early 20th century until 1926, the influence of mutual societies can be seen, as well as the development of early cooperatives, some of which operated according to certain principles brought to Rochedale. Furthermore, the impact of emigration played a role in the establishment of mutual aid societies and the subsequent formation of cooperatives, particularly in the realm of healthcare. Rural cooperatives were more prominent in that period than urban cooperatives, with agricultural cooperatives taking the lead. Moving into the 1950s, more significant organisational structures like Cooperativa de San Genaro began to take shape. This cooperative, operating in the province of Santa Fe, focused on providing telephone services (ECyT-ar, 2017). The National Institute of Cooperative Action (INAC) was formed in 1971, and its task was to deal with the legal work of cooperatives. The Honorary Consultative Council was formed to fulfil its function, an organisational unit within this institute with the main task of proposing legal solutions. The result was already in 1973 when law 11,388 was put *ad acta* and replaced by the law under number 20,337, which still retained the essence of the previous law (Trevisan, 2009).

During the early 1990s, President Carlos Saúl Menem implemented new policies that closed many cooperatives. It was a period of crisis not only in Argentina but also in other Latin American countries. That crisis highlighted the challenges health systems faced in meeting the growing demands of the populations they serve. In various countries, there is an ongoing debate on the necessity of significant changes in healthcare system financing and organisational models. Those systems were compelled to navigate a complex situation characterised by dilemmas. On the one hand, they had to adapt to the new financial conditions resulting from the financial crisis and decreased social security resources. On the other hand, they had to address the rising healthcare needs of the population, particularly those with critical conditions (Belmartino, 1991).

However, following the latter half of the 1990s and particularly during 2001–2002, a significant number of companies in Argentina came under workers' control after their previous private owners abandoned them. Subsequently, these companies transformed into cooperative organisations on a large scale.

During that period and in light of the state of health and the imperative need to establish health-focused cooperatives, the President of the Administrative Council of Coopescrevi in San Gregorio, Province of Santa Fe, and Treasurer of the Administrative Council of FAESS (the Argentine Federation of Solidarity Entities of Health Cooperativa Ltda.) explained the significant challenges faced by the country during the 2001–2002 crisis, particularly regarding the establishment of Primary Care Centres since the inception of FAESS in 1999. That coincided with a wider national crisis within the healthcare sector and political turmoil that had enduring consequences. One of the consequences of the crisis was the implementation of an emergency decree in 2002, which remained in effect until the end of November 2004. As a result, the country had a national health emergency for three years, which severely strained the response capacity of the nation-state and the private sector, including mutual crisis and healthcare providers. Addressing this situation became imperative. Amidst those circumstances, efforts were made to confront the challenges and the ongoing outcomes resulting from those efforts. The underlying objective has been to pursue social equity and achieve a more equitable healthcare system (Giribaldi, 2007).

In modern times, Argentina has over 20,000 operating cooperatives with diverse purposes. The most notable associations include the Asociación de Cooperativas Argentinas (founded in 1922), the Federación Argentina de Cooperativas Agrarias, the Unión de Cooperativas Agrícolas Algodoneras (founded in 1905), the Federation of Agricultural Cooperatives (founded in 1963), the Federation of Agricultural Missions Cooperatives (founded in 1939, a union type of an organisation focused on implementing healthcare systems for the protection of members and their families), and Coninagro (an oversight organisation) (Confecoop, 2023).

Health cooperatives development in Argentina

The Argentina Federation of Solidarity Entities of Health Cooperativa Ltda. (FAESS) is a prominent organisation in Argentina renowned for its commitment to promoting health equity. It was established through collaborative efforts between the Mobilising Institute of Cooperative and Cooperative Funds and the Confederation of Cooperatives of the Argentine Republic (Cooperar). The establishment of FAESS was inspired by successful health cooperative models in Spain and Brazil, which have achieved notable progress in the field. Addressing the distinct challenge of inadequate healthcare access faced by nearly 50% of the population in Argentina, FAESS strives to contribute to developing a more inclusive and equitable healthcare system in the country. Such health cooperatives offer various health services, encompassing preventive and curative care. These cooperatives prioritise addressing inadequacies in medical services, such as prosthetics provision, emergency aid for residents in remote areas, and timely surgical interventions. Before 2007, the federation comprised 54 institutions that delivered various services beyond healthcare. These institutions encompassed both mutual societies and cooperative organisations. FAESS advocates for integrating users and service providers within the healthcare sector through the Unisol Salud brand. Unisol Salud comprises medical centres that deliver primary healthcare, incorporating cooperatives, mutual societies, and other solidarity organisational forms. Their goal is to achieve adequate healthcare, increase health equity and health equality, and actively work on proposals for new policies that would enable such a thing in practice.

The first medical centre was established in Mariano Acosta. Regarding this centre at the beginning, when it was still an abandoned hospital, and before the formation of the cooperative, the hospital in their local community was in a deplorable state, representing a healthcare facility in dire conditions, primarily serving underprivileged individuals. It was heart-wrenching for them, as it was their place of birth, upbringing, and where their children currently reside. However, they took it upon themselves to initiate a restoration process for the hospital. The extent of neglect was so severe that providing healthcare services seemed impossible. Although they do not delve into the intricate political factors contributing to the widespread deterioration of public hospitals, including insufficient investment, logistical support, infrastructure, and the provision of essential materials, their determination to address these challenges and revive the hospital for the betterment of their community was unwavering (Giribaldi, 2007). Other centres were primarily established in rural areas with a considerably smaller population of around 5,000 residents. We should also mention the most complex centres with the most comprehensive medical services, such as Rufino and Venado Tuerto. The characteristic of these cooperatives is the funeral services provided by various other cooperatives founded in the 1970s. Another characteristic of these cooperatives is their multi-disciplinary approach. Organised cooperatives formed the first sector for the provision of services in the field of electrical services and also for the establishment of sanitary conditions in the community, which did not exist. Subsequently, those cooperatives expanded their scope to encompass significant hospital capacities, serving over 2,000 patients monthly across more than 20 specialised areas such as radiology and neonatology and took a significant role in the community in health education. One such example is sexual education for adolescents, psychological and social support, and vaccination (Giribaldi, 2007). To raise the vaccination rate in the communities, they organised vehicles to initially visit the place and detect public health problems and residents who were not vaccinated according to the national vaccination plan. Efforts were made to seek out individuals who have not received vaccination if they do not come forward voluntarily. Instead of relying on a single visit, there were follow-up attempts to reach out to these individuals (Giribaldi, 2007). The aim is to educate and raise awareness among the population, emphasising their responsibility to ensure vaccination.

In Argentina, various organisations dealing with health cooperatives were founded: CAMI (Cooperativa Argentina de Medicina Integral), ACA – SALUD (Cooperative of Health Services for agricultural producers associated with the Agrarian Cooperatives nucleated in the Association of Argentine Cooperatives), COMI (Cooperativa Médica Integral, Cooperative of service providers of health in the Federal Capital and the Buenos Aires suburbs), and COMACO (Cooperative of Public Works and Services, Housing and Services) (CAMI, 2023).

In recent decades, there has been an ongoing discussion among various alternative forces regarding the existing healthcare model, both theoretically and practically. The Conference on Health Cooperativism, held in 1993 and 1996, played a significant role in shaping this debate, with substantial participation from Dr Espriú from Spain and collaboration with Unimed. Moreover, establishing the Integrated Health System (SIS) and the Red SIS demonstrated a collective effort by COMI, the Mutual of Municipal Doctors, the Company Health Programs, and others to actively engage in this initiative. Another notable accomplishment was the involvement in deregulating social work, primarily through OSPESGA (Obra Social Del Personal De Estaciones De Servicio,

Garages, Playas y Lavaderos Automaticos), a social work organisation. As a result of these achievements, the focus has shifted towards the establishment of the Obra Social de los Médicos (Healthcare of Doctors), which involves collaboration between the Union of Mutual Cooperatives, the health union sector, and the progressive strengthening of ties with the cooperative banking and financial sector. These endeavours signify ongoing efforts to shape and improve the healthcare system through cooperative initiatives (Revista de la Cooperativa de Trabajo Idecoop, 1997).

In line with enhancing healthcare, a solidarity and cooperative management model emerged in Argentina after 2001. This goal attracted the attention of the experts and the public, and one of the examples was later organised the "Cooperativism in Health, a necessary presence" meeting in 2004, organised by the Argentine Federation of Health Solidarity Entities Coop. Ltda. (FAESS) and the Instituto Movilizador de Fondos Cooperativas y Cooperar (Cooperative Confederation of the Republic of Argentina). As a response to the problematic situation in local communities (a year earlier, the financial report of local governments reported that more than 50% of them are in a state of economic uncertainty), the financing of healthcare is also threatened. Joint forces with political orientations in power at the time agreed on the development of primary healthcare in particular (interestingly, more than 80% of political platforms before 2004 defined the obligation to strengthen healthcare). Then the model in development was connected to the primary service model and included general practitioners, clinicians, and paediatricians providing free access to ophthalmology and obstetrician gynaecology services. The approach to medicine is evidence-based, utilising formularies and prescribing generic and cost-effective medications. National emergency and urgent care services coverage focus on health promotion and primary healthcare education. Preventive campaigns are conducted to raise awareness and promote good health practices. Both healthcare providers and users have a solid educational background. A minimal coinsurance requirement is in place to encourage responsible healthcare utilisation, ensuring that visits to the doctor are not solely driven by social factors but rather for specific medical needs or consultations related to a particular condition (López, 2004).

In 2015, health cooperatives in Argentina provided services to more than two million members out of a total population of 56 million, and 1,056 organisational units were formed, comprising 195 cooperatives and 861 mutual societies. This includes organisations that provide the most diverse healthcare, prevention, curative care, and pharmaceutical services. In terms of organisation, a large number are workers' cooperatives. FAESS is primarily responsible for health cooperatives, while the Argentina Federation of Mutuals is responsible for mutual societies. Interestingly, unlike Brazil and Spain, which advocated for forming FAESS based on their model, in Argentina, universal healthcare preceded the development of health cooperatives.

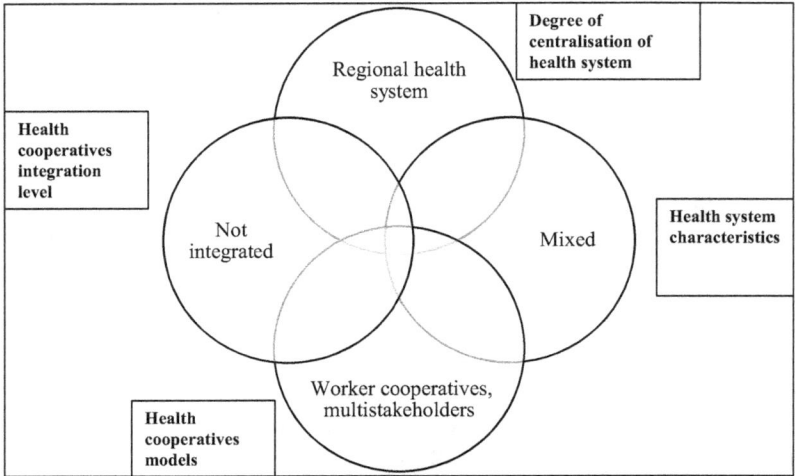

Figure 5.1 Overview of cooperative health types in the healthcare system set up in Argentina, created by the author.

In recent times, when these cooperatives have been formed and are stable in their development, the development plan also refers to developing new technologies that can help, such as tele-education and telemedicine.

Besides Argentina, health cooperatives were formed and strengthened in several other countries following similar models, including Spain and Brazil, with the aim of establishing universal healthcare. One country declares the achievement of the right to universal coverage, while the other focuses on the practical circumstances, such as financial, organisational, and legal aspects, necessary to implement universal coverage in practice.

Brazil

Healthcare system development in Brazil

The Brazilian health system is a complex network of public and private organisations that have evolved over different historical periods. During the early 1900s, strict and organised public health campaigns were implemented, often encountering opposition from population segments, politicians, and military leaders. Notably, in 1904, a vaccine revolt was sparked by a mandatory smallpox vaccination campaign led by Oswaldo Cruz, who served as the Director General of public health then.

The intervention model in social policies by the Brazilian state emerged in the 1920s and 1930s, linking an individual's social and civil rights to their position in the labour market. Social protection expanded during the presidencies of President Vargas (1930–1945) and the military regime (1964–1984). However, with limited public involvement, decision-making and management processes were centralised, resulting in a fragmented and unequal social protection system. The healthcare system relied on an underfunded Ministry of Health and the social security system, which provided medical care through retirement and pension institutes, each offering different services and coverage levels. Those with casual employment faced challenges accessing public services and often resorted to philanthropic care or private healthcare services (Braga & Paula, 1981).

Following the military takeover in 1964, government reforms facilitated the expansion of the predominantly private healthcare system, especially in major urban centres. The coverage expanded rapidly with the inclusion of rural workers in the social security system. From 1970 to 1974, federal funds were allocated to reform and construct private hospitals. Moreover, healthcare provision was extended to trade unions and philanthropic institutions that served rural workers. Direct subsidies to private businesses for healthcare provision were substituted with income tax discounts, which resulted in the proliferation of private health insurance plans and growth in the healthcare market (M. H. Almeida, 1996).

The combination of increased social security coverage and fee-for-service payments from the private sector created a funding crisis within the social security system, exacerbated by the economic recession in the 1980s, which intensified the need for reforms. In Brazil, the health sector reform diverged from the post-welfare health sector reforms globally during that period. It emerged as a response to the struggle to restore democracy in the mid-1970s and gained momentum through a social movement encompassing grassroots sectors, middle-class populations, trade unions, and left-wing political parties (C. M. Almeida, 1981). The reform movement regarded health not solely as a biological matter to be addressed by medical services but as a social and political issue that demanded public attention. Health professionals, progressive public health professors, and researchers from the Brazilian Society for the Advancement of Science actively participated in grassroots and trade union struggles. The Brazilian Health Studies Centre (CEBES) was established in 1976 to coordinate the health reform movement, followed by the Collective Health Postgraduate Association (ABRASCO) formation in 1979. Those organisations played a crucial role in advancing the reform agenda.

The health reform movement expanded its reach and formed alliances with progressive members of Congress, municipal health officials, and other social movements. Municipal health officers started holding meetings in 1979, and in 1980, the National Council of State Officers (CONASS) was established. In

1986, the 8th National Health Conference marked a significant milestone by recognising health as a citizen's right and laying the foundations for the Unified Health System (SUS) (Médici, 1990). This conference led to the developing of strategies that promoted coordination, integration, and resource transfers between federal, state, and municipal health institutions. These administrative changes set the stage for future actions by the SUS. Despite strong opposition from the robust private health sector, the health reform movement and its allies managed to secure approval for reform during the National Constituent Assembly (1987–1988). The 1988 constitution was enacted during economic instability, decreasing influence.

The Brazilian health system is a complex network comprising various complementary and competitive service providers and purchasers. It operates as a mixture of public and private sectors, with private funds serving as the primary source of financing. The system consists of three subsectors: the public subsector (SUS), which offers services financed and provided by the state at federal, state, and municipal levels; the private subsector (for-profit and non-profit), which receives funding through different public or private sources; and the private health insurance subsector, which encompasses various health plans with different premiums, coverage levels, and tax subsidies. Although these subsectors are distinct, they are interconnected, enabling individuals to access services based on their ability to pay or the convenience of access. The National Health Council, National Health Conference, and executive bodies facilitate social participation and inter-managerial coordination in policymaking. The Ministry of Health, along with tripartite and bipartite committees, state health authorities, and municipal health councils, play crucial roles at the federal, state, and municipal levels. The public healthcare subsystem was implemented in 1990, coinciding with the inauguration of President Fernando Collor de Mello.

Despite Collor de Mello's reluctance to commit to healthcare sector reform due to his neoliberal agenda, a framework healthcare law (Law 8080/90) was approved. The healthcare sector reform gained momentum in 1992 after the president's impeachment for corruption. Decentralisation efforts were reinforced, and the Family Health Program (PSF) was launched. Economic stabilisation plans and privatisation processes were promoted by subsequent presidents, such as Fernando Henrique Cardoso and Luiz Inácio Lula da Silva (Ministério da Saúde, 2006).

Although the healthcare sector reform became less of a political priority during the 1990s, several initiatives were undertaken. Those included the development of a national HIV/AIDS prevention and control program, tobacco control efforts, establishing the national sanitary surveillance agency, creating the National Supplementary Health Agency, and improving Indigenous healthcare. During President Lula's administration, initiatives like the Mobile Emergency Care Service and the National Oral Health Policy (Brasil Sorridente) were implemented. Decentralisation and participatory management were essential aspects of the health system's reform. This process was part of a broader political transition and the redesign of the Brazilian Federation initiated by democratic movements in the 1980s.

The decentralisation of the health system involved the introduction of complementary legislation, new rules, and administrative reforms at all levels of government. The Ministry of Health played a crucial role in defining funding mechanisms, establishing representative councils and management committees, and redefining responsibilities. Those structures have evolved over time to promote social participation and decision-making at the federal, state, and municipal levels.

The private healthcare subsystem in Brazil has historically thrived with state protection and support. It encompasses private medical practices, specialist clinics, private hospitals, and private health insurance companies (Côrtes, 2009). This subsystem interacts with the public sector by providing services contracted out by the SUS, out-of-pocket hospitals, ambulatory services, drugs, and private health plans. While the SUS finances some services, others rely on private funding.

Private health insurance is primarily sought by public and private company employees offering such coverage. The private health plan and insurance market is concentrated in the southeast region of Brazil. A few companies dominate the market, with commercial firms accounting for most private plans and insurance policies (Miranda, 2007). Private health plans cater to different socio-economic and occupational groups, offering varying levels of care quality and amenities. Also, people with private health plans generally report better access to preventive services and higher utilisation rates than those without such plans. However, individuals with private health plans may still access certain high-cost services and procedures through the SUS.

As mentioned, the Brazilian constitution of 1988 recognised health as a fundamental right of every citizen and a responsibility of the state. This recognition led to the establishment of the SUS (Unified Health System), which was built on the principles of universality, comprehensiveness, and social participation. The inclusion of healthcare as a constitutional right resulted from extensive political struggles and the efforts of the Brazilian Health Reform Movement. However, the implementation of a universal health system in Brazil faced challenges due to an unfavourable political and economic climate favouring a neoliberal approach over a universal one. International organisations also discouraged publicly funded national health systems, advocating for intermediate steps.

In recent decades, progress has been made in implementing the SUS. Significant institutional innovations have been introduced, including a substantial decentralisation process that granted municipalities greater responsibility for health service management and facilitated formalised social participation in health policymaking and accountability. The SUS significantly improved access to healthcare for a large portion of the Brazilian population, universal coverage of vaccination and prenatal care, increased public awareness of health as a fundamental right, and investments in human resources and technology, including domestic pharmaceutical production.

However, the SUS remains a health system in ongoing development, facing challenges in achieving universal and equitable coverage. The growing private sector market share has led to contradictions and unfair competition when interacting with the public sector. Conflicting ideologies and goals, such as universal access versus market segmentation, have a negative impact on the equity of healthcare access and outcomes. Although federal funding has increased in recent years, the health sector's share in the federal budget has yet to grow proportionally. This has resulted in limitations in financing, infrastructure, and human resources.

Additional challenges arise from the changing demographics and epidemiological characteristics of the Brazilian population. These changes require a transition from an acute care model to one focused on intersectoral health promotion and the integration of health services. The Pact for Health, with its proposed healthcare network based on primary care and recommendations from the National Commission on Social Determinants of Health to address the root causes of ill health, may contribute to developing more comprehensive care models. However, significant challenges must be overcome to implement these initiatives successfully.

Ultimately, addressing the challenges facing Brazil's health system requires a revised financial structure and a comprehensive reassessment of public–private relations. The greatest challenge for the SUS is considered political. Issues related to financing, the composition of the public–private mix, and persistent inequities cannot be resolved solely through technical means. While the legal and regulatory foundations have been established and valuable operational lessons have been learnt, ensuring the SUS's political, economic, scientific, and technological sustainability is essential.

Cooperatives development in Brazil

Since the time of colonisation by the Portuguese, one can see the first hints of ideas that later led to the formation of cooperatives in Brazil. In 1889, the Economic Cooperative of Public Employees of Ouro Preto (Minas Gerais region) was formed and engaged in agriculture as an early organisational form (coops4dev, 2017). On the other hand, historians see the development of cooperatives in Brazil as a consequence of the early work (17th century) of Jesuit missionaries and the communities they originally formed (which followed the idea of social collectivism) (Burke & Finan, 2017).

More modern cooperatives were founded in the late 19th and early 20th centuries and were based on the principles of the Rochdale Pioneers. Of course, it cannot be said that all principles were respected comprehensively, but they were respected to a significant extent. Thus, it was possible to create a good foundation for the further development of cooperatives in Brazil (e.g. there was no institutionalisation in the operation of cooperatives at that time) (Noronha, 1976). The areas of Brazil that emigrants inhabited were particularly prominent in the early development of cooperatives. Among them, it is essential to mention the region of Parana, where cooperatives were founded as early as 1847 following these international cooperative principles, while the first modern agricultural cooperatives were formed in Minas Gerais (1907) (Burke & Finan, 2017, p. 86). The first savings and credit cooperatives were formed as early as 1902 thanks to emigrants from Germany and especially to a priest Theodor Amstad from Switzerland (Mladenatz, 2003). We should also mention the Japanese emigration, especially from 1890 to the 1930s, and their advocacy and promotion of agricultural cooperatives. The law from 1932 (Decree no. 22,239) established the cooperative as an institution with associated rights and obligations.

In Brazil in 1935, a total of 179 cooperative associations were identified, of which the most were consumers associations (22 in total with 26,214 members), then followed by productive and credit associations (36 in total, with 5,691 members), school cooperatives associations (94 in total with 14,960 members), agricultural associations (a total of 26, with 1,037 members) and building associations (1 such association that had 2,682 members). That made a total of 50,584 cooperative community members (Development of Cooperatives in Latin America, 1941, pp. 810–816).

After that period, in 1938, the fellowship was under the significant influence of politics (during Getúlio Vargas and the last military dictatorship until 1985). In 1971, the General Law for Cooperativism (Law no. 5764-71) was passed, which created the body CNC (the National Council of Cooperativism) and created a register at the national level that included cooperatives (Burke & Finan, 2017, p. 91). In 1988, a new constitution was adopted that is still in force today (additional: Provisional Law 1.715, Decree no. 3.015 for providing support to cooperatives, including education and promotion of activities). As part of this recent solution, the Frente Parlamentar de Cooperativismo was formed, enabling independent and autonomous organisational forms in Brazilian cooperatives and enabling each cooperative to be formed without state influence. In 2002, the Civil Code was formed, which did not affect the changes to the previously adopted Law no. 5,764 of 1971, which has already introduced the novelty. There are also special legislations such as the previously mentioned Law no. 5.764, of 16-12-1971; Law no. 9.867, of 10-11-1999; Law no. 12.690, of 19-07-2012; Complementary Law no. 130, of 4.17/2009 (Cooperativas de las Americas, 2020). Law no. 9.867/99 defines social cooperatives but also the organisation and management of health cooperatives (Law no. 9.867/99, Article 1).

In Brazil today, there are more than 2,000 credit and agricultural cooperatives, boasting a membership of over a million individuals. The cooperative movement in the country operates at both local and national levels. The prominent institution overseeing cooperatives in Brazil is the Organisation of Brazilian Cooperatives (Organizacao des Cooperatives Brasileiras, OCB), headquartered in Brasilia. The Department of the Ministry of Agriculture (DENACOOP) provides additional support to cooperatives, which plays a significant role in further developing this type of association in Brazil, with the aid of state funds. Also, Frencoop (Frente Parlamentar do Cooperativismo) emerges as a crucial player within the cooperative landscape of Brazil. As of 2017, Frencoop had 238 members and 23 senators, and it maintains a close collaboration with the Organisation of Brazilian Cooperatives. Furthermore, it operates across Brazil (Burke & Finan, 2017, p. 92).

In addition, Brazil has eight members of the International Cooperative Alliance (coops4dev, 2023b):

- Organización de Cooperativas de Brasil (OCB) is a full member and is the apex organisation in Brazil;
- Confederación Nacional de Cooperativas Médicas (Unimed) is a full member in the health sector;
- Central Nacional das Cooperativas Odontólogicas (UNIODONTO do Brasil) is a full member of the health sector;
- Central de Cooperativas e Empreendimentos Solidários do Brasil (UNISOL do Brasil) is a full member and an intersectoral national organisation;
- Central Nacional Unimed – Cooperativa Central (CNU) is a full member of the health sector;
- Seguros Unimed is a full member of the insurance sector;
- Cooperativa de Trabalho Médico de Ribeirão Preto (COMERP) is a full member and an intersectoral national organisation;
- Cooperativa de Crédito de Livre Admissao de Associados Pioneira da Serra Gaucha – SICREDI Pioneira RS is a full member in the finance sector.

When observing the various sectors within the cooperative system of Brazil, we can identify savings and credit cooperatives, consumer cooperatives, infrastructure cooperatives, housing cooperatives, labour cooperatives, and health cooperatives. In 2021, Brazil had 6,828 cooperatives with 425,318 employees and 14,618,720 members (coops4dev, 2023b). Health cooperatives accounted for approximately 226,000 members, whereas the savings and credit cooperatives were the most populous, with around 3.5 million members.

Health cooperatives development in Brazil

Health cooperatives in Brazil have been active for over 50 years. The initiative, launched by Sistema OCB (Organisation of Brazilian Cooperatives) in Brasilia, is reaching out to policymakers and representatives from financial institutions to highlight the significant role of cooperatives in enhancing health indicators in the country.

The most significant area of the historical development of Brazilian health cooperatives was seen in the second period of the 20th century and with the development of the Unimed health cooperative. Today, according to the statistical data of the Organisation of Brazilian Cooperatives (OCB), it can be seen that public cooperatives are present in 83% of urban areas in Brazil. The federal agency regulates health cooperatives in Brazil for supplementary health and can be classified into two directions as worker cooperatives and consumer cooperatives.

In 2019, the United Nations, together with ESCOOP Saude (Faculty of cooperative technology), made a cross-section of the state of health cooperatives in the territory of Brazil and pointed out significant development components (De Conto, 2019). In 2018, there were 813 health cooperatives with 225.191 associates and 98.230 employees in Brazil. The prominent health cooperative in Brazil is Unimed, consisting of 115,000 members (medical specialists) and about 18 million users. Unimed owns a large number of hospitals, and in 2018 the turnover was US$ 1.33 billion with a 37% market share (IHCO, 2015).

Regarding the work of health cooperatives in Brazil, a notable contribution comes from the first resolution, CFC 944/2002, titled "Entidades Cooperativas de Assistência à Saúde" (Cooperative Entities for Health Assistance), which approves the Brazilian Accounting Standard for health cooperatives (NBC T 10.21). This standard was established by the Accounting Council (CFC) in 2002 (CFC, 2002).

The second resolution is CFC 1.013/2005, also known as "Cooperative Entities," which provides clarification on the technical interpretation of the Accounting Council regarding specific criteria and procedures for the valuation and recording of changes in equity and the structure of Financial Statements (CFC, 2005). Additionally, this resolution outlines the minimum information that should be included in explanatory notes concerning NBC T 10.8 – Cooperative Entities. These resolutions are presented and discussed within the context of this work.

Over time, health cooperatives in Brazil have expanded their presence, with public cooperatives now being present in 83% of urban areas across the country, according to statistical data from the Organisation of Brazilian Cooperatives (OCB). These cooperatives operate under the federal Agency for Supplementary Health regulation and can be categorised into worker and consumer cooperatives.

The significant development of health cooperatives in Brazil was highlighted in a cross-sectional study conducted by the United Nations and ESCOOP Saude, the Faculty of Cooperative Technology, in 2019. This study shed light on essential growth factors and provided a comprehensive overview of the state of health cooperatives in the country.

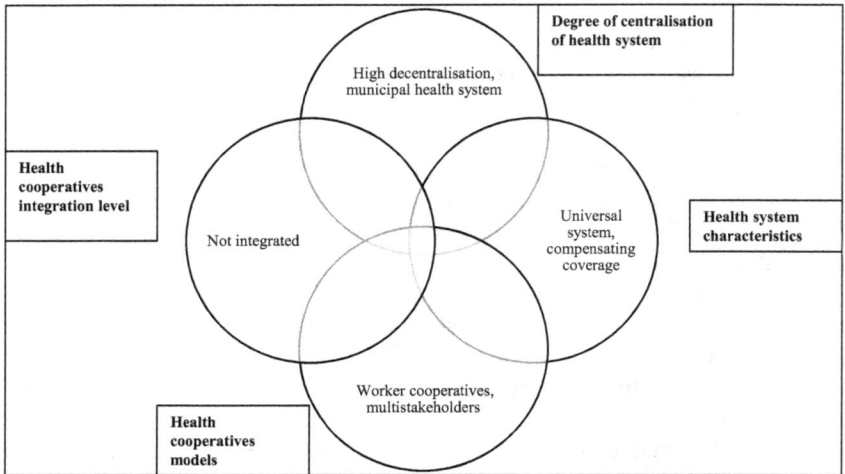

Figure 5.2 Overview of health cooperative types in the healthcare system set up in Brazil, created by the author.

One standout health cooperative in Brazil is Unimed, boasting an approximate membership of 115,000, consisting of medical specialists, and catering to around 18 million users. The cooperative's extensive scale and influence in the healthcare sector position it as a prominent player in Brazil. Unimed's noteworthy presence is further strengthened by its ownership of numerous hospitals. In 2018, Unimed achieved a turnover of US$ 1.33 billion, capturing a 37% market share.

Health cooperatives have a rich history in Brazil, making substantial contributions to improving health indicators in the country. In line with the initiative by Sistema OCB, policymakers and representatives from financial institutions are being informed about the crucial role that cooperatives play in the healthcare system. Through their governance, strategic planning, and the adoption of innovative technologies, health cooperatives can enhance services, processes, and outcomes, ultimately benefiting the communities they serve. The collaborative efforts of stakeholders and a supportive legal framework will further promote the growth and sustainability of health cooperatives in Brazil.

Case study – Unimed

The largest healthcare network in Brazil, known as Unimed, operates as one of the world's largest systems of medical cooperatives. Founded in 1967, Unimed consists of 354 medical cooperatives that provide health services to over 20 million customers, making it a crucial player in Brazil's healthcare sector (Duarte, 2001). With more than 110,000 active physicians, 113 hospitals, and additional services like emergency care, laboratories, and ambulances, Unimed focuses on improving medical working conditions and patient care (Unimed, 2023). Collaborating with the doctors' union in Santos, São Paulo, they explored alternatives and proposed the creation of a co-op, which was accepted and resulted in the establishment of the first cooperative.

Approximately 12% of Brazil's population relies on Unimed, covering 83% of the national territory and accounting for 32% of the health insurance market. Unimed aims to offer a valuable service as a distinct provider, particularly in areas where the public system faces limitations. Unimed's focus is not profit-driven but on reinvesting revenues in infrastructure and extensions to hospitals and laboratories. Furthermore, Unimed seeks to prioritise primary care and enhance preventive medicine to adapt to changing demographic trends (The News Cooperative, 2022; Voinea, 2015).

While Unimed's growth has been impressive, it encounters certain challenges. Adhering to the guidelines set by the National Health Agency, which regulates health providers in Brazil and imposes limits on insurance coverage prices, requires careful investment in the sector. Additionally, Unimed aims to address the evolving healthcare landscape, shifting away from hospital-centric care and prioritising preventive medicine. Considering the patient's family history, community, and region, Unimed's dedication to providing comprehensive and integrated services has yielded positive outcomes for over 100,000 patients. Although Unimed's success offers valuable lessons, mutualising the healthcare sector on a broader scale remains complex. Scaling such initiatives requires careful consideration, innovative approaches, and potential legislative support to integrate mutuals into the national healthcare system.

Another example is related to Seguros Unimed, the insurance arm of Brazil's largest medical work cooperative and health insurance provider. Seguros Unimed has partnered with Dacadoo, a digital health platform provider, to offer digital health and wellness services to its 18 million beneficiaries and 120,000 physicians across Brazil.

Seguros Unimed, the largest Brazilian medical work cooperative and health insurance operator globally, aims to enhance its services by integrating Dacadoo's technology and functionalities through an Application Programming Interface (API). This collaboration will enable Seguros Unimed to provide Dacadoo's digital health services to its customers and affiliated physicians via mobile applications starting in 2020.

Seguros Unimed, focusing on transforming healthcare, originated as a medical work cooperative and has expanded its services. It serves six million clients in health, dental, life, and other insurance segments, including professional liability insurance. With revenues of BRL 3.26 billion in 2018 and growth of over 14% in 2019, Seguros Unimed is recognised as one of the most significant and vital players in the Brazilian insurance market.

Dacadoo is the developer and operator of the Dacadoo digital health engagement platform, which empowers users to manage their health conveniently. By combining motivational techniques derived from behavioural science with elements from online gaming and social networks, Dacadoo engages users holistically in managing their bodies, mind, and lifestyle through different programs. The platform uses its patented Dacadoo Health Score and AI-based health coaching to achieve long-term user engagement and produces positive health outcomes (Decadoo, 2023). Their technology is available in over 13 languages and can be provided as a fully branded, white-label solution or integrated into customer products through their applications showing a high diversity level in health cooperative operations.

Colombia

The healthcare system development in Colombia

Situated in South America, the Republic of Colombia has a vast territory, making it one of the largest countries in the region. With nearly 51 million inhabitants, it has the third-largest population in Latin America. The country has been focusing on ensuring universal healthcare services for its citizens. In 2022, the Colombian government dedicated approximately 9% of its GDP to current health expenditure, and this level of investment was expected to be maintained in the years to come. While this percentage falls below the allocation of 10% seen in countries like Argentina and Brazil, it exceeds the 6% reported by neighbour countries Mexico and Peru (Statista, 2022b).

Colombia has a long history of precolonial and later periods of healthcare service development. The 16th century captured the initial development of healthcare, and the further development of Colombian healthcare is connected with the colonial period. The first formally educated medical doctor, Alvaro de Aunón, arrived in New Granada from Seville, Spain, in 1597 but stayed briefly. Around the same time, the first pharmacy in Colombia was established in the main square of Bogotá by Pedro Lopez Buiza. In 1636, Rodrigo Enriquez de Andrade established the first medical faculty in New Granada at St Bartholomew's College. However, most medical practice in the country was conducted by individuals without formal education.

In 1740, Don Vicente Tomás Cansino initiated the medical program at Our Lady of the Rosary University. Medical care at that time primarily took place in the homes of the sick due to the lack of healthcare institutions. The first hospital in Colombia was San Pedro Hospital in the capital city of Bogotá. The hospital, built by Bishop Juan de los Barrios, began operating in 1564. In 1739, the Hospital San Juan de Dios in Bogotá was opened and built by Friar Pedro de Villamor.

The emergence of medicine during the colonial period in Colombia took place between 1758 and 1810, driven by principles of authority and order with scholastic influences. Baltasar Masi Burgués, a Jesuit, established the first medical school at the University and Academy of San Francisco Javier, later known as Universidad Javeriana, in 1767 (Ministerio de Educación, 2009). The inaugural medical lessons were given on April 1, 1636, by Rodrigo Henríquez de Andrade, a licensed physician who graduated from the University of Alcalá.

In 1653, Friar Cristóbal de Torres founded the Colegio Mayor de Nuestra Señora del Rosario, which offered instruction in philosophy, theology, jurisprudence, and medicine. This marked the increasing influence of the Catholic Church in the country's educational system. Don Vicente Román Cansino, a regent of medicine at the Colegio Mayor del Rosario, oversaw the recognition and licensing of "popular doctors" such as barbers, tegus, midwives, and bleeders prevalent in the old Santa Fe.

In 1802, Mutis and De Isla presented a study plan for medical students, resembling the ones at Spanish universities, to gain approval from Spanish authorities. The plan consisted of five years of theoretical study covering anatomy, medical institutions, general pathology, and Hippocratic doctrine, followed by three years of practical training at the Hospital de la Caridad, focusing on the practical study of operations. This curriculum formed the foundation for medical classes at the Colegio del Rosario, establishing the first Faculty of Medicine in the country.

Medicine at that time was limited to and practised by recognised individuals, representing a social class art form. In 1653, the King of Spain delegated the establishment of the Colegio Mayor del Rosario, following the model of the University of Salamanca, to the fiar Cristóbal Torres, providing a platform for those interested in studying medicine, jurisprudence, and the teachings of Santo Tomás. However, the college was closed in 1810 by Vicente Gil de Tejada due to a lack of support for the cause of emancipation.

In 1815, the Military Hospital was founded to provide care for the wounded in combat, and doctors from San Tafereños were compelled to offer their services under strict military control to prioritise the care of those supporting the cause of liberation. Similar developments were observed in other Colombian cities. For instance, in Santa Marta, General Mariano Montilla appointed Alejandro Próspero as the Reverend doctor of the garrison and hospital (Ramírez, 2007, pp. 55–65).

A devastating smallpox epidemic occurred in 1782 in the Viceroyalty of New Granada, encompassing present-day Colombia, Ecuador, and Venezuela. Although variolation was practised, the epidemic revealed deficiencies in medical knowledge and training within New Granada, a region that lacked its own medical school. This event marked a turning point, leading doctors and government authorities to call for medical reforms to reshape and improve the Spanish colonies.

In the following years, doctors, intellectuals, and government officials on both sides of the Atlantic proposed and implemented measures to enhance public health. These measures included reforms in urban hygiene and sanitation, burial practices, the introduction of the smallpox vaccine, and improvements in medical education. Additionally, botanical expeditions were organised to study the medicinal plants of the New World (Quevedo et al., 2008).

The European Enlightenment strongly influenced the reform-minded doctors of New Granada. Moreover, many of their reform initiatives were implemented during intense political upheaval, characterised by the decline of royal authority in Madrid under Charles IV, the Napoleonic invasion of Spain, and the subsequent calls for independence in the colonies.

A significant achievement highlighted in this volume is the meticulous reconstruction of the politics of medical reform and the involvement of Creole doctors in politics during the turbulent period from 1802 to 1822. Figures like José Celestino Mutis led the rise of an enlightened medical movement within New Granada and are considered the pioneers of modern Colombian medicine and science. Before the Napoleonic invasion, these individuals extensively published and advocated for plans to reform medical education. They continued their medical work and gained political influence as the crisis of royal authority and the wars of independence unfolded (Quevedo et al., 2008).

After gaining independence from Spain, there was a growing influence of French medical thought on Colombian medicine, facilitated by the travel of Creole scientists and intellectuals to France (Ramírez, 2007). Notably, Francisco Antonio Zea organised a crucial mission to bring doctors, scientists, and intellectuals from France and other countries to Colombia to improve scientific knowledge and reform medical education. While the mission had mixed outcomes, it significantly contributed to disseminating French scientific knowledge in the region. French doctors introduced the teachings of Francois Broussais and engaged in conflicts over authority with local doctors.

Despite enduring political instability, doctors successfully established a medical school at the University of Bogotá in 1826 and initiated comprehensive medical reforms. In the 1840s, they further expanded university-based medical education (Ministerio de Educación, 2009).

In 1849, when José Hilario López abolished universities and university degrees, medicine, which was considered an elitist science, was affected. Consequently, pseudo-medical doctors emerged from private universities. However, qualified hospital doctors were responsible for mentoring young individuals eager to study medicine. These apprentices lived and practised together, learning under the guidance of their supervising doctor. Once the doctor deemed their apprentice ready, they would grant them the endorsement to practice.

During the 19th century, discussions began about establishing the Faculty of Medicine at the National University of Colombia.

Considering the present day and education establishment, 47 state and private universities throughout the country offer Medicine Programs. The Ministry of Education required all programs to have a Qualified Registry and accreditation. The Cooperative University of Colombia offers a medicine program across four locations: Santa Marta, Pasto, Villavicencio, and Medellín. Similarly, the University of San Martín has five medicine campuses in Sabaneta, Bogotá, Cali, Pasto, and Puerto Colombia. Traditional amphitheatres have become a thing of the past as students now prepare themselves using online resources and large simulation rooms equipped with anatomically correct manikins. These manikins are preprogrammed to simulate patient scenarios, enabling students to practice various medical procedures, experience simulated deaths and resuscitations, and even practice childbirth.

The establishment of welfare services in Colombia can be traced back to the 1930s. These social security programmes encompass various benefits, such as health and maternity benefits, workers' compensation, and allowances for individuals unable to work. However, like many Latin American nations, housing scarcity poses a significant challenge, particularly in large cities where a substantial migrant population settles in slums. The Housing Institute focuses on building affordable housing for low-income individuals in rural and urban areas to address this issue. In addition, through independent efforts, the Ministry of Public Health aims to generate community interest in finding solutions to health issues. These initiatives include developing drinking water systems and public education on basic sanitation, home maintenance, balanced nutrition, and personal hygiene.

Additionally, the ministry regulates industries and organisations that may pose health hazards. Common health problems in rural areas, mainly poorly drained lowlands, include malaria and dysentery, with occasional cholera epidemics. Hookworm infections are prevalent in the humid environments of shaded coffee plantations. Thankfully, yellow fever, which used to be a significant concern in port cities, has been successfully eradicated. While there have been improvements in health conditions, significant challenges persist, particularly among the impoverished population and in remote areas, including malnutrition-related issues.

In the modern period, Colombia operates a hybrid healthcare system that combines medical and health services provision, parallel public and private financing, and Health Promoting Enterprises (EPS) involvement as insurance intermediaries responsible for managing resources. Despite significant progress, the nation faced challenges in achieving its UHC goal in 2001, with only 60% of the population covered. However, as of July 2020, the coverage reached an impressive 96.33% indicating a substantial improvement in the performance of the health system (Ministerio de Salud y Protección Social, 2018). Despite the advances, there are persistent concerns raised by different sectors of Colombian civil society regarding the structure and organisation of the healthcare system. These criticisms stem from the disparity between UHC data and accessibility to health services. Three key factors contradict the notion of equal access to UHC and health services. Firstly, ample scientific evidence highlights various economic, geographical, administrative, cultural, regulatory, and supply-related barriers hindering healthcare access. These barriers, referred to as "bureaucratic itineraries" by experts, result in complex administrative procedures, delays in medical appointments, diagnosis, treatment, and authorisation for medication delivery (Bello & Bonilla, 2008).

Secondly, there has been a surge in legal actions, known as Tutelas, against the health system due to inadequate access to healthcare services, with a record of 617,071 cases in 2016. These legal actions reflect the dissatisfaction and challenges faced by individuals seeking healthcare. In 2018, there were recognised 207,734 unresolved claims related to lack of access to health services.

Thirdly, the Ministry of Health and Social Protection, Colombia's highest health authority, encounters difficulties regulating and ensuring the fundamental human right to health within a fragmented system involving multiple public and private actors (Domínguez et al., 2017). Data on health services accessibility in Colombia are fragmented and sourced from various information systems. The Integral Social Protection Information System (SISPRO) contains records of the number of people affiliated with the system, healthcare facilities, hospital beds, operating rooms, physicians per 1,000 people, and prenatal care and births in health facilities (Ministry of Health and Social Protection, n.d.). In addition, the Quality of Care Observatory provides indicators of timely access to medical appointments. However, obtaining complete and reliable information on accessibility to health promotion and disease prevention programs remains challenging. The fragmented nature of the Colombian health system, with involvement from both public and private health insurers and service providers, hinders the availability of comprehensive accessibility data beyond the indicators mentioned and UHC reports (Guerrero et al., 2011). While global efforts strive for equity in healthcare accessibility, Colombia faces significant challenges in achieving this objective. Although incomplete and difficult to interpret due to varying methodologies, the existing evidence highlights the magnitude of inequalities in health services accessibility.

Colombia operates a healthcare system that combines public and private insurance coverage. While official data indicates a high UHC rate of over 96%, the persistence of barriers hindering access to healthcare services is identified and raises questions about the equity and universality of the healthcare system in Colombia.

Cooperatives development in Colombia

Modern cooperatives in Colombia began with the formation after the efforts of General Rafael Uriba (1904), who advocated for cooperative organisations.

After that, in 1916, the first state cooperative project was formed by President José Vicente Concha in cooperation with the Ministry of Agriculture. In 1920, the Priest Adán Puerto advocated promoting cooperative development after visiting Europe (coops4dev, 2023a). At the beginning of the 20th century, associations were formed in Colombia, whose economic activity was predominantly agricultural. One of the most significant such associations was the FNC (National Federation of Coffee Growers of Colombia), which was formed as early as 1927 and represented more than 500 families engaged in this type of production (Burke & Finan, 2017, p. 161).

In Colombia, the significant development of cooperatives began after the introduction of the law related to cooperatives (1931). This law primarily encouraged the development of cooperatives in the urban sector. Later, it also strengthened cooperatives in rural areas, becoming essential to Colombia's social and economic trends in the 1960s following the Cuban revolutions. The state primarily focused on agricultural reforms, which influenced the development of cooperatives in this economic sector. Meanwhile, the Church played a role in establishing savings and credit cooperatives (Burke & Finan, 2017, p. 157). By 1933, there were only four cooperative associations with 1,087 members, and in 1934 there were already 16 (with 3,380 members); in 1935, there were 25 (with 5,519 members); and in 1939, there were 170 with 36,808 members (Development of Cooperatives in Latin America, 1941). In 1939, there were 68 consumer cooperatives (business worth 2,583,932 pesos), 56 credit associations (16,495,090 pesos worth), 9 agricultural organisations (5,123,322 pesos worth), 23 worker cooperatives, 7 dealer cooperatives, and 4 housing associations (1939 exchange rate of one Colombian peso was 57.1 dollar cents). Since the 1980s, these activities have multiplied as a result of the development of the socio-economic idea, particularly due to the development of laws related to the solidarity economy and defining cooperative principles aiming to provide the framework for the cooperative sector and establish those organisations as fundamental in the national economy enacted in 1998. (coops4dev, 2023c).

Thanks to Law 100 from 1993, health cooperatives were defined as organisations providing social protection, including healthcare. Of particular interest is Article 181, which addresses the promotion and acceptance of healthcare services and states that non-governmental organisations and the social-solidarity sector are established with the specific aim of serving as Health Promoting Entities. This category encompasses solidarity health companies, organisations within Indigenous communities, and private or public entities formed solely to promote health and well-being.

Today in Colombia, there are 3,205 cooperatives with 139,093 employees and 6,290,927 members. Among these, the largest number of cooperatives is found in the banking sector (27%), followed by administrative and other services (17.9%). Cooperatives engaged in the transport field also have a notable presence, while cooperatives involved in agriculture account for 6.8% of the total.

Colombia has 11 members of the International Cooperative Alliance, including organisations such as the Asociación Colombiana de Cooperativas (ASCOOP), apex organisation; Casa Nacional del Profesor (CANAPRO) in the finance sector; Confederación de Cooperativas de Colombia (CONFECOOP), apex organisation; Cooperativa Empresarial Multiactiva Popular (COEMPOPULAR), a national intersectoral organisation; Cooperativa del Magisterio (CODEMA), a national intersectoral organisation; Cooperativa Médica del Valle y de Profesionales de Colombia (Coomeva), a national intersectoral organisation; and La Equidad Seguros in the insurance sector.

Health cooperatives development in Colombia

In 1964, Dr Uriel Estrada Calderon spearheaded the establishment of Coomeva, a health cooperative in Colombia. Initially, the organisation primarily focused on the insurance sector, aligning with the growth of savings and credit cooperative organisations in the country. However, from 1967 onwards, Coomeva expanded its membership to include professionals from various fields. Today, Coomeva has evolved into the Business Cooperative Group, operating across approximately 1,000 municipalities and boasting 265,000 members. The organisation's activities encompass finance, logistics, and the health sector.

In 1975, Coomeva made a significant breakthrough by pioneering health insurance through its Medical Propaganda sector. This marked a pivotal moment in the cooperative's history as it ventured into providing comprehensive health coverage to its members.

Through this initiative, Coomeva aimed to ensure accessible and quality healthcare services for its growing membership base (Coomeva, 2023). Over the years, Coomeva has emerged as a prominent player in Colombian healthcare, becoming a well-established and trusted institution known for its commitment to meeting the diverse needs of its members. By combining the principles of cooperation and solidarity, Coomeva strives to enhance its beneficiaries' overall well-being and quality of life.

The reach of Coomeva extends far and wide, with a presence in numerous municipalities across the country. The organisation strives to bring healthcare services closer to its communities through its extensive network. By maintaining a strong presence in both urban and rural areas, Coomeva aims to bridge the gap in healthcare access, ensuring that individuals from all walks of life can avail themselves of the necessary medical assistance.

As Coomeva continues to grow and evolve, it remains dedicated to its founding principles of cooperation, inclusivity, and community engagement (Coomeva, 2023). The cooperative's unwavering commitment to providing comprehensive health services reflects its ongoing efforts to contribute to the well-being and development of the Colombian population.

Since 1984, this large organisation has become a system of integrated management, with a current worth of approximately US$ 2.5 billion in assets (Coomeva, 2023). It generates about 40,000 jobs and has approximately 250,000 members (Coomeva, 2023). Today, they advocate for their organisation's digital transformation and alignment with Industry 4.0. They also aim to generate 20% of their revenues through digital services in the coming period.

SaludCoop EPS (Entity for Health Services) is another example of a health cooperative in Colombia. Its establishment in 1994 marked its initial focus on rural areas, intending to provide healthcare services to underserved communities. Two years later, SaludCoop expanded its operations to include urban areas, recognising the need for accessible healthcare in both settings. The cooperative's commitment to growth and innovation led to the opening of the first specialised clinic in Bogotá in 1998, further enhancing its service offerings. In 2000, SaludCoop was strategically invested in developing computing centres to support its expanding infrastructure. These technological advancements allowed for streamlined processes and improved service delivery across its network of clinics.

Additionally, SaludCoop diversified its portfolio by offering a range of services and products to supplement the healthcare provided in its facilities. This expansion culminated in the acquisition of Cruz Blanca in 2002, propelling SaludCoop to become one of Colombia's most prominent business organisations in the healthcare sector. However, starting in 2011, SaludCoop encountered financial difficulties that would ultimately have legal ramifications. These challenges posed significant obstacles for the cooperative, which had amassed seven million members and employed approximately 30,000 individuals. Unfortunately, financial obstacles were not overcome by this cooperative giant leading to the closure of the facilities and liquidation, causing further government audits and legal actions.

The health cooperatives sector in Colombia comprises approximately 4% of the total number of cooperatives in the country. However, it plays a significant role in the economy by employing around 9% of the population within the sector. With a count of 156 health cooperatives, these organisations collectively provide employment opportunities for 15,598 individuals. Furthermore, the membership base of these cooperatives is substantial, with 55,973 individuals benefiting from the services and support offered by these cooperatives (Coomeva, 2023). These health cooperatives serve as vital contributors to the healthcare system in Colombia, offering accessible and inclusive services to a significant portion of the population. Placing emphasis on the cooperative model, these organisations prioritise the well-being and needs of their members, fostering a sense of community and shared responsibility in providing healthcare services. Through their collective efforts, health cooperatives contribute to the overall development and sustainability of the healthcare sector in Colombia.

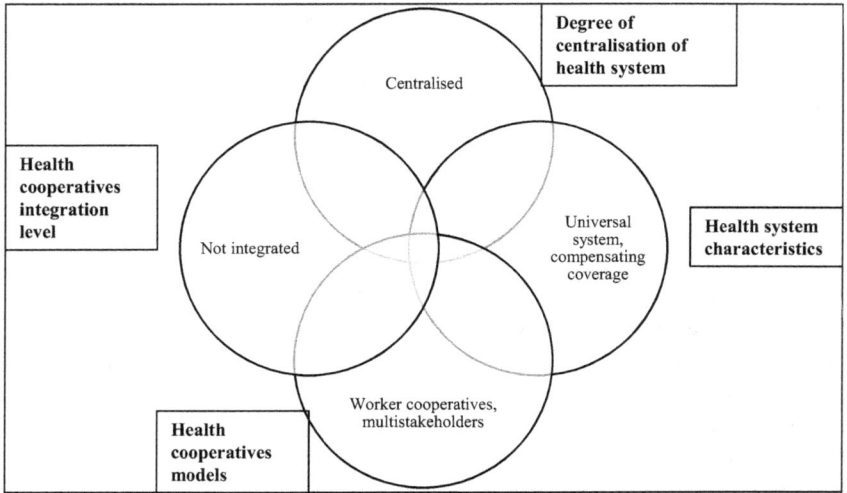

Figure 5.3 Overview of cooperative health types in the healthcare system set up in Colombia, created by the author.

The employment opportunities provided by health cooperatives contribute to the country's economy and positively impact the livelihoods of thousands of individuals. By offering stable and meaningful employment, these cooperatives contribute to their employees' well-being and financial stability. Additionally, their membership base reflects the trust and confidence placed in these cooperatives by individuals seeking quality healthcare services.

6 Historical and modern aspects of health cooperatives development in Asia (Japan, China, and India)

Japan

Healthcare system development in Japan

Japan has an extraordinarily healthy population and ranks among the highest globally in terms of life expectancy for both women and men. The country exhibits low rates of infant mortality and maternal mortality. Age-related illnesses, such as malignant neoplasms, heart diseases, and cerebrovascular diseases, are Japan's predominant causes of death. Particularly noteworthy is Japan's achievement of the lowest mortality rate from heart disease among OECD countries, with approximately 29.4 deaths per 100,000 population (Statista, 2022a).

The healthcare in Japan has evolved throughout history, starting from the Middle Ages when it was rudimentary. During that time, most people depended on traditional healing methods like acupuncture and herbal medicine to address their health issues. However, due to the Japanese government's isolationist policies, individuals could not study traditional medicine techniques abroad. As a result, they had to rely solely on their existing knowledge

Japan's modern healthcare system began to take shape during the Meiji period when the country opened itself to Western influences. The introduction of Western medicine, including antibiotics, had a profound impact on healthcare in Japan and contributed to the enhancement of the quality of life for millions of Japanese citizens.

The establishment of the Japanese health insurance system can be traced back to the drive for industrialisation and progress. A pivotal moment in the history of the Employee's Health Insurance system occurred with the introduction of the Health Insurance Act in 1922. This act was developed by both the government and the industrial sectors to provide health insurance to workers, with the primary objectives of safeguarding employees' health and preventing their inclination towards socialist ideologies (Sakamoto et al., 2018).

Before the 1920s, private and public mutual aid associations provided health and life insurance to workers in the private and public sectors, respectively.

DOI: 10.4324/9781003183068-6

This system transitioned to the current government-regulated employment-based health insurance system in 1927 following the implementation of the Health Insurance Law. In 1938, the National Health Insurance Law was passed, establishing residence-based National Health Insurance (NHI) and assigning healthcare governance to each prefecture. However, it was not until 1958 that the law mandated municipalities to establish residence-based NHI programs, leading to complete population coverage by 1961 (Health and Global Policy Institute, 2018).

Significant improvements have been made in reducing disparities between the wealthy and the poor in Japan's healthcare system. Agricultural land reforms and the implementation of a graduated income tax played a role in narrowing these gaps. Since the 1960s, Japan has maintained a universal health insurance system that ensures comprehensive coverage for all its citizens. This system has played a crucial role in achieving health successes, including the control and eradication of common infectious diseases, significant reductions in transport accident deaths, and the achievement of having the world's highest life expectancy.

The period of strong economic growth from the mid-1950s to the early 1970s also witnessed significant improvements and expansions in social welfare services, including social insurance programs, services for the elderly and disabled, and care for disadvantaged children. However, concerns about increased healthcare spending for the older population in the 1970s raised sustainability issues, leading to the passage of the Health Care for the Aged Law in 1982.

The healthcare system in Japan in contemporary times is characterised by the Statutory Health Insurance System (SHIS), which covers 98.3% of the population. The SHIS consists of employment-based plans covering approximately 59% of the population, residence-based insurance plans covering non-employed individuals under 75 (27%), and health insurance plans for adults aged 75 and older (12.7%) (Tikkanen, 2020). All SHIS plans provide a standardised benefits package, including hospital visits, primary and speciality care, mental healthcare, approved prescription drugs, home care services, hospice care, physical therapy, and dental care. The system is mostly publicly financed through general tax revenue, with self-pay accounting for a smaller portion.

The healthcare system in Japan is regulated by the national government, which sets policies, regulations, and fee schedules. Local prefectures implement national regulations and manage residence-based insurance plans, while municipalities organise health promotion activities and manage beneficiaries. Government agencies, such as the Ministry of Health, Labour and Welfare, the Social Security Council, and the Pharmaceutical and Medical Devices Agency, play critical roles in policy development, regulation, and quality control.

Japan's population has aged significantly, resulting in a shift in healthcare demand towards the elderly. Low birth rates and high life expectancy contribute to the ageing population. Health indicators in Japan, such as fertility rate, life expectancy, and mortality rates, reflect the demographic and health characteristics of the country. The majority of the population is of Japanese ethnicity, and strict immigration policies contribute to its racial and ethnic homogeneity.

The Japanese government has implemented several service delivery and financing reforms to address these challenges since the year 2000. These reforms include establishing the Long-Term Care Insurance System in 2000, implementing the Integrated Community Care System in 2006, the Comprehensive Reform of Social Security and Tax in 2010, and introducing the Regional Healthcare Vision in 2014.

However, Japan faces significant structural challenges in its healthcare system due to negative population growth, a low fertility rate, an ageing population, a shrinking economy, and rising unemployment. These factors have led to a mismatch between the demand for healthcare resources and their supply and a decline in accountability for the quality of care. Japan's economic slowdown, prolonged life expectancy, and increased utilisation of expensive medical technologies have escalated healthcare expenditures. As a result, providing high-quality care at an affordable price has become increasingly difficult.

Furthermore, young healthcare leaders in Japan have proposed the Japan Vision: Health Care 2035, which advocates for a paradigm shift in the healthcare system. This vision aims to establish a sustainable healthcare system that prioritises better health outcomes, provides responsive and equitable care to all members of society, and contributes to the overall prosperity of Japan.

Cooperatives development in Japan

The early development of cooperatives in Japan dates back to 1800 and began with the establishment of mutual societies. The first cooperatives are primarily related to agriculture, consumer, and credit, but also forestry and fishery. One of Japan's first private mutual societies was Kanebo Mutual Association (Kanebo Kyosai Kumiai), which produced textiles (Takakazu, 2011, pp. 22–25).

According to historical data, the development of cooperatives as an organisational model in Japan can be traced back to the tanomoshi-ko forms, which were primitive associations primarily focused on facilitating credits and loans. Research suggests that this organisational form was adopted from China during the Middle Ages (Fisher, 1938). Other, more recent organisational models known as *mujin* have also been documented (Takakazu, 2011, pp. 22–25).

These organisational forms were predominantly found in rural areas, where farmers participated by sharing in cooperatives. Over time, they were able to obtain loans or bonuses periodically.

In 1843, the first organisational form resembling a more modern understanding of cooperatives emerged. It was called Hotokusha and was founded by Ninomiya

Sontoku. This cooperative continued the tradition of providing credit and loan services to rural farmers (Yamauchi, 2015).

During the years 1878–1880, two additional trading cooperatives were established in Gunma-prefecture. A thesis suggests that these cooperatives were the first ones founded in Japan based on the Rochdale principles. S. Maruoka (1927, cited in Fisher (1938)) claimed that the association formed in Tokuyu (around 1879) was organised in a manner very similar to the Rochdale cooperative. Dr Kiyoshi Ogata (1923, p. 6) wrote about it and confirmed this discovery. This association had approximately 500 members and distributed rice, beans, and soy sauce but was disbanded after only three years.

The modern form of cooperatives in Japan developed through the efforts of Viscount Y. Shinagawa and Count T. Hirata. They stayed in France and Germany around 1870 and introduced the Reiffessen savings and credit cooperative model and the Schultz-Delitzch model. These contributions led to the proposal of the Cooperative Credit Society law. Subsequently, Japanese cooperatives expanded their scope beyond credits and loans to include food, tools, seeds, and technology provisions.

The credit society bill 1891 entered into force in an amended form only in 1900. Then the Industrial Cooperative Law, or Sangyo Kumiai Ho, was passed, which contributed to the support of health cooperatives, mainly since 1922

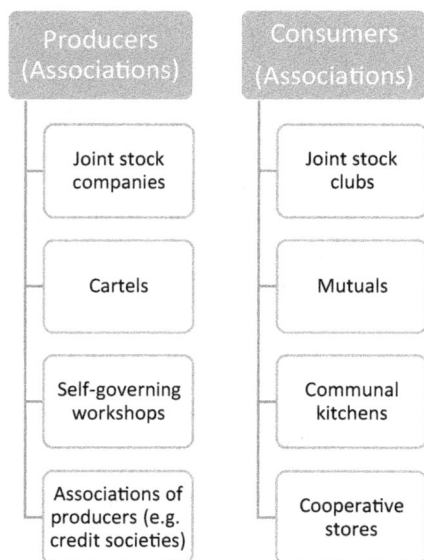

Figure 6.1 Cooperatives development at the beginning of the 20th century in Japan, created by the author.

(that law was based on German law) (Takakazu, 2011, pp. 22–25). It can be said that many cooperatives, before WWI, functioned outside the framework and guidelines agreed upon in Rochdale due to the interference of politics, partisanships, and so on. After the war, the first cooperative was founded that included housewives in Kyoekisha, and after the establishment of the Kateikai sector, which was taken over based on the British Cooperative Women's Guild. Researchers report that in 1936, 15,457 organisations were organised with 6,197,000 members and over two billion yen in capital. However, it is essential to note that the development of health cooperatives in Japan was facilitated because there were already institutionalised principles in the work of mutual aid societies and the Jyorei model, especially in rural areas. The Jyorei model has been in operation since 1835, and its roots were in Munakata and Kurate on the island of Kyushu.

Medical Cooperative Societies were also established based on this model to provide healthcare to impoverished farmers and ensure their financial independence. The government played a role in this by promoting the rapid formation of agricultural cooperatives in nearly all rural areas to stimulate agricultural production and other goods. Consequently, these newly formed Medical Cooperative Societies granted their members access to public healthcare. However, unlike previous Jyorei organisational forms, healthcare cooperatives completely shifted to monetary payments. In the 19th century, Jyrei also facilitated bartering among peasants in rural areas. For instance, northern regions commonly exchanged rice (Sugita, 2012).

Before WWI, Japanese cooperatives were booming, showing their contribution to society in different areas. After WWII, that trend continued, and we can conclude that the Japanese history of cooperatives has lasted from the earliest period of the 19th century until today, with a pause caused by wars. In contemporary times, cooperatives are very developed and operating successfully in different sectors. This development can be seen as in 2013; there were 41,610 cooperatives in Japan, consisting of 40,252 primary cooperatives and 1,358 federations. These cooperatives accounted for 1.1% of the country's total legal entities, which amounted to 3,856,457. Small and Medium-Sized Enterprise Cooperatives constitute the largest category, with 34,971 cooperatives, making up 86.9% of the total. The other categories, in descending order, were Fisheries Cooperatives (1,779 or 4.4%), Agricultural Cooperatives (multi-purpose and specialised, 1,206 or 3.0%), Consumer Cooperatives (820 or 2.0%), Forest Owner Cooperatives (617 or 1.5%), and Worker Cooperatives (442 or 1.1%) (JCA, 2018). The Consumer Cooperatives showed 26.74 million members for purchasing, 36.78 million for insurance, and 2.98 million for health and welfare (127 cooperatives). The total number of cooperatives members increased for the observed year with membership increases observed in Health and Welfare Cooperatives (13.2%).

Health cooperatives development in Japan

Drawing inspiration from Germany, where Western-style medicine was predominantly practised in urban areas due to wealthier patients, advanced medical technology, and more significant financial resources, Japan faced similar challenges. The scarcity of doctors in rural regions and the rising costs of medical care prompted the formation of farmers' medical cooperatives. In 1919, Shimane Prefecture established the first medical cooperative, catering primarily to farmers. Some cooperatives even built their medical facilities and recruited doctors temporarily or permanently. The growth of medical cooperatives gained momentum with the inclusion of medical cooperatives under the Industrial Cooperative Law in 1922, modelled after the German system. Prominent Christian reformers Nitobe Inazō and Kagawa Toyohiko played a significant role in expanding medical cooperatives, with the Tokyo Medical Cooperative, founded in 1932, becoming the most prominent (Takakazu, 2011, p. 25). As a result, the number of medical cooperatives emerged from four in 1924 to 22 in 1931 and increased to 819 by 1936.

In 1937, the Health Insurance Act was passed in Japan, which brought healthcare throughout Japan for the first time, especially to farmers. Among other things, the leaders of the cooperative movement are responsible for this law. Also, it was noted that Kagawa (the father of the cooperative movement) held discussions with the Cabinet Minister in 1936, thereby aiding in a better understanding and acceptance of the idea of health cooperatives. This law allowed the Japanese government to instruct the rest of the population to join a health cooperative after 2/3 of the population voted in favour of its formation. This approach highlighted the importance of politics in the further development of cooperatives in Japan, and this was recognised by the Central Union of Cooperatives and the Young Men's Cooperative Alliance, who at that time decided to support and vote for any politician committed to working towards the development of cooperatives in Japan in accordance with their principles. Politics in Japan have often significantly influenced the cooperative movement's development, particularly in terms of massification, the need to increase production, and the impact on the labour market. Due to massification, cooperatives also encouraged health programs and became leading centres for organising specific population segments. While not classified as health insurance, urban clinics emerged to provide medical care at lower costs. Although the goal was similar to health insurance, these clinics aimed to improve access to medical services. In 1911, Suzuki Umeshirō and Katō Tokijirō were granted permission by the Home Ministry to establish an "actual expense" clinic in Tokyo. These clinics set lower doctors' fees for medicine and medical care, initially about one-third of those set by local medical associations. Initially, the medical associations took a wait-and-see approach, underestimating the impact of these clinics. However, as the actual expense clinics spread to other regions, medical associations grew more resistant, fearing patient diversion and declining average doctors' fees. In 1915, the medical associations successfully lobbied the Home Ministry to restrict further expansion of these clinics. While the growth of private actual expense clinics was curtailed, existing private clinics were permitted to continue, and public actual expense clinics were established, resulting in a total of 153 clinics by 1929.

Private initiatives emerged in the early 20th century to protect people from medical catastrophes. First, private health insurance schemes in firms were developed in response to the inadequacy of the existing healthcare system in meeting people's needs. Concurrently, medical cooperatives and actual expense clinics were established with similar objectives. Initially, medical associations held varying attitudes towards these developments.

Additionally, private health insurance was strengthened in rural areas through health cooperatives known as *iryo riyo kumiai*, which allowed peasants to seek medical care from village doctors (Kanpo). The scarcity of doctors in rural regions posed a significant problem at the beginning of the 20th century. One of the reasons was that doctors knowledgeable in "Western medicine" were more likely to remain in cities where the population was wealthier. Another reason was the implementation of a state act that limited the number of doctors (Kanpo) in rural areas. As a result, in 1919, the first health cooperative was established in Shimane Prefecture, pioneering this approach.

In the period before WWII, specialised health cooperatives appeared more and more frequently for the provision of various health services, especially in rural areas of Japan.

State associations operated in rural areas before and during WWII and were especially characteristic of Aomori Prefecture, while ten were in the Tohoku region and later spread to other areas. Through joint efforts with the Ministry of Agriculture and Forestry, these organisational entities have become of great importance for the entire healthcare system of Japan. These organisations worked during the war as well as after WWII. After the Law on Cooperatives reconstruction, the Association of Agricultural Hospitals was established as a new Agricultural Welfare Cooperative, which continued as a federation known today as Koseiren. The number of health cooperatives grew from four (in 1924) to 22 (1931) up to 819 (1936) (Ministry of Health and Welfare Medical Bureau, 1976).

The Ministry of Health and Welfare was established in 1938 when the First National Health Insurance Law was approved. The benefits of this regulation were related to establishing an NHI system that enabled the management of individual prefectures. After an amendment to this law in 1958, total healthcare coverage in Japan was achieved in 1961 (Shimazaki, 2013).

As mentioned earlier, cooperative models were formed in Japan that provided healthcare under the name Koseiren. These models emerged from agricultural cooperatives and were based on community principles developed earlier in the history of Japan. Also, other models of health cooperatives were studied, with the fact that they primarily provided healthcare in urban areas, while Koseiren was represented in rural areas of Japan. In addition to the forms mentioned above of cooperative organisations, Zenkyoren, also known as JA Kyosai, represents the National Mutual Insurance Federation of Agricultural Cooperatives. Today, this organisation has a representative office in Tokyo and representative offices in 47 prefectures in Japan. Known as "JAs," Japan Agricultural Cooperatives group also includes other organisations like Zenkyoren. This organisation is proud of the work of Toyohiko Kagawa, previously mentioned as one of the initiators of cooperatives in Japan. He was also the first Japanese nominated for the Nobel Prize for Literature, a fighter for social justice who spoke about insurance at that time (1945) in the following way: "Life insurance is managed by capitalist commercial insurance and does not aim for the benefit of the working masses. Not limited to life insurance, insurance itself is by nature mutually supportive, and all insurance should be cooperative" (Zenkyoren, 2020). From then (1954) to today, these cooperatives have worked and function with many benefits for their members and users of their services. In 2020, it was the 20th anniversary of integrating the Zenkyoren Federation within JAs.

JAs include Chuokai (prefectural Unions of Agricultural Cooperatives) and Zenchu (Central Union of Agricultural Cooperatives) organisational forms responsible for policy proposal/change, organisation and cooperation on an international level. Yen-Noh (Agricultural Cooperative Associations) and Keizairen (Prefectural Economic Federations of Agricultural Cooperatives) are responsible for logistics to consumers, where they transport agricultural products. In addition, marketing is their field of action within the JA group. Shinren (Prefectural Credit Federation of Agricultural Cooperatives) and Norinchunkin Bank (Central Cooperative Bank for Agriculture, Forestry, and Fisheries) finance cooperatives; cooperative members and other users operate through loans and other banking instruments.

As we mentioned earlier, Zenkyoren (National Mutual Insurance Federation of Agricultural Cooperatives) is part of the JA group and is particularly interesting because it deals with the mutual aid approach, which enables its users to be insured against the most various risks that can affect them and their lives. In addition, Zenkyoren is involved in planning, product development, public health, and other education, development of information systems, and management of investment funds (Zenkyoren, 2020).

The crucial segment of insurance in JAs is related to life insurance policies that include important public segments through whole life insurance, term life insurance, endowment life insurance, medical insurance, and nursing care insurance. JA comprehensive life insurance this organisation had 21.6 million policies in 2020, with a total value of 245 trillion yen.

In 2018, there were 41,610 cooperatives in Japan, and the Health and Welfare Cooperatives grew by 6.7%, while Insurance Cooperatives and Purchasing

Coops also experienced an increase. Among Consumer Cooperatives, there were 2.98 million members for purchasing health and welfare within 127 cooperatives. In addition to this, there is a trend of increasing memberships in the Health and Welfare Cooperatives in Japan; based on historical knowledge, those types of organisations are deeply part of Japan society today, and their further development should be expected.

China

Healthcare system development in China

People's Republic of China, the world's most populous country, had a population of 1.35 billion in 2012, accounting for 19% of the global population showing a further significant increase with approximately 1.45 billion people in 2023. The country is currently facing the challenge of rapid ageing, with 8.7% of its population aged 65 or older. Urbanisation has been a significant trend, with 51.8% of Chinese citizens residing in cities. In conjunction with China's economic advancements, there has been an improvement in the general public health of the Chinese population in recent decades. Currently, China boasts a comprehensive healthcare system that reaches 90% of its citizens, resulting in increased life expectancy and enhanced accessibility to affordable, high-quality healthcare services. Although significant progress has been made in preventing infectious diseases, managing chronic illnesses and providing healthcare for the ageing population, significant obstacles remain for the country's healthcare system (Statista, 2022c).

The history of medicine in China extends back to thousands of years, with Traditional Chinese Medicine (TCM) having a lineage of at least 23 centuries. TCM aims to prevent and treat diseases by restoring the balance of yin and yang. China boasts one of the world's oldest medical systems, with practices like acupuncture and Chinese herbal remedies dating back to over 2,200 years. The Huangdi Neijing (The Yellow Emperor's Inner Classic), written in the third century BCE, serves as the earliest known written record of Chinese medicine and forms the basis of TCM's theoretical concepts that continue to be followed today. Traditional Chinese healers strive to achieve harmony between two complementary forces, yin (passive) and yang (active), believed to exist within the human body and the universe. According to TCM, good health is maintained when these forces are in balance, while illness arises from an imbalance between yin and yang. In 1578, Li Shizhen published his well-known work, the *Bencao Gangmu* (Compendium of Materia Medica), and meticulously catalogued 1,892 drugs and over 11,000 formal prescriptions for specific ailments (Britannica, 2023). Three decades later, in 1601, the *Zhenjiu dacheng*, a comprehensive work on acupuncture, was published following the appearance of the *Bencao gang mu*, an extensive pharmaceutical encyclopaedia. With the rise of the Ming dynasty in the 15th century, Chinese nationalists began questioning the reasons behind the perceived decline in Chinese intellectual history. When the Manchu conquest overthrew the Ming dynasty, establishing the Qing dynasty in 1648, a movement emerged in the 17th and 18th centuries advocating a return to earlier Chinese perspectives. Medicine was not exempt from this trend. While some schools adhered to theoretical models developed between the 12th and 15th centuries, many authors sought to reclaim the presumed advantages of ancient untainted knowledge. They engaged in philological reconstructions of ancient medical and pharmaceutical texts or sought to present ancient wisdom as a framework for contemporary knowledge. Others explored new paths, such as investigating folk healing practices and conducting systematic examinations of human anatomy, previously inaccessible to physicians of earlier centuries. One example of this exploration is the Chuanya, compiled by Zhao Xuemin in the late 18th century, based on the notes of a travelling healer, which provides insights into common medications and medical techniques. In the 19th century, when Western medicine was introduced to China, it encountered diverse ideas and practices encompassing both ontic and holistic perspectives. Ontic theories attributed illness to the invasion of the body by pathogenic agents. At the same time, holistic ideas viewed disease as a deviation from a harmonious state maintained by a lifestyle aligned with the fundamental laws of the universe. However, in the 20th century, the further development of Chinese medicine within its traditional theoretical foundations stopped. As the ancient doctrines of yin-yang and the five phases lost prominence in everyday life, each new generation in China became increasingly disconnected from the worldview based on systematic correspondences.

More robust primary care has been associated with significant contributions to health system performance, yet many countries need help adequately resourcing it due to competing hospital demands. In China, despite having originated influential models of primary healthcare in its history, the country continues to grapple with the dominance of hospitals in health service delivery. The first hospital in China was established on the mainland in 1825. In the period until 1949, when the People's Republic of China was founded, the main characteristic of healthcare was the hospital-centric model, established during the early institutionalisation of Western medicine in China (Xu et al., 2019).

Before 1949, areas under Chinese Communist Party (CCP) control provided free medical treatment. Following the CCP's rise to power in 1949, national "patriotic health campaigns" and local government initiatives successfully implemented essential sanitary measures and preventive hygiene education. The provision of healthcare was linked to individuals' places of work, such as government bureaucratic units, enterprises, factories, schools, cooperatives, or communes in rural areas. In 1951, labour insurance regulations were introduced to address medical issues among workers in the industrial and mining sectors. Free medical treatment was also experimented with in northern

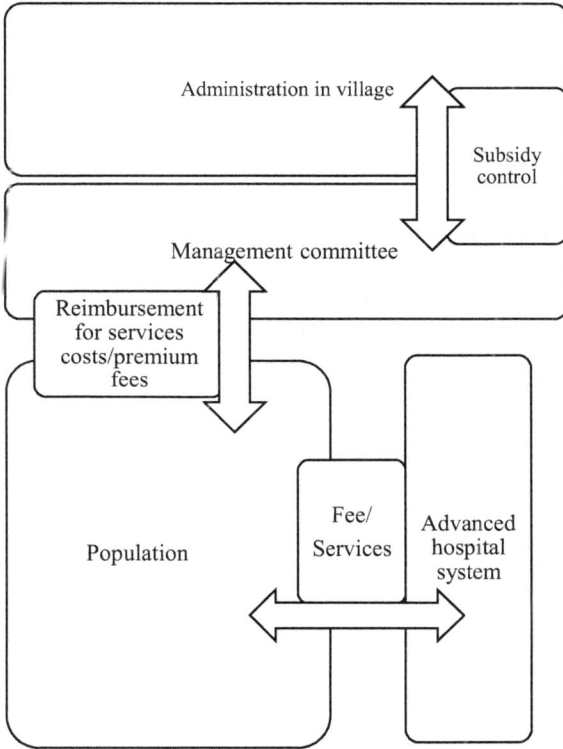

Figure 6.2 Development of health cooperatives before the 1950s in China, created by the author.

Shaanxi and certain ethnic minority areas during the same year. On June 27, 1952, the Administration Council issued instructions for implementing free medical treatment and prevention for government officials, political parties, organisations, and affiliated institutions at all levels. Subsequently, the CCP government gradually collectivised and modernised the medical and healthcare system, modelling it after the Soviet Union. Under the planned economy, a three-tier hospital structure was established, consisting of municipal and district hospitals and sub-district outpatient services. A three-level healthcare network was created in rural areas, with county hospitals as leaders, township (town) health centres as hubs, and village clinics forming the foundation (Leow, 2014). During the Cultural Revolution (1966–1976), Mao Zedong's followers targeted medical professionals as part of their attack on elitism. Basic primary care services were extended to rural areas through programs like the deployment of barefoot doctors and other state-sponsored initiatives. Urban healthcare systems were also streamlined in addition to rural areas (Andrews & Bullock, 2014). The Cultural Revolution further emphasised rural healthcare, prioritising healthcare and medicine for rural people nationwide in Mao's June 26 Directive.

Consequently, clinics and hospitals dispatched their staff on medical tours to rural areas, and cooperative healthcare initiatives in rural regions expanded. Barefoot doctors were crucial in delivering healthcare services to areas where urban-trained doctors were reluctant to settle. They promoted basic hygiene, preventive healthcare, family planning, and treated common illnesses. However, with the onset of economic reforms in 1978, significant disparities in health standards emerged in China, between urban and rural areas and between coastal and interior provinces. This led to the privatisation of much of the healthcare sector. The closure of communes and state-owned enterprises and declining state employment for urban residents resulted in reduced access to social security and health benefits. Consequently, urban residents have increasingly had to bear out-of-pocket healthcare costs since the 1990s. On the other hand, many rural residents faced challenges affording the expenses of seeking healthcare in urban hospitals.

China's administrative system consists of the Central Government, known as the State Council, and local governments at various levels, including provinces, cities, counties, and townships. The country's economic system transitioned from a planned economy between 1949 and 1978 to a market-based system following economic reforms in 1978. Since then, China has experienced economic growth and became the world's second-largest economy in 2010. However, regional disparities and inequalities persist between urban and rural areas.

The health status of the Chinese population has significantly improved over the years. Life expectancy at birth has increased from 35 in 1949 to 75 in 2012. The disease profile has also shifted from infectious diseases and high birth and death rates to chronic diseases and low birth and death rates. Chronic diseases now account for 85% of China's approximately 10.3 million annual deaths, contributing to 70% of the country's total disease burden.

China has established a comprehensive health system with various health laws and administrative regulations. The National Health and Family Planning Commission (NHFPC) and the State Administration of TCM are critical health authorities at the national level. Other government departments, such as the National Development and Reform Commission, Ministry of Civil Affairs, Ministry of Finance, and Ministry of Human Resources and Social Security, also play roles in planning, funding, and managing the health system.

The health administration in China operates at four levels: the NHFPC, provincial health bureaus, municipal health bureaus, and county health bureaus. Despite several reforms to streamline administration and decentralise power, the Central Government retains significant influence in lawmaking and decision-making. Local governments implement plans and decisions within their jurisdiction based on principles established by the Central Government. Different government sectors, including the party, the government, the military, and mass organisations, collaborate through patriotic health campaign committees at various levels to coordinate nationwide health campaigns. Governments carry out the regulation and oversight of health service delivery in China at different levels.

Regarding health financing, China employs four main methods: tax-based funding, social health insurance, private insurance, and out-of-pocket payments. Health expenditure has increased with the rapid development of the market and technological progress. In recent years, the government has made greater investments in health and established basic medical insurance to reduce out-of-pocket payments, improve accessibility, and promote equity. The proportion of out-of-pocket payments in total health expenditure has significantly decreased from 59.0% in 2000 to 34.4% in 2012. China has implemented basic medical insurance systems to cover both urban and rural residents. Urban Employee Basic Medical Insurance (UEBMI) is compulsory for urban workers, while Urban Resident Basic Medical Insurance (URBMI) is available for those whom UEBMI does not cover. Rural residents can enrol in the New Rural Cooperative Medical Scheme (NRCMS). Government subsidies are crucial in financing URBMI and NRCMS, ensuring that low-income individuals have access to primary healthcare (Meng et al., 2015).

The Chinese health system operates under a legislative framework consisting of three interconnected subsystems: health financing, health service delivery, and health supervision. Although these subsystems maintain a certain level of independence, they are interrelated and function together. Various actors play specific roles within these subsystems.

Since 2009, China's healthcare financing has predominantly relied on social insurance. By 2013, more than 95% of the population was covered by the three insurance schemes, albeit with varying benefit levels due to differences in funding. The delivery of healthcare services has traditionally relied heavily on public hospitals and other public healthcare facilities, including traditional medicine hospitals. However, the private sector has increasingly played a supplementary role in healthcare financing and delivery. In 2013, private health insurance accounted for 3.55% of total health expenditure, and private health institutions comprised 45.09% of all health institutions (Meng et al., 2015).

Regarding health legislation, China has established a unified system integrating multiple laws and regulations, with the Chinese Constitution as a guiding principle. Laws issued by the National People's Congress (NPC), administrative regulations, and local laws significantly contribute to the legislative system. Various legal departments constitute this system, such as Constitution Related Law, Civil and Commercial Law, Administrative Law, Economic Law, Social Law, Criminal Law, Procedural Law, and Non-Procedural Law.

China has implemented a three-tier legislative system following the Constitution and the Law on Legislation. This system consists of the NPC, the State Council and its affiliated departments at the national level, provincial People's Congresses and governments at the provincial level, as well as People's Congresses and governments in capital cities and major cities approved by the State Council. At the provincial level, the authority to formulate provincial laws and regulations is granted, provided they align with the Constitution, other laws, and administrative regulations. They are acknowledged by the NPC's Standing Committee. Provincial governments can establish regulations, while city-level People's Congresses and governments possess the power to enact local regulations and rules, which must not contradict other regulations, laws, and the Constitution.

The Constitution explicitly outlines the health rights of Chinese citizens, affirming their entitlement to material assistance from the state and society in the event of old age, illness, or disability. The state is responsible for developing social insurance, social assistance, and health services to ensure citizens can exercise this right. In China, health laws and regulations cover many areas, including legislation for health institutions, medical practices, public health, and health services. These laws provide standards and guidelines for specific aspects of the health system. However, no comprehensive overarching health law directly links the Constitution to specific health legislation, although efforts are underway to develop such legislation. The majority of health legislation in China consists of administrative laws and regulations. Alongside the laws issued by the NPC's Standing Committee, there are 38 administrative regulations enacted by the State Council. These regulations encompass various aspects, including managing health facilities, handling medical malpractice, regulations on TCMs, management of public health emergencies, and nurse regulations. Furthermore, ministries or local governments issue numerous local laws, regulations, and documents. Over the years, the healthcare system in China has experienced significant transformations including further changes.

Health cooperatives development in China

During the Sino-Japanese War, health cooperatives were established in the Shanxi-Gansu-Ningxia region to realise fundamental rights to healthcare. The number of cooperatives at that time was small, but they still had a contribution to preserving healthcare for their users. During this period, there was a noted visit of Chinese experts to health cooperatives in Yugoslavia to assess the health cooperatives model, and later it was transferred to China (Stamenovic, 2020). They also expressed keen interest in developing and functioning health cooperatives at that time. According to Xingzhu and Huaijie, the Cooperative Medical System (CMS) has existed since the 1950s and was developed primarily for rural areas of China, especially for farmers.

The period from 1955 to 1959 is considered the beginning of significant growth of cooperatives to provide health services and health insurance. Along with the development of agricultural cooperatives, other areas of cooperatives also grew. In that development process, CMS was also created, and the first one was formed in 1955 in Wangdian, Zhengyang Country, and then they were founded in Henan, Jiangsu, Hubei, and Shanxi.

Thanks to the high level of representation, health cooperatives in 1960–1979 reached about 90% coverage in rural areas (1979). Mao Zedong and the Communist Party consider health cooperatives as a valid organisational option to support significant rural healthcare issues. This is another example of the flexibility of health cooperatives to be used within the scope of different political and ideological systems and incorporated to resolve practical healthcare issues. In order to improve further, new regulations were needed, so the Ministry of Health, Finance and Agriculture jointly enacted the Regulation of the Rural Cooperative Medical System in 1979. Several reports showed that after 1980 there was a dramatic decline (from 90% to 5%) in the number of cooperatives and that one of the main reasons was the unpredictable economic reform that was in force at the time, but also certain ideological political positions that looked at CMS as a product of the Great Leap Forward (Han, 1991; Zhou, 1987).

After 1986, the most significant number of services were provided through direct forms of payment, although CMS survived in certain countries such as Shangdong, Jiangsu, Hubei, and Shanghai. Interestingly, they managed to keep the number of users at 80% or more in these areas. Also, it is interesting that these provinces were among the first in the initial establishment of this system. Hence, the population's habits and good organisation at the organisational level also influenced their sustainability.

Since the 1970s, there have been more significant changes in China's reforms that have affected the healthcare sector in one way or another. All changes were made through new laws and regulations, and the essence was related to the greater responsibility of the individual concerning the collective, especially in the context of the social and health sectors. In the public sector, this contributed to the development of preventive and curative healthcare so that the cooperative health system became increasingly difficult in rural areas.

Concerning health insurance, in the 1970s, there was a collapse of the health cooperative system. However, in later years, the reorganisation of the CMS was carried out, for example, CMS reform in 2002 (thanks to funds from the Ministry of Finance and Department of Finance of the Provincial Government), which until 2003 covered approximately 10% of the population.

The primary rationale for reintroducing health cooperatives was related to the fact that it is necessary to strengthen the healthcare sector in Chinese villages. At the beginning of the new millennium, there was discussion about advanced medicine and the existence of technologies (medicines, medical devices, therapeutic procedures) that are significantly more advanced and can treat those diseases for which there was no cure in the previous settings. The new therapies are also expensive, bringing new challenges in financing healthcare in China and throughout the world. However, China's rapid economic development since 2000 has made it possible to create additional finances to start strengthening healthcare in rural areas. It is important to note that there is a specific geographical diversification in the development and coverage of rural areas with healthcare. Still, the People's Republic of China, as a country that was transitioning from a centrally planned to a market economy, looked for an answer here in the centralisation of its activities and the creation of central plans (Ministry of Health of China, 2003; Ministry of Health, Ministry of Finance, & Ministry of Civil Affairs, 2012; Sun et al., 2009).

As a result, the Ninth Five-Year Plan (1996–2000) for National Economic and Social Development was issued on September 28, 1995, and aimed to cover the population in rural areas with healthcare quickly. This plan led to a significant revival of the Chinese State because its primary goal was modernisation in important segments for development.

After that, in 2002, the Decision of the Central Committee of the Communist Party and the State Council of China on Further Strengthening Rural Health Work was adopted. In 2003, a document called Notice of the General Office of the State Council on Forwarding the Opinions of the Ministry of Health and Other Departments on the Establishment of a New Rural Cooperative Medical System was adopted (Ministry of Health of China, 2003).

This program had significant government support, which is realised through various subsidies that are very significant, and the goal of this program was to cover about 800 million people in rural areas with healthcare, including cooperatives (Liu & Cao, 1992; Liu & Tsegai, 2011).

The document states:

> Establishing a new type of rural cooperative medical system is an important content of rural health work in the new era. It significantly improves farmers' health, promotes rural economic development, and maintains social stability. The new rural cooperative medical system is a system of mutual medical assistance and mutual aid for farmers, organised, guided, and supported by the Government, farmers voluntarily participate, individual, collective and Government financing and major illnesses are coordinated.
>
> (Wang et al., 2014)

Therefore, it was planned that starting in 2003, all provinces, according to the planning work of the government, would select two to three cities for pilot projects to implement the new health cooperative scheme.

A rural cooperative medical management committee was formed, consisting of representatives of farmers who are interested in membership in health cooperatives. A financing system based on individual payments, government funding, and collective support has been implemented, where individual payments should not be lower than ten yuan, and rural collective economic organisations should support this system, both financially and educationally, to support individuals to join this system for providing healthcare. On the other hand, the state provides subsidies according to the 1:1 system, so for ten yuan paid, subsidies of ten yuan per capita are given. The rural cooperative medical fund, part of the New Medical Cooperative Scheme, is more precisely organised by the rural cooperative medical management committee, into which farmers voluntarily contribute funds and funds from collective organisations, and the Chinese Government supports the fund. Also, the New Medical Cooperative Scheme provided health protection from 11.63% to 21% at the level of the entire nation in 2005. It was below expectations, but it still showed specific results. During the same year, healthcare costs for older people were, on average, at US$ 204.77, while reimbursement for the same population was 30.6%. In 2014, the percentage of the population receiving healthcare through the New Medical Cooperative Scheme increased to 80.34%. However, the costs for the elderly population that year amounted to US$ 696.23. During the same year, healthcare costs for the elderly population were, on average, at US$ 696.23, while reimbursement for the same population was 56.1%. By the end of 2014, about 736 million people participated in this organisational model (Zhang et al., 2016; Ma et al., 2016).

Another crucial role of the New Medical Cooperative Scheme is that it optimised out-of-pocket healthcare costs. However, even today, this type of expense exhibits a growing trend and poses a severe challenge to the Chinese State (Zhang et al., 2016; Ma et al., 2016). The policy development of the NCMS clearly demonstrates an improvement in the financing level and reimbursement from 2005 to 2014. Nonetheless, in 2011, the actual reimbursement ratio fell significantly below the nominal reimbursement ratio of the NCMS plans (Ma et al., 2016). Furthermore, the NCMS was influenced to provide financial protection to the impoverished population in rural areas and ensure their access to healthcare services. This initiative has had a significant impact on reducing healthcare inequalities and improving healthcare accessibility.

The goal was to enable almost complete coverage of rural areas with healthcare by 2020 while the establishment of a new rural CMS must follow the following principles: volunteer participation, multi-party fundraising, expenditure as determined by revenue, pilot projects, and continuous evaluation. This was not achieved completely, but significant success was achieved.

Today's problem in the healthcare system of the People's Republic of China is related to the significant differences in the healthcare processes in urban and rural areas. Modern economic-technological trends that entail a transition in terms of the characteristics of the labour market, increased urbanisation, and accelerated development of China in recent decades are also essential factors for the development of the health system. Accordingly, the necessary work on the contribution of health-oriented benefits to the economic development of rural areas was identified, regulation of the health market in rural areas, a plan for the development of the health system in a populous country like China, and development of the system for social and health insurance and continuous evaluation of the work of Basic Medical Insurance and Cooperative Medical System. Currently, health cooperatives are considered part of the solution to the rising challenges of the China healthcare system and, considering historical and modern developments, they would be expected to play an important role in further developments too.

India

Healthcare system development in India

Before gaining independence from British colonial rule in 1947, the responsibility for legislation and implementation of public health activities in India was delegated to the states through the Montagu-Chelmsford Reforms of 1919 and the Government of India (GoI) Act of 1935. Those reforms aimed to introduce self-governance institutions in colonial India gradually. In that era, modern health services, including hospitals and dispensaries, were mainly developed in major presidency towns such as Madras (now Chennai), Bombay (now Mumbai), and Calcutta (now Kolkata). Those services primarily catered to British officers, troops, their families, and to some extent native princes and elites. The commoners and poor people of colonial India primarily relied on traditional systems of medicine like Ayurveda and Unani, as well as mission hospitals.

In 1943, the Health Survey and Development Committee, chaired by Sir Joseph Bhore, remodelled health services in India. The committee aimed to integrate curative and preventive medicine at all levels. It is important to note that the establishment of the Bhore Committee coincided with the rise of Keynesian economic policies and the emergence of welfare states in many parts of the Western world. Those policies emphasised the government's responsibility for providing public services. In this context, the Bhore Committee envisioned a three-tier public health system in India, funded and delivered by the government, focusing on integrated and universal access to healthcare (Bajpai & Dholakia, 2011). However, India did not achieve the short-term goals outlined in the Bhore Committee report during the first ten years. The committee recommended that each district in India should have approximately 25 primary health centres (PHCs) serving a population of no more than 40,000, along with a 30-bed hospital to cater to two PHCs. Each PHC was proposed to have a staff of 15, including two medical officers, four public health nurses, one nurse, four midwives, four public health inspectors, two pharmacists, one clerk, and other support staff (Bajpai & Dholakia, 2011).

At the time of independence, the private healthcare sector in India was relatively small and comprised allopathic and alternative medical providers who mainly offered outpatient care services. National health policies at that time focused on vertical disease control programs, such as eradicating smallpox and polio, as well as family planning. The promotion of primary care services was not a high priority. Public-sector facilities dominated the hospital sector until the early 1980s, with limited private-sector involvement.

In 1983, India introduced its first National Health Policy (NHP) following the Alma-Ata Declaration in 1978. The NHP 1983 emphasised primary healthcare, focusing on preventive, promotional, and rehabilitative aspects. However, this policy deviated significantly from the ideals outlined in the Bhore Committee report. While the Bhore Committee recognised healthcare as a public good and placed the responsibility of providing it on the government, the NHP 1983 explored approaches that aimed to reduce government expenditure by leveraging the private sector, involving voluntary agencies, and transferring knowledge and expertise to health volunteers at the grassroots level to provide low-cost primary care.

The introduction of Auxiliary Nurse Midwives, Community Health Workers (CHWs), and other initiatives under the Minimum Needs Program increased investment in primary care. However, these initiatives faced challenges and declined in the late 1980s due to structural adjustment policies. From the 1980s, limited funding, policies favouring the private sector, and rising incomes led to the rapid growth of the private health sector. This resulted in serious challenges for people experiencing poverty to access affordable and high-quality care. Rural–urban disparities also worsened.

In response to the growing rural–urban health disparities, the NHP of 2002 aimed to strengthen the health system and implement specific vertical disease control programs (Ministry of Health and Family Welfare (MoHFW), 1983; MoHFW, 2002). The NHP 2002 recognised the need for increased public-sector investments in health and committed to allocating 2% of gross domestic product (GDP) to the government health sector by 2010. The goal was to improve the existing public health infrastructure and increase the utilisation of outpatient health services provided by public-sector facilities from less than 20% to over 75% by 2010. The NHP also emphasised the importance of an integrated system for surveillance, health accounts, and health statistics to inform and enhance program planning. Around the same time, regulatory changes in the health insurance sector allowed private-sector competition and foreign direct investment, marking a shift influenced by international trade negotiations and service trade liberalisation.

A significant development following the publication of the NHP in 2002 was the National Rural Health Mission (NRHM), launched in 2005. The NRHM operationalised the policy objectives outlined in the NHP 2002 and focused on improving maternal and child health indicators. It aimed to increase institutional deliveries, promote universal immunisation, address micro-nutrient deficiencies, and allocate an expanded budget to train and deploy frontline workers. The NRHM, designed as a centrally sponsored scheme, required state governments to contribute matching funds (10% for priority states and 40% for others), with the remaining funding provided by the Central Government. This led to a prioritisation of health spending in government budgets. In 2005, India's public-sector spending on health was only 0.9% of its GDP, one of the lowest among developing nations. However, funding for the NRHM helped increase budgetary allocations, and by 2014–2015, public-sector spending on health rose to 1.1% of GDP, even as India's GDP growth remained one of the highest in the world. The NRHM targeted 18 "high-focus" states with inadequate health infrastructure and poor health outcomes. In addition to supporting public-sector health infrastructure, NRHM funding led to the emergence of a workforce of female health activists/volunteers in villages known as Accredited Social Health Activists, as well as decentralised community planning and monitoring through Village Health and Sanitation Committees (Selvaraj et al., 2022).

During the 2000s, extensive research highlighted the significant role of poor health in driving high out-of-pocket health spending and causing impoverishment. Publicly funded health insurance schemes, particularly those targeting the poor and vulnerable populations, became recognised as important mechanisms for providing financial risk protection. Several countries, including Mexico, China, Colombia, the Philippines, Vietnam, and Thailand, implemented publicly funded insurance programs with varying degrees of success. India also joined this group by introducing a fully subsidised health insurance scheme called the "Rajiv Aarogyasri" in 2007 in Andhra Pradesh. Subsequently, the Ministry of Labour and Employment launched another publicly funded insurance scheme for people experiencing poverty, the "Rashtriya Swasthya Bima Yojana" (RSBY), in 2008. Other Indian states, such as Tamil Nadu, Maharashtra, Karnataka, Himachal Pradesh, and Kerala, also introduced publicly funded insurance programs (Karan et al., 2017).

In 2018, the GoI replaced RSBY with a more comprehensive health insurance scheme called the Pradhan Mantri Jan Arogya Yojana (PM-JAY), the world's largest publicly funded health insurance scheme. The accessibility and affordability of medicines, vaccines, and diagnostic facilities pose significant challenges in the healthcare system. Insufficient government funding and weak procurement and logistics systems have resulted in poor access to medicines and medical equipment in government health facilities. However, a few states in India have successfully funded and established efficient mechanisms for the procurement and supply of medicines and diagnostics. Physical access to medicines is relatively easier in the private sector, but affordability remains a hindrance. Also, many essential medicines remain expensive, making them unaffordable for numerous households. Despite India's reputation as the "pharmacy of the global south," the branded generics market remains elusive and costly for most of the population. Inadequate regulatory oversight has also limited the control over inappropriate prescription and use of medicines.

As mentioned, several policy initiatives have been introduced to address the challenges in the Indian health system. The NRHM and National Health Mission (NHM) were launched to strengthen the health systems of state governments, with a primary focus on maternal and neonatal conditions, infectious disease control programs, and the expansion of institutional deliveries. While there has been progress in some states, concerns persist regarding the quality of delivery services, emergency obstetric care, the availability of essential medicines and diagnostics, and data quality in the Health Management Information System. Government health programs have faced significant underfunding at national and state levels. Although efforts have been made to increase tax devolution from the Central to state governments, the funds allocated to health have not substantially increased. State treasuries often allocate tax funding to other priority areas, thereby limiting the resources available for health.

The subnational drug regulatory system needs better infrastructure; there is a lack of skilled personnel, and the legislation is confusing, hindering the effective implementation of rules and regulations, although in the last years, there has been significant improvement noticed. The current price ceiling mechanisms for medicines aim to balance the interests of drug makers and patients but have resulted in limited coverage and price reduction of essential drugs in the private market. The NHP 2017 provides a framework for achieving universal health coverage through prevention, promotion, and affordable and comprehensive primary care. Policies and plans emphasise the need to increase public spending on health to 2.5% of GDP by 2025. Integrating urban health plans with the NHM and scaling up insurance models like the Pradhan Mantri Jan Aarogya Yojana (PM-JAY) aims to improve access to healthcare services and financial risk protection for households. Strengthening public-sector health services requires focusing on resources, governance, and quality. Increasing public health spending, recruiting and training health professionals, implementing pooled procurement and improved supply chains, and effectively regulating the for-profit private care sector are essential steps. Additionally, improving governance and accountability in healthcare delivery is crucial to meeting citizens' needs and aspirations and ensuring high-quality care.

Cooperatives development in India

The earliest origins of certain organisational forms that can be compared to cooperatives can be traced back to the Moghul dynasty (15th to 16th century), which offered specific financial services to peasants who were struggling with insolvency, debt, and their desire to break free from feudalism and regain ownership of their land. Unlike some other territories of that time, cooperative organisations did not exist. The history of cooperatives in India has primarily been influenced by the former British Empire and the cooperative work conducted within the United Kingdom. This knowledge and experience were transferred from Britain to India, which was then one of its colonies. Sir Frederick Nicholson, who resided in Madras, is considered the pioneer of the modern cooperative movement in India. In the 19th century, rural areas of India faced numerous challenges, particularly those related to agricultural financing, to facilitate what is now known as sustainable development. Two laws, namely The Land Improvement Loans Act of 1883 and The Agriculturalist Loans Act of 1884, were enacted to provide the necessary financing. During the agrarian movement in the Deccan, a significant historical event unfolded as peasants revolted against moneylenders who imposed exorbitant interest rates on loans obtained during times of desperate need. With no alternative, the peasants took matters into their own hands by confiscating promissory notes and mortgage deeds from these moneylenders. This chaotic situation led to the government implementing the Taccavi Legislation, which subsequently led to the formation of cooperative societies. In the ensuing years, a series of famines occurred in India, starting from 1875. Such devastating famine compelled the government to establish a Famine Commission to explore ways to alleviate the effects of famine and improve the economic conditions of peasants.

Hence, the early forms of cooperatives in India were the organisation of Nidhis and Chit Funds in Southern India. In 1892, the Madras Presidency sent a Civil Servant named Sir Frederick Nicholson to study European cooperative structures. His findings led to the recommendation of forming Rural Cooperative Credit Societies based on the German Raiffeisen model. Subsequently, the government formed a Law Committee in 1901, which drafted a blueprint for cooperative laws. In 1904, the GoI enacted the Cooperative Credit Societies Act, leading to the establishment of Primary Credit Societies. However, in addition to these laws, it was essential to develop cooperatives, and work was started with thrift and credit cooperatives thanks to Sir Frederick Nicholson and his report from 1895. After the beginning of the 20th century, the first Cooperative Act (The Cooperative Credit Societies Act) was promulgated (1904), enabling modern cooperatives' organisation in that area. Then in 1912, the Second Law on Cooperatives was passed, which enabled and recognised the formation of other cooperatives such as housing, insurance, and production.

The Cooperative Societies Act of 1912 facilitated the establishment of non-credit societies and federal cooperative organisations throughout the country. In 1915, the Maclagan Committee highlighted the significance of limited and small operational areas for cooperative societies to foster mutual knowledge, social cohesion, and closer connections among their members. The committee also recommended that membership in a cooperative society should be accessible to all individuals irrespective of their caste and creed. With the enactment of the Government of India Act in 1919, cooperative societies became a transferred subject, leading to the introduction of Cooperative Societies Acts by various provinces.

The Government of India Act in 1935 designated cooperative societies as a state subject. In 1945, the Cooperative Planning Committee declared that Village Primary Credit Societies should engage in activities directly impacting the daily lives and businesses of agriculturists, artisans, and others by operating as Multi-Purpose Societies. The committee also recommended the establishment of societies catering to fruit and vegetable growers, land reclamation, animal husbandry, fisheries, agricultural marketing and processing, minor and subsidiary industries, labour, consumers, housing, urban credit, and more. In 1951, the Reserve Bank of India appointed the All India Rural Credit Committee. The Committee suggested expanding the operational areas of Village Societies to enhance their economic viability and proposed the reorganisation of small societies through mergers. Moreover, the committee proposed government participation in the equity of cooperative societies.

After its independence in 1947, India enacted two five-year plans; the second one, from 1956 to 1961, emphasised the development of industry, education, and population health. Impressions about the work of cooperatives and their general influence on the emancipation of the population at that time are the same in many countries. Namely, just as the cooperative newspapers of Poland, Yugoslavia, Switzerland, and other countries had an impact on public health and wrote about it, Indians also spoke about the impact of cooperatives on emancipation and public health.

Over the years, several committees have extensively examined the functioning of cooperatives in India, aiming to strengthen them as powerful instruments for socio-economic upliftment. These committees have recommended measures such as providing financial and managerial assistance from the government, strengthening infrastructure and developing professional skills, ensuring democratic management, and promoting open membership. Despite experiencing quantitative growth, the cooperative sector in India faces various challenges, including legislative and policy constraints, limited resources, inadequate infrastructure development, institutional deficiencies, lack of awareness among members, erosion of democratic management, excessive bureaucratic and governmental controls, and unnecessary political ore requisites. In 2009 and 2010, 610,020 cooperatives of various organisational forms and activities operated in India. The number of women's cooperatives (like SEWA, Self-Employed Women's Association) was 11,615 (2% of total number of cooperatives). There were 147,991 agricultural and credit cooperatives, or 24% of the total number of cooperatives. The fact that the total number of members in all cooperatives for 2009–2010 amounted to 249,367,000, and 0.4% of that is in women's cooperatives, while agricultural and credit cooperatives make up about 73% of the total number of all members speaks about development and specific diversity of the cooperatives organisational forms in India (International Labour

Organization (ILO), 2018). Considering the long history of health and other cooperatives development, and the current strong presence in India, it would be expected to see further growth of those organisational forms, but also its replications to the other countries, especially in resolving diversity-related issues and costly healthcare services.

Health cooperatives development in India

Health cooperatives in India were developed after WWI when ideas about this type of association began to find fertile ground. Health cooperatives came to India mainly through the transfer of ideas and mechanisms of operation of health cooperatives in China and Yugoslavia. Considering that China has implemented the Serbian model (later developed in Yugoslavia), we recognise this geographical cluster of Asian countries in spreading the organisational form and accepting it and adopting later to the local requirements. The first health cooperatives were formed on the territory of the Indian states of Gujarat and Kerala. In these areas, health cooperatives mainly dealt with primary healthcare and healthcare financing, a characteristic of most Chinese health cooperatives. In the Kerala area, health cooperatives were mainly engaged in providing curative healthcare services, and this area is one of the first where health cooperatives were conceived.

The state cooperative idea spread throughout India in the 1920s and 1930s and found its refuge in parts of India, Punjab (including Better Living Cooperative Society), Bengal (preventive care), and Chennai. As mentioned, health cooperatives from the Kingdom of Yugoslavia have become a model for health cooperatives in other countries, including India, before WWII. After WWII, health cooperatives were developed in Goa, Kerala, and Maharashtra. Initial development was supported by visits from Indian experts to Yugoslavian health cooperatives before developing in India (Stamenovic, 2020).

After the Indo-Pakistan conflict, Kerala's medical cooperatives began to take shape in the early 1970s, and it was one of the few states in India where medical cooperatives were re-established in substantial numbers under government sponsorship (Nayar, 2000). When they emerged in Kerala in the 1970s, health cooperatives contributed to the 450 villages in this area that had inadequate healthcare. That influenced the redevelopment of health cooperatives in this area (Government of Kerala, 1998). A positive aspect was the employment of young doctors who then had the opportunity to provide care to the population of the rural areas of this Indian state through the work of health cooperatives. A severe economic recession that followed the war led to a serious financial crisis in the social sectors and an increase in unemployment among graduates of the state's publicly funded medical colleges. Cooperatives were considered a feasible alternative strategy for delivering essential medical treatment to the people and, simultaneously, for accommodating the approximately 450 villages in Kerala that were medically under-served (Government of Kerala, 1998).

Considering what happened during cooperative rural dispensaries in the early years, self-contained healthcare facilities were developed in numerous districts in the late 1970s to contain spending by the government on social areas. Developed pharmacies were supposed to complement the FHCs' work and publicly accessible government dispensaries at a lower cost exchequer. This system lasted until the 1980s, when the state public health system strengthened and enabled more robust healthcare in rural areas, and the state's interest in health cooperatives also declined. On the other hand, the private sector continued to grow (Panikkar & Soman, 1984).

Health cooperatives in India are sponsored by the non-governmental sector in certain Indian states. At the same time, there are also health cooperatives sponsored by the state (e.g. in Kerala), so those organisations are state-dependent, but also there are many examples when the ownership is in the hands of health workers within "workers" cooperatives or in the hands of women in case of the significant health cooperative SEWA. Their orientation ranges from primary care to curative care. Governance goes from the self-assistant model to the model of private companies that offer service according to the fee-for-service system, while they are the first to work on the social security approach (Rajasekharan Nayar & Razum, 2003).

Health cooperatives were recognised and developed both in India and Sri Lanka based on the influence of the Serbian model of health cooperatives, later developed in Yugoslavia and many other countries globally. On certain occasions, it was considered that health cooperatives were opened for political reasons rather than to articulate community health problems (Hyden, 1988). This arguably could be considered for any type of state intervention, but the health cooperatives globally and historically offered many solutions which are beyond the politics and the ideology, showing their flexibility to function in a variety of systems, from entirely market economies to communist societies with centralised economies.

Case study – SEWA

SEWA is an acronym for the Self-Employed Women's Association, which originated from a textile organisation formed in 1920 by Anasuya Sarabhai and Mahatma Gandhi. In 1972, SEWA was established to promote self-employment opportunities for women in Ahmedabad, Gujarat, India. Presently, SEWA offers various services such as healthcare, childcare, insurance, legal assistance, and housing for disadvantaged women. The organisation encompasses SEWA Bank, Health Care, Child Care, Insurance, Legal Services, Capacity Building, and Housing sectors. SEWA's foundation is built upon four pillars: planning, monitoring, and implementing diverse programs for workers' associations; capacity building; social security (including basic healthcare and childcare); and capital formation (household level, providing financial support). Elaben Bhatt, a professional lawyer, deserves to be mentioned as the pioneer of SEWA, an organisation that today includes over 1.5 million women across 14 states in India (ILO, 2018).

Although SEWA operates among different sectors, for this research, the most relevant aspects are related to healthcare, and the division within the SEWA organisation that focuses on healthcare is known as the Lok Swasthya Health Cooperative. Its full name is Shree Gujarat Mahila Lok Swasthya SEWA Sahakari Mandali Ltd (LSM). The cooperative was established in 1990 and reached 1,800 members by 2018. It operates in both rural and urban areas of India. In 1986, Childcare Services were founded under the name Sangini Childcare Cooperative. This cooperative, which exclusively serves urban areas of India, started with 624 members.

According to the International Labour Organization, in 2018, the Lok Swasthya Health Cooperative provided healthcare services to approximately 150,000 women in the Indian state of Gujarat (ILO, 2018). Mirai Chatterjee, the Chair of the Lok Swasthya Health Cooperative, reported that it had 1,800 members in the same year. Membership in this cooperative is open to those employed in some capacity in the healthcare sector, although the number of public health experts, doctors, and pharmacists is relatively small (below 5%). Nevertheless, attention is given to individuals who have recently obtained their qualifications and are entering the workforce, thus becoming financially independent women.

This health cooperative provides services in prevention and health promotion (care education, immunisation, adequate nutrition, demand and formation of public health centres, and population health monitoring centres). It is significant that in 2017, through the development of IT support for education, this organisation reached 460,000 people in 110 villages. The curative medical services reference diseases that are potential causes of epidemics and all other diseases and available drugs and medical treatments. In addition, mental health, occupational health, and the promotion of more accessible and cheaper public healthcare are part of their activities and the production and sale of medicines (by 2018, about 35 medicines were registered).

Financial aspects of the cooperative SEWA since 1984 began its health initiatives to create a core staff of 50 CHWs. These women became suitable promoters and contributed the initial share capital in 1990. LSM started a drugstore with INR 70,000 from this initial investment, and after a year, the business was profitable. LSM opened a large Ahmedabad hospital pharmacy with the help of start-up funds provided by the Ahmedabad Municipal Corporation. Currently, LSM is a cooperative that can support itself financially by selling its manufactured ayurvedic goods from the medicine shops it operates.

The cooperative encountered some significant obstacles. It took time to overcome the first difficulty, which was persuading members of the informal economy that they could provide appropriate healthcare for their communities.

Similarly, initially, residents of their urban and rural communities did not trust them, commenting that they did not have sufficient education.

The second obstacle was opening low-cost drug stores in some places where drug store owners or private and public doctors already had established interests. Aggressive strategies forced SEWA to leave these areas eventually. Additionally, recent competition resulting from a government initiative has presented another difficulty.

SEWA's extensive and complex organisational structure includes an apex union, cooperatives, and support services. It comprises 85 cooperatives, most of them engaging in production-related activities (SEWA, 2000). Women employees join cooperatives, contribute to share capital, and find employment there. In addition, women are eligible to join one or more cooperatives.

The cooperatives are overseen by a democratically elected executive committee of workers. SEWA has established schools to train nurses and midwives. Trained personnel from these institutions perform health-related tasks in nine districts nationwide.

Cooperatives between health professionals and midwives have also been established to enhance the health of female employees. SEWA offers community-based integrated primary healthcare with a particular emphasis on women, referral services, health education, cataract surgeries, immunisation, and case detection and treatment for tuberculosis, as part of its multifaceted and multipurpose approach (Vyas, 1992).

However, even with the substantial organisational structure, the initial full coverage of the members could not be realised over time (Jhabvala & Bali, 1993). Through analyses of work, it was demonstrated that the SEWA community-based health insurance strategy could serve as a risk-pooling effort, particularly for shielding low-income households from high medical costs.

7   Health cooperatives

Geographical and historical dispersion of the model

This monograph provides an overview of 20 countries related to healthcare development, cooperative development, and health cooperative development. These countries were chosen based on their historical accomplishments in health cooperatives. Additionally, we have presented several other instances of cooperatives or cooperative practices from African countries like Benin, Zimbabwe, South Africa, Cameroon, and more. These examples serve to confirm their presence in diverse regions across the globe. The countries examined in this monograph are distributed across five continents: Europe (including Eastern and Western Europe), Asia, North America, and South America, with specific illustrations provided for African countries. Moreover, this research encompasses eight case studies of organisations from various countries and continents. Alongside enabling assessments of the scale, importance, and patterns of cooperatives in most of the examined countries, the analysis of case studies has revealed factors that contribute to variations in the roles of health cooperatives. These factors include the degree of integration of cooperatives and mutual aid societies within public health systems and the extent of centralisation or decentralisation in the health systems. These criteria assist in explaining the distinct roles and functions of health cooperatives across countries.

Furthermore, the case studies reveal significant diversification in the organisational characteristics among organisations concerning governance, financing, and the services they provide. When analysing health cooperatives, their development includes various types, including user-owned and provider-owned health cooperatives, cooperative insurance enterprises offering health insurance, and cooperative pharmacies. After the analysis, it was confirmed that health cooperatives were ultimately established to meet the healthcare needs of the people that could not be satisfied by different organisational models (public/private). One of the secondary findings of this study was to demonstrate the potential of cooperatives over time and determine if these organisational forms exhibit an upward trend. Historically, in many countries, there were specific periods of more substantial growth in these movements and periods of decline

DOI: 10.4324/9781003183068-7

in their development. The scope for cooperative enterprises expanded with the restructuring and downsizing of public sectors. However, in some countries, the availability of these opportunities fluctuated with changes in government and varying perceptions of the cooperative alternative. The crisis within the hybrid public/private structures in the United States also presented significant opportunities for cooperative initiatives to make meaningful contributions. Additionally, wars significantly impacted health cooperatives in different regions, particularly during WWI and WWII (mentioning other conflicts such as the Indo-Pakistani war and others where the impact on the development of health cooperatives was significant).

In the analysis of the 20 countries, welfare states in market economies (WE region), transition economies (EE region), Japan, Latin American countries, and developing countries in Asia were included. This revealed a significant concentration of affected countries in specific geographical clusters. A correlation exists between the type of cooperative engagement, the overall societal structure, and the organisational configuration within the health and social care sectors, which is also presented graphically. In addition to the previous development analysis, it is worth considering the general trajectory of historical evolution to address how health cooperatives and health services have evolved in the sector.

In the 19th century, cooperative and mutual involvement primarily focused on social security measures, with some health and social care provisions mainly driven by the consumer cooperative movement in Western, Northern, and Central Europe. The Rochdale Pioneers significantly influenced the emergence of modern cooperative organisations worldwide. This period marks a shift towards modern concepts of cooperatives, contrasting with older forms that were not driven by cooperative principles. While the monograph presents various organisational forms involved in healthcare services throughout history, we primarily view them as potential evolutionary models for emerging forms of health cooperatives. Pharmaceutical cooperatives, mutuals, family cooperatives, and other forms discussed in the monograph were developed in the 19th century and, in some cases, even earlier. However, the development of modern health-oriented cooperatives can be traced back to the 1844 Rochdale Pioneers and later the International Cooperative Alliance's first Congress in 1895, held in London. These milestones provide a more solid foundation for aligning the work of cooperatives with cooperative principles, particularly in the healthcare context.

In the late 19th century, the public sector began partnering with cooperative and mutual insurance enterprises to expand social security in certain European countries. Retail cooperatives contributed significantly to improving nutrition, while housing cooperatives played a crucial role in enhancing sanitation, considering their broader impact. However, engagement in health service delivery was limited during this period, with a stronger emphasis on social care by the consumer cooperative movement. By the beginning of the 20th century, more initiatives were developed supporting the ideas of social welfare and considering cooperatives in healthcare as valid solutions. Throughout the research, we focused on the initial forms of cooperatives and later periods during the 20th century up to the current time, which we elaborate in further text.

Initial modern health cooperatives

Looking into the first modern health cooperative globally, we noted the early health cooperative movement from Serbia in the 19th century. At the same time, we noted the very early development in Japan in the 20th century, where Nitobe Inazō and Kagawa Toyohiko played a significant role in expanding medical cooperatives. In Japan, having roots in mutuals societies, the inaugural health cooperative was established in Shimane Prefecture in Aohara Village in 1919. The community members collaborated to initiate a small clinic and recruited a medical doctor from the nearby town. That grassroots initiative subsequently expanded to other rural regions throughout Japan. The basic difference between the Japanese 1919 health cooperative from Shimane prefecture and the first health cooperative developed in Serbia in 1921 in Požega is that the Japanese health cooperative was operated by industrial unions, while in Serbia in Požega, the health cooperative was an independent entity. In addition, the Health Cooperative Union in Serbia was formed in 1922 based on the initial ten health cooperatives operating independently and modern health cooperative principles that occurred before such initiative in Japan. Agricultural cooperatives providing health support were initiated in Serbia in 1985, and some examples existed through the period (e.g. in Krupanj around 1915) until the forming of the independent health cooperative operating on the basis of the modern cooperative principles in Požega.

It is important to recall the initial steps taken in relation to the early movement in Serbia (later Yugoslavia). Serbian society in the 19th century had its foundations in family cooperatives and the early development of agricultural cooperatives. While the first Serbian health cooperative, commonly referenced in literature, was established in Požega in 1921, earlier models of health cooperatives in Serbia can be traced back, with initiatives halted by the wars preceding WWI. During the First Congress of Agricultural Cooperatives in 1895, discussions were held on implementing innovative healthcare solutions. These cooperatives even established hospital funds. Also, mass health cooperatives were introduced during the same Congress. The proposal aimed to address the rural population's health and social protection issues through cooperatives based on agricultural principles. The idea was to create cooperatives that would offer mutual support during illness. At the IV Congress of the Main Union of Serbian Agricultural Cooperatives in 1901, there was recognition of the need to review the work of village and county doctors. The proposal suggested that doctors should visit patients directly instead of patients having to travel for medical care. This progressive system emerged through collaboration between the General Federation of Cooperative Unions, Dr Kojić (a Serbian doctor), and representatives from the Serbian Child Welfare Association of America. The movement focused on improving health conditions, particularly in rural areas, which required active involvement and community support, including providing information and education, even in schools. Health cooperatives were also established in collaboration with the Serbian Welfare Association, and a health insurance/hospital fund was established in Krupanj. It is also significant to mention that the third world modern (agricultural) cooperative was founded in Bački Petrovac in 1846, and the first acknowledgement of the collaborative law in Serbia was in the same year as the Rochedale Pioneers (1844).

By looking into another example of an early modern health cooperative from Japan, we can notice certain similarities in the developmental model. Developing cooperatives in Europe influenced the establishment of health cooperatives in Japan. Reports on consumer-owned cooperatives were introduced as early as 1878, with more comprehensive reports in 1902. In the following years, intellectuals, labour leaders, and members of Christian communities attempted to create health facilities as part of the cooperative consumer movement. The concept spread rapidly within the agricultural cooperative movement during the 1920s and 1930s. Urban consumer cooperatives began establishing health cooperatives to serve low-income households excluded from public programs, providing affordable health services. Based on those and multiple other examples from the monograph, connection between the development of cooperatives, its international movements, and the development of health cooperatives is confirmed. Although this might be expected, we should also acknowledge the long history of different social organisations and cultural and other specifics of the different societies globally contributing to developing cooperatives for health provision.

The period between WWI and WWII and health cooperatives' global development

Following the formation of health cooperatives after WWI, health service delivery began to expand in various parts of the world. In Japan, both agricultural and consumer cooperative movements played a role in providing health services. Similarly, farmers' organisations in the United States conducted early experiments with user-owned cooperatives. Additionally, agricultural cooperative movements in Canada initiated support for the community-based health services. In Israel, joint trade unions and cooperative enterprises were integral to health services within Jewish settlements in Palestine.

Rural user-owned and community-based health cooperative systems emerged and experienced significant growth in Eastern Europe, particularly in former Yugoslavia based on the Serbian model. This model also spread to countries like

Poland. Additionally, in India, Sri Lanka, and China, a range of rural community-based experiments in cooperative health service delivery was undertaken, partly influenced by the former Yugoslav model. We have provided literature-related evidence from archives in the country's overview sections for those transfers.

During the same period, government-cooperative/mutual partnerships continued to develop, particularly in European countries where welfare state elements were gradually established. A similar partnership was formed in the United States as part of the New Deal's support for rural cooperative development. Spain had a unique proto-cooperative movement with provider ownership and specific characteristics. However, in the former USSR and Mongolia, any inclination towards cooperative engagement, if it existed, ceased with the establishment of socialist enterprise-based service provision.

Thus, at the onset of WWII, significant cooperative activity in health and social care was observed in various parts of Asia, Europe, and North America. These cooperatives were predominantly user-owned, operating as health cooperatives or consumer-owned retail and housing movements, along with their associated mutual insurance enterprises that were similarly user-owned.

The period after WWII and health cooperatives' global development

The wartime and immediate post-war conditions profoundly impacted the expansion of cooperative engagement, particularly in direct service delivery and insurance. The socialist systems in Eastern and Central Europe and China impeded further development, leading to the public sector replacing previous cooperative movements in China, Poland, and the former Yugoslavia.

In Western European countries, where comprehensive welfare states were established based on the Beveridgean model, most existing cooperative enterprises were absorbed, thus preventing further expansion. Similar limitations occurred in other countries, such as Canada, during the 1950s and 1960s as the public sector expanded. In developing countries with a history of colonial or semi-colonial experience, colonial welfare systems and centrally planned public-sector monopolies also prevented the emergence of cooperative engagement in service delivery or other sectors. Consequently, early autonomous cooperative movements were often incorporated into state-controlled structures.

The United States and Japan were the only countries where expansion continued. In the United States, urban-based user-owned health cooperatives could develop, while rural experiments declined. In Japan, agricultural and consumer movements gained strength and increased their commitment to health and social care in the immediate post-war period. Consequently, the trade union/cooperative system became the de facto national system in Israel. However, the late 1940s and 1950s can be characterised as a period when previous cooperative expansion globally stalled and possibly even declined.

In the late 1960s, a new development emerged with the establishment of provider-owned health service delivery cooperatives in Latin America. These cooperatives experienced expansion during the 1970s, although political upheavals in some countries affected their progress. Additionally, they underwent various phases of interaction with national social security systems as these systems were implemented. In the United States, favourable economic conditions encouraged further expansion of user-owned health delivery and health insurance cooperatives, benefiting from the development of enterprise-based health insurance and public-sector programs that supported people experiencing poverty and older people.

During the 1980s, there was a growing concern about environmental pollution and an increased focus on improved nutrition and healthy living. Consumer-owned retail cooperatives took the lead initially, followed by agricultural cooperative movements that joined the effort. Housing cooperatives significantly contributed to preventive health initiatives, particularly in Japan and Western Europe. Towards the late 1980s and increasingly in the following decade, housing and insurance cooperatives and user-owned health cooperatives joined forces with other movements to advocate for improvements in the public-sector provision, which had become inadequate in several developed countries with welfare states. Public authorities sometimes yielded to establishing cooperative partnerships, as seen in Italy. As public sectors underwent adjustments and retrenchment, opportunities for cooperative enterprises expanded. However, in certain countries, these opportunities experienced cycles depending on changing governments and perceptions of the cooperative alternative. The crisis in the mixed public/private structures in the United States also created openings for cooperative contributions.

During this period, numerous developing countries experienced severe cutbacks in their public sectors, presenting significant opportunities for cooperative health and social care organisations. However, capitalising on these prospects proved challenging due to the weakened state of the cooperative movement following previous periods of close collaboration with the public sector. Nonetheless, restructuring, deregulation, and privatisation opened up new avenues for cooperative insurance enterprises, including those providing health insurance. This new landscape offered substantial opportunities, even within well-established systems of provider-owned health cooperatives system.

In transitional economies, genuine engagement in cooperatives has potential, yet practical constraints have thus far impeded substantial development. Nevertheless, the opportunities persist, and finding solutions to the current difficulties remains crucial. Throughout the 1980s and 1990s, cooperative contributions to health and social welfare expanded However, this expansion took on a more diverse nature compared to the past, primarily due to the dominance of the public sector. Furthermore, cooperatives had to navigate intense

Table 7.1 Health system and health cooperatives characteristics matrix

No.	Country	Healthcare system characteristics	Co-payment required	Health cooperatives present (significant development)	Health cooperatives models identified in the observed countries within the scope of research
1	UK	Beveridge model, national health system, financed predominantly through taxation	yes	yes	Worker cooperatives; mutuals
2	Spain	Mixed model, financed through taxation and mandatory insurance	yes	yes	Worker cooperatives; mutuals; multistakeholder model
3	France	Compulsory health insurance	yes	yes	Insurance, mutuals
4	Italy	Compulsory health insurance	yes	yes	Worker cooperatives, mutuals, multistakeholder cooperatives (e.g. social cooperatives)
5	Belgium	Compulsory health insurance	yes	yes	Worker cooperatives, mutuals
6	Sweden	Strong public health, high level of decentralisation	no	yes	Worker cooperatives, mutuals
7	Serbia	Compulsory health insurance, Bismarckian model	yes	no	Not applicable
8	Croatia	Compulsory health insurance	yes	no	Not applicable
9	Bosnia and Herzegovina	Compulsory health insurance	yes	no	Not applicable
10	Slovenia	Compulsory health insurance	yes	yes	Worker cooperatives
11	Poland	Compulsory health insurance	yes	yes	Worker cooperatives
12	Romania	Compulsory health insurance	yes	yes	Worker cooperatives
13	US	Market-based, predominant private insurance	yes	yes	Worker cooperatives, insurance, multistakeholders

14	Canada	National health insurance, decentralisation high	no	yes	Worker cooperatives, multistakeholders
15	Argentina	Public and private mixed system	no	yes	Worker cooperatives, multistakeholders
16	Brazil	Public and private mixed system	no	yes	worker cooperatives, multistakeholders
17	Colombia	Public and private mixed system	no	yes	Worker cooperatives, multistakeholders
18	Japan	National health system	no	yes	User cooperatives, agricultural cooperatives (e.g. Koseiren)
19	China	Public insurance	yes	yes	National scheme, subsidies based; agricultural community; workers cooperative
20	India	Public and private mixed system	yes	yes	Worker cooperatives, user cooperatives

Source: Created by the author.

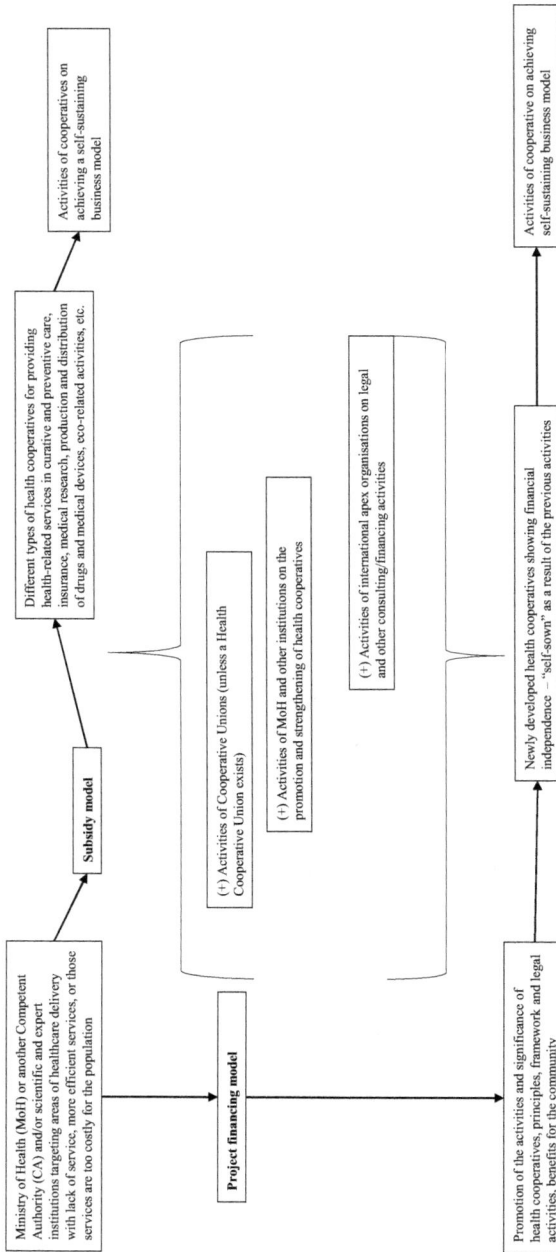

Figure 7.1 Comprehensive model of health cooperatives development, created by the author.

competition from the private for-profit sector and widespread disruptions in the labour market.

In contemporary times, thanks to the work of the International Health Cooperative Organisation and affiliated international and national apex organisations and institutes, we can see specific progress regarding major obstacles to the further development of cooperatives. Progress was visible in the statistical country reporting as it was very challenging to statistically distinct health cooperatives from similar organisational forms and track their work and progress nationally and internationally. In addition, another relevant challenge is related to laws and regulations where the guidance is more streamlined.

Considering the urgent need to address the growing challenges faced by healthcare systems worldwide and the various market failures within the healthcare sector, such as affordability issues and information imbalances, it is not surprising that the significant role of healthcare cooperatives and the call for their revitalisation have emerged.

Historically, even during the establishment of public healthcare systems, mutual aid societies and cooperatives have remained active. They have also continued to operate in countries that have developed universal public health systems, indicating that health cooperatives can provide services to the population regardless of the level of development of the healthcare systems.

By modifying public health models, one of the potential models to be used in the development of health cooperatives is presented in Figure 7.1, showing the importance of the approach in which health cooperatives target unavailable medical services or those demanded by the population. If the state recognises interest, a holistic approach might be considered, and health cooperatives might be subsidised or project financed until they achieve a point in development when they become self-sustainable financially. With preliminary analysis, such development would support the decentralisation of the healthcare system, engage various communities, and support vulnerable groups in addition to other populations. Also, project financing is one of the options where health cooperatives would provide particular healthcare delivery segments, especially in public health and medical research considering benefits for society. A prerequisite in those cases would be that subsidies or project financing would cost the state less than other types of involvement, especially public ones. However, for a comprehensive revival of health cooperatives to occur, healthcare authorities and relevant stakeholders must better understand the role, significance, and potential of health cooperatives.

8   Why do we need health cooperatives in the modern era?

Views on the modern healthcare systems globally

According to the World Health Organization (WHO), health is not only the absence of illness and disability but also a state of complete physical, mental, and social well-being. The right to health encompasses access to various forms of assistance, products, services, and conditions necessary to achieve the highest possible standard of health. As a complex subsystem, the healthcare system has evolved over centuries through various factors, including beliefs, scientific advancements, commercial influences, and social forces. Despite its intricate development, there is a transparent interconnection between the healthcare system and other sectors, such as education, industry, and agriculture. By examining the chronological presentation of the ideological concept of social organisation and its relationship to the economy, healthcare, and humanity, we can better understand the current global position of healthcare and how it is affected by significant challenges. Throughout history, healthcare models have been intertwined with economic views, aiming to maximise benefits for stakeholders and society. These connections are explored by primary economic theorists, especially in the social economics model of globalisation and neoliberalism, which are considered powerful frameworks for developing healthcare systems. When examining the development of health cooperatives, their impact differed in market-oriented societies and societies in transition (Stamenović, 2019d).

For instance, when we look at the historical evidence, despite facing opposition from contemporaries in the mercantilist and physiocratic camps, Adam Smith recognised the importance of a well-functioning division of labour in increasing production and, ultimately, the wealth of a nation. This understanding laid the foundation for capitalism, which forms the ideological basis of today's neoliberal concept and its derivatives. While capitalism has been shown to create significant class disparities that favour the wealthy, it has also provided historically marginalised individuals with access to a higher quality of life. However, capitalism tends to deepen class differences, and developed capitalist states are

DOI: 10.4324/9781003183068-8

hesitant to challenge this status quo as it would require increased state intervention, contradicting the principles of a free neoliberal market.

In the healthcare sector, attitudes have evolved within different ideological frameworks, including communism, socialism, capitalism, and derivatives of neoliberalism ideologies (Cuzovic et al., 2019, pp. 205–211). Interestingly, health cooperatives have achieved success in all types of societies, demonstrating their flexibility to adapt to the interests of their members. Today, economic theory is rapidly developing, particularly in behavioural economics. This approach, exemplified by Nobel laureate Richard Thaler, seeks to understand the decision-making process by exploring the internal psychology of human behaviour. As behavioural economics aims to identify profitable solutions and gaps by quantitatively measuring consumer and company behaviour, it leads to higher profits and could substantially support the complex activities within healthcare systems.

Also, society's attitude towards individuals, as reflected in philosophical and economic principles, significantly shapes healthcare. The patient-centred nature of healthcare necessitates an understanding of philosophical viewpoints and the foundational principles on which healthcare is built. Therefore, a patient-centric model is urged for all healthcare systems globally, and a holistic approach to healthcare is required. Historically, health cooperatives have offered holistic models to their members (Stamenović, 2019b). One example is the health cooperatives developed in Yugoslavia in 1921 (Stamenović, 2021a). Specifically, these cooperatives included agricultural, veterinary, and educational components alongside healthcare services. In this way, they aimed to provide medical education and cure and address socio-economic and cultural aspects of the individuals using their services (Stamenović, 2019c).

The health system comprises interconnected components within educational institutions, workplaces, communities, and various healthcare sectors. It encompasses the infrastructure required for delivering a wide range of health programs. Furthermore, the health system is a complex socio-economic entity vital in promoting, preserving, and improving the nation's health. However, historical health systems were often designed to fulfil diverse and sometimes conflicting social and political goals, leading to inconsistent substructures or subsystems. From a historical perspective, there are five types of health systems:

- Bismarck's model (1883) of basic social (health) insurance;
- Semashko's model (1918) of the national health system in centrally planned economies;
- Beveridge's model (1948) of the national health service in market economies;
- Voluntary/private market-oriented model of insurance (the 1960s and 1970s);
- Mandatory opening of medical/health savings accounts (Singapore 1984).

In addition to the models presented above, mixed variants are implemented to achieve better results in the required areas. The objective of a health system is to improve overall health and achieve the highest possible level of health while reducing disparities between individuals and groups. Health policy aims to bridge the gap in healthcare quality between the affluent and the impoverished (Stamenović et al., 2017). The OECD provides intriguing health expenditure statistics highlighting the need for levelling. For instance, comparing the United States' annual per capita health expenditure of £12,914 to Myanmar's £72 expenditure in 2020 reveals the stark disparity (World Bank, 2023). OECD countries, known for their high healthcare standards, spend an average of £4,380 per person per year, despite comprising only 18% of the global population. However, the health system must appropriately structure and align with a country's needs and resources. It should be grounded in realism while considering cultural, traditional, and philosophical perspectives on healthcare provision. Political decisions often influence the organisation and functioning of healthcare systems, resulting in significant and ongoing compromises. Adequate funding is essential, but an effective health system should consider the broader context and societal attitudes towards healthcare.

Public health is another emerging area, defined as presenting a complex and multifaceted field, with its concepts spanning a wide range of areas in countries where it has been established or is under development. To remind of the commonly accepted definition of public health, coined by Winslow in 1920, describing it as the science and art of preventing diseases, prolonging life, and improving physical health and efficiency through community efforts. These efforts include rehabilitating the environment, preventing and controlling infections, educating individuals about personal hygiene, organising medical and nursing services for early diagnosis and prevention of diseases, and developing social mechanisms to ensure every individual has a suitable standard of living that preserves health and longevity.

While health systems and government policies differ across countries, the general goals of public health policy remain consistent, encompassing the availability of healthcare, equality of access, material security for users, economic efficiency, freedom of choice, and autonomy for healthcare providers. The National Institute of Health in the United States identifies three core functions of public health: assessment, policy development, and assurance (Cuzovic et al., 2018, pp. 205–211). Public health has had to establish its role in medicine over the 20th century, and the recent proliferation of public health schools and programs underscores its importance as a medical and interdisciplinary field. Concurrently, public health has developed alongside the boom of economic globalisation, suggesting that globalisation has played a role in its significant advancement as a science. International institutions, such as the WHO, address global public health issues and promote various forms of public health promotion. The WHO acknowledged that chronic non-communicable diseases, including cancers, diabetes, and obesity, account for approximately 60% of the disease burden. Lifestyle and dietary factors influenced by globalisation are implicated in the rise of these diseases, along with market freedom, skilful product branding, and aggressive marketing. Aspects of globalisation significantly impact public health and formulating appropriate public health policies (Rabrenović & Stamenović, 2018). Understanding the influence and challenges posed by the global economy on health is crucial, including the identification of global public health priorities that may conflict with prevailing economic or trade interests.

Moreover, recognising how trade agreements affect access to affordable medicines, medical devices, and other vital health services is essential for maintaining population health. This extends to the state's involvement with products like tobacco and alcohol and food procurement. Prevention is another significant segment of the public health and overall healthcare systems that requires additional attention globally.

Whether targeting individuals or populations, the primary objective of preventive interventions is to enhance overall health and maintain low disease risk. Implementing effective preventive care policies can limit the occurrence of new diseases, and the incidence of existing communicable and non-communicable diseases can be reduced. The Covid-19 pandemic highlighted the significance of a robust public health surveillance system in enhancing preparedness (Stamenović, 2021b). Monitoring and controlling the spread of infectious diseases require a well-functioning national and regional public health infrastructure equipped with trained personnel, diagnostic laboratory resources, and the ability to rapidly scale up testing and monitoring capabilities during future

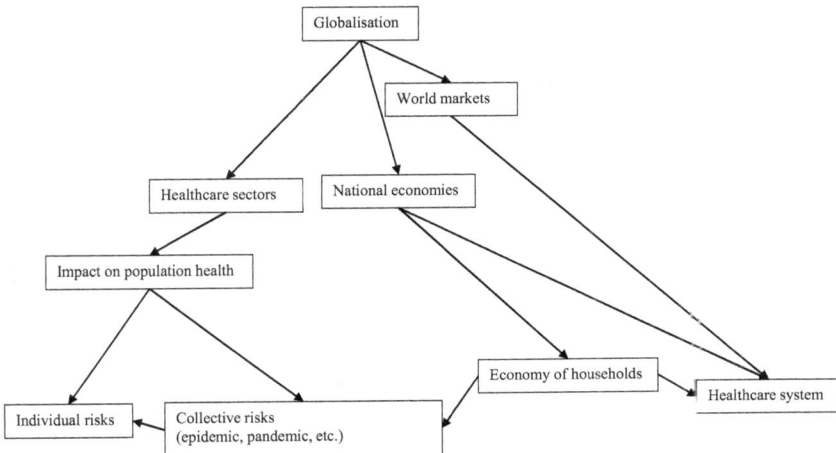

Figure 8.1 Conceptual framework of globalisation in healthcare, created by the author.

health crises. Although a growing body of evidence demonstrates that health promotion and disease prevention measures can significantly improve health outcomes at a relatively low cost, health spending data indicates that only a small portion (approximately 2.7%) of overall health expenditure is allocated to prevention activities. Considering a set of population health measures, a modest increase in the allocation of resources to prevention (to 0.3% of GDP) would bring the expenditure in line with higher-performing public health systems observed in OECD countries (OECD, 2020). This additional investment in prevention would better equip health systems to address future crises effectively. Examining the relationship between global trade and public health reveals a need for an adequate representation of public health concerns and insufficient consideration of sustainable economic development through a public health lens (Gmeinder, 2017). Also, Health diplomacy is a specialised discipline that deserves much more attention, not only in crisis times.

An example of an international agreement dealing with healthcare provision is the Agreement on Trade-Related Aspects of Intellectual Property Rights (TRIPS), connected with public health issues in global trade. TRIPS significantly impacts global public health aspects, clinical studies, and medical research in healthcare, particularly regarding patent protection and its impact on achieving favourable public health outcomes (Stamenović & Trosic, 2023; Stamenović, 2021a). The World Trade Organization, as an advocate for liberal market flows, supports the liberalisation of healthcare and the reduction of state interventionism in the sector, aligning with the neoliberal concept that some authors argue provides the framework for globalisation (Jelisavac Trošić et al., 2018). Additionally, TRIPS requires a 20-year patent protection period before adequate generic production is allowed (Stamenović, 2021d).

The impact of globalisation on international standards and the availability of medicines can be observed from a global perspective, especially in the context of healthcare as a public interest. While global companies manufacture drugs and medical devices, regulations still predominantly function nationally. Consequently, access to medicines and their transportation relies on local regulations, customs policies, and other measures. Some argue that the demarcation between domestic and foreign is now perceived as illusory, necessitating national regulations that align with global business frameworks.

Although it is inevitable to restrict access to generic products, trademark owners of pharmaceutical product patents must actively strengthen their marketing efforts after the expiration of the patent protection period. While the quality of generic drugs is often inferior to innovative ones, purchasing a drug is typically driven by price considerations, making generic drugs preferable over expensive innovative alternatives (Stamenović & Ćuzović, 2018). When the exclusivity provided by patents expires, pharmaceutical companies must enter into fierce competition with generic manufacturers, enhancing their marketing and sales strategies to secure a substantial and anticipated market share (Stamenović, 2019a; Stamenović, 2023).

The economic aspects of pricing, market behaviour, planning, and budget size (also political) are crucial for finding solutions to improve the availability of medicines. However, legal aspects also play a significant role, as regulations and legislation at national and international levels provide the work frame. Inadequate regulation can significantly impact price increases when drugs are brought to the market, as exemplified by the lengthy regulatory approval process during clinical trials (Rabrenović et al., 2016). Considering that a drug's clinical trial costs, on average, $2.4 billion, the economic importance of every moment spent in the trial process becomes apparent. Some studies indicate that one month of a clinical trial results in a million-dollars net loss in case of unreturned investment. When considering that clinical trials, especially Phase II and III, are conducted globally across multiple centres and often in numerous countries, the wider-scale repercussions become evident (Stamenović et al., 2018). Modern hospitals and professional networks, similar to health cooperatives, frequently operate in many countries to increase efficiency (please refer to the French-based network case study explained in this monograph) (Stamenović, 2021c).

Healthcare systems might be significantly more efficient by advancing health economics and management knowledge. Health economics is a relatively new field of study that emerged primarily in the latter half of the 20th century, with notable contributions from economists such as Milton Friedman, Selma Mushkin, and Michael Grossman. In her paper "Towards a definition of health economics," Dr Mushkin identifies two key factors that led to the establishment of this discipline (Mushkin, 1958). Firstly, introducing numerous drugs into the market and transforming previously incurable infectious diseases into curable ones created a demand for new medicines. This necessitated the consideration of advance payments through health insurance and health planning. Secondly, there was a significant change in demand for healthcare services. Mushkin also notes that economists historically paid relatively less attention to health issues, likely due to the unique nature of the healthcare market compared to classical economic markets. While this discrepancy may not be as pronounced today as it was in the 1950s, economists still face challenges in understanding and addressing healthcare-specific issues, including health policy. health system development strategies, and subsystems. The importance of health economics as a field of study continues to grow due to the increasing need for healthcare providers in a world with a rapidly expanding population. The pharmaceutical industry, in particular, is experiencing significant growth.

Furthermore, employee migration in the healthcare sector is a direct conse-quence of globalisation, facilitated by market liberalisation, including the labour market, the international recognition of qualifications, and increasing standard-isation in healthcare provision. Developed countries greatly benefit from such migrations as they receive educated professionals who can start working and contributing productively quickly, often with minimal additional training or none. Education costs are borne by the professionals' countries of origin, often significantly higher in developed countries. Some countries intentionally classify medical workers as deficit occupations and simplify migration through visa facilitation (e.g. Germany).

Moreover, the costs associated with medical research are high globally, but they are notably lower in underdeveloped and developing countries compared to developed countries. This enables the globalisation of this form of business to disperse costs and reduce them in regions with lower income levels (Stamenović & Dobraca, 2017).

Healthcare systems development in today's society has far-reaching implications for health from an economic perspective, impacting nations, institutions, and individuals. It drives changes in healthcare quality, coverage extent, and overall quality of life. Technological advancements and the increasing availability of medications and medical devices mean significant historical progress. However, the globalisation of healthcare also presents complex ethical, legal, economic, cultural, and moral challenges that warrant careful attention and consideration. Figure 8.2 shows a multidimensional overview of the health cooperative organisation in the globalisation landscape. The determinants are divided into institutional, economic, and environmental determinants, while each was fragmented into proximal, distant, and contextual levels depending on the type of impact the determinant has on the health cooperative as an organisation. Compared with other organisational forms, health cooperatives have coverage in all those dimensions, implying a holistic approach to society guided by globalisation changes.

Considering that the patient-centric model is critical to achieving better healthcare and empowering both organisations and individuals, we consider health cooperatives as the organisational entities that can significantly address those elements. Individual and organisational empowerment are incorporated in the health cooperative's work by both management processes and outcomes, while patient-centricity is interconnected with empowerment provided by both organisation and individual levels. However, further research should be done on the limitations of organisational empowerment to further contribute to developing the patient-centricity model and improving healthcare delivery.

Another contribution might be going in the direction of popularisation of the health cooperatives in countries that specifically target medical services that need to be covered or are too expensive when provided by other healthcare delivery entities (please refer to the model presented in Figure 7.1). Massing the health cooperative entities would increase contribution to society, which would be an additional benefit.

In addition, a holistic approach to patients is increasingly important in recent periods when specialisation as the model is highlighted in every area of life. Also, further consideration of value-based healthcare might lead to complementary

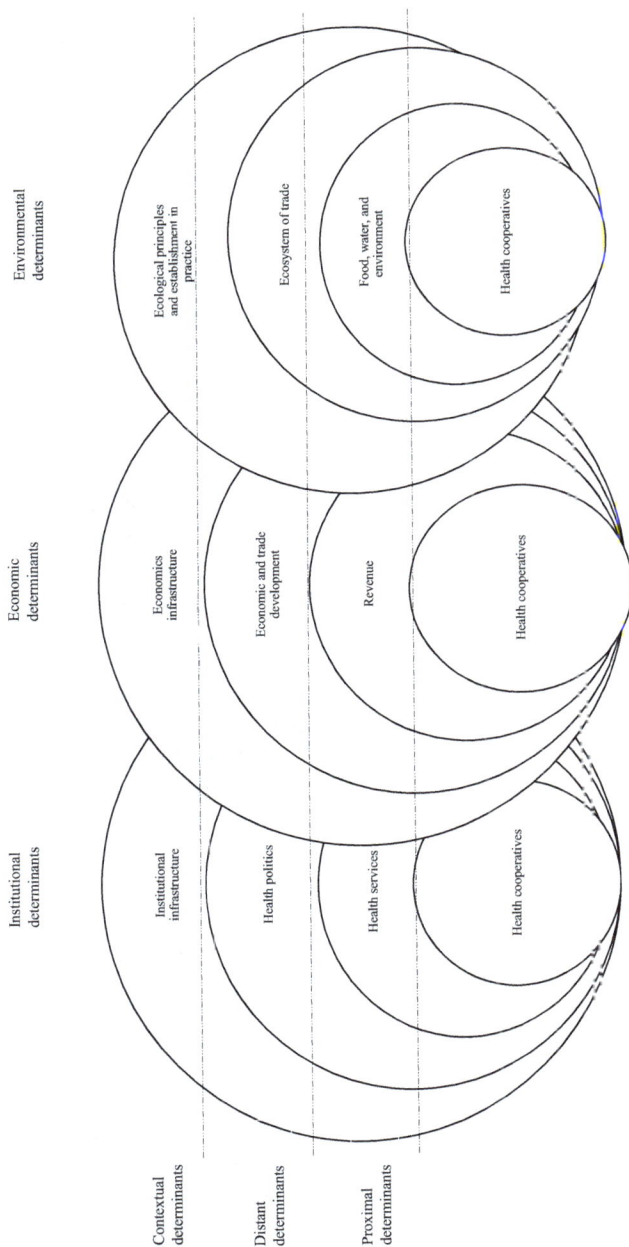

Figure 8.2 Holistic approach in health cooperatives within proximal, distant, and contextual determinants of globalisation, created by the author.

support for developing health cooperatives considering their role in different countries. In 2023, fee-for-service seems overrated compared to the fee-for-value mechanism, which will implement a more holistic and valuable approach to the patients and reduce unnecessary specialisation and segmentation of the services leading to higher costs.

Challenges of healthcare systems and health cooperatives

According to the WHO, the global healthcare sector faces several significant challenges, among which the climate crisis stands out as a major threat to both the planet and human health. Emissions contribute to the premature deaths of around seven million people annually and are responsible for over a quarter of deaths from heart attacks, strokes, and lung cancer. Moreover, extreme weather events, including droughts and floods, worsen malnutrition rates and facilitate the spread of infectious diseases such as malaria. Therefore, it is crucial to address the climate crisis to protect the environment and public health.

Additionally, healthcare delivery becomes particularly challenging in conflict-affected regions. Countries experiencing conflicts witness numerous attacks on healthcare workers and facilities, resulting in casualties and hindering disease containment efforts. Displaced populations often lack access to healthcare services, further exacerbating their health challenges. To ensure health equity, bridging the gap between different socio-economic groups and improving access to healthcare, particularly for marginalised populations, is essential. Expanding availability and affordability of medicines is also crucial, as many individuals worldwide lack access to essential medications. Efforts to combat substandard and counterfeit medical products are necessary to protect lives and build trust in healthcare systems. By addressing these challenges, promoting health in the face of climate change and enhancing access to healthcare, we can work towards a healthier and more equitable future (WEF, 2020).

According to WHO, health services encompass three fundamental components: promotion, prevention, and rehabilitation. However, developing a sustainable health promotion and disease prevention business model poses challenges. These activities often rely on volunteer support or dedicated funding, as the results may only be evident in the long run. In addition, individuals are generally not inclined to pay for health promotion, considering that lifestyle changes require time and effort.

Nevertheless, cooperative models may allocate surplus funds from other activities or donation campaigns to support such initiatives, even if they are not self-sustaining. Furthermore, the cooperative model proves valuable when combining health and social care, recognising the importance of improving members' social well-being alongside healthcare provision (Gabriele, 2006). Determining the funding base for cooperatives or mutuals engaged in healthcare is a complex issue. The roles and regulations set by the state and related organisations heavily influence this domain. Governments are encouraged to play an active role in the health system, particularly in achieving Universal Health Coverage (UHC) to ensure equitable access to health services without causing financial hardship. In countries where the public sector's involvement is substantial, the scope for cooperatives may be limited. However, in low-income countries, there is room for a mix of affordable health plans and external support. The state's engagement in providing health services varies, including staffing, clinic and hospital ownership, and management.

Cooperative and mutual models must design their business models and revenue sources based on their relationship with the state and prospective beneficiaries, considering the presence or absence of a third-party payer. Funding for healthcare activities within cooperatives or mutuals can come from various sources, such as contracts or service agreements with the state or public bodies, individual billing (out-of-pocket or insurance covered), provider billing (charging fees to healthcare professionals), insurance system billing (user fee or reimbursement), and donations or grants.

Regarding health insurance, cooperatives and mutuals have made significant progress over the past two centuries, aligning with the development of the welfare state. Health insurance schemes can be categorised as compulsory or voluntary within national welfare systems. Compulsory health insurance provides primary coverage through a national health service or health insurance funds. Voluntary health insurance can be substitutive (offering the same coverage as compulsory insurance), supplementary (providing additional services on top of compulsory insurance), complementary (covering co-payments or additional services not included in the statutory system), or duplicative (offering services alongside national health systems).

The role of mutuals in health insurance varies depending on the country and the type of insurance scheme. In low-income countries with limited resources, the state's role is more limited, and achieving UHC through general taxation is often not yet accomplished (Rainhorn, 2003). A significant portion of the population relies on out-of-pocket payments as the primary financing method. However, in some countries, Mutual Health Organizations (MHOs) provide small-scale, pre-paid, or risk-pooled systems based on membership. MHOs are voluntary associations founded on solidarity among members and offer affordable health plans that cover essential services. They can be structured based on territorial or professional affiliations, such as civil servants.

Business models of health cooperatives are very diverse. They range from isolated health cooperatives with no integrated network to large cooperative networks such as Unimed in Brazil, Espriu in Spain, and HeW in Japan, some of the world's largest health cooperative networks. Additionally, Colombia has lesser-known but extensive networks such as Coomera. Operating within a network enables cooperatives to exchange ideas, share resources, collaborate on development projects, and have a more substantial lobbying presence.

Regarding development, a health cooperative can choose to grow into a large organisation by attracting new members and creating new services. Alternatively, it may prefer to maintain a certain level of development and pool resources with other health cooperatives. This approach allows members to maintain a sense of intimacy with the organisation rather than adjusting to a larger and less personal enterprise. Some insurance or pharmacy cooperatives have even expanded their activities to other countries.

Another example is seen in Canada's oldest health cooperative in Saskatoon. By combining health and social care expertise, these cooperatives adopt a broader understanding of health that aligns closely with the social determinants of health concept.

In some countries, such as Costa Rica and Uruguay, public authorities explicitly recognise the cooperative model as a strategic business model for providing healthcare to citizens. In countries such as Italy, Spain, and Portugal, the contribution of the cooperative model is even acknowledged in the state constitution. In Spain, doctor cooperatives that are part of the Espriu Foundation network manage several public hospitals. In the United Kingdom, Out-Of-Hours (OOH) GP practices, which operate based on the worker cooperative model, are formally integrated into healthcare delivery, offering various services such as emergency care, primary care, minor surgery, and dental care.

Some cooperatives may not directly deliver health services but contribute to the health sector through various means. Additionally, some cooperatives in France and Finland use IT solutions within the health sector. The Finnish Innovation Fund initiated a project in 2010 to establish a Personal Health Record platform and ecosystem in Finland (Taltioni). It was created to operate the technical platform and form the business ecosystem. The cooperative model was chosen due to its easy accessibility, allowing companies to join or resign from the ecosystem effortlessly. This user-based cooperative aims to provide citizens with a lifelong personal health account.

Also, this business model thrives in Spain, Portugal, Greece, and Malta by combining a solid social commitment with diverse stakeholders. In Canada's Quebec province, solidarity cooperatives specialise in providing home care for seniors, achieving notable success. Social care cooperatives exist in other Canadian provinces and the United State as well. For instance, Cooperative Home Care Associates in New York employed 2,000 staff members in 2006 (Gabriele, 2006), while today, they have around 1,600 employees. The recently established HomeCare Coop Foundation in the United States supports in-home care cooperatives by offering capacity-building resources to enhance the skills and well-being of caregivers and ultimately benefit their clients. However, there is limited information on social care cooperatives in South Africa. These cooperatives, likely multistakeholder or producer-oriented, offer services to elderly individuals, including fitness programs associated with care and health, massage therapy, home-based care, and assistance for those with disabling diseases. Evidence from around the world underscores the significant role played by the state in developing social care cooperatives, which bridge economic and social concerns. The state can enact relevant laws or regulations, establish programs dedicated to social care cooperatives, or create protected markets. The Coopérative de solidarité de services à domicile du Royaume du Saguenay in Quebec provides services such as personnel management, stewardship, cafeterias, and overall support to seven nursing homes for older people. It also owns one of these homes.

Considering those examples from the world, it is feasible to generate another model applicable for use and user-oriented, satisfying the population's requirements in specific domains. Of course, additional effectiveness analysis should be done. However, looking historical relationship of the population connected with health-related cooperatives and their health satisfaction, this might be another benefit in the modern society aligning with the patient-centricity model and moving towards a more holistic approach in healthcare delivery.

Considering these global examples, it is possible to develop an alternative model suitable for user-oriented applications, meeting the specific needs of the population in particular domains. Naturally, further effectiveness analysis needs to be conducted. However, examining the historical connection between the population and health-related cooperatives and their satisfaction with healthcare could present an additional advantage in contemporary society. It aligns with the patient-centric model and signifies a shift towards a more comprehensive approach to delivering healthcare.

Sustainability of healthcare systems and health cooperatives

The impact of human activities on the environment continues to escalate, leading to various hazards that have a detrimental effect on human health and well-being. These risks include the emergence of diseases and injuries, decreased productivity, and increased strain on healthcare systems. While hygiene and pollution reduction advancements have improved health outcomes in affluent nations, global challenges such as contaminated water, food, and air persist, contributing to suffering and mortality. Climate change further compounds these issues, necessitating substantial adaptations within healthcare systems to mitigate the risks posed by rising temperatures and extreme weather events (WHO, 2019). Climate change is intricately connected to several health-related risks, including injuries caused by storms and floods, the spread of insect-borne diseases, and the aggravation of chronic illnesses such as respiratory, cardiovascular, and kidney diseases (Carnell et al., 1999).

Moreover, extreme weather events and changing climate patterns indirectly disrupt healthcare delivery and jeopardise food security, thereby impacting human health. Vulnerable populations, mainly those already disadvantaged, will experience more severe health consequences from climate change, exacerbating health disparities and inequality. To tackle these challenges, there is an opportunity for countries to develop national climate adaptation plans with a specific focus on health. In addition, both the public and private sectors should increase investments in health-related adaptation financing.

Low- and middle-income countries, which bear the most significant health burden, face additional challenges due to weaker healthcare systems and limited resources for long-term resilience building (Cummings, 2019). Understanding the intersection between climate change mitigation and human health is crucial for effective action in both areas. In addition, healthcare systems are significant contributors to environmental pollution and carbon emissions, necessitating efforts to reduce their ecological footprint.

When considering the cooperative model, they play a crucial role in achieving sustainable development goals. One area where cooperatives excel is the reduction of poverty and exclusion, as recognised by various actors such as the United Nations, the International Labour Organization, and the International Cooperative Alliance. Cooperatives contribute to poverty reduction by identifying economic opportunities for their members, empowering the disadvantaged, providing security through collective risk-sharing, and facilitating member access to assets for livelihoods. For example, savings and credit cooperatives enable financial access, agricultural cooperatives provide inputs and market access for farmers, and consumer cooperatives ensure affordable household supplies. Such services help lift members out of poverty (Lemma, 2008).

Furthermore, cooperatives play a significant role in promoting gender equality. Women's participation in cooperatives enhances their economic and social engagement in local economies and societies worldwide. For example, in Africa, in consumer cooperatives, most members are women, and they are increasingly represented in the governance structure. Women also demonstrate a strong presence in worker cooperatives, holding directorial positions at higher rates than in non-worker-owned enterprises. Women's participation in financial and agricultural cooperatives in East Africa is on the rise, with an increasing number of women joining and assuming leadership roles. Women-led cooperatives have emerged in various countries, addressing challenges in accessing fair prices and capital, and such cooperatives offer self-employment opportunities and contribute to social inclusion and empowerment.

However, persistent challenges remain, particularly concerning the representation of women in traditional cash/export crop-related cooperatives, where male ownership prevails. Women play a more significant role in subsectors such as fruits, spices, cereals, and dairy, where land ownership and capital requirements are less important. In larger financial cooperatives, women tend to be in the minority, whereas, in smaller savings and credit cooperatives that offer microfinance schemes, women are more likely to constitute the majority.

The occupational gender division within cooperatives is also evident, with women predominantly involved in service cooperatives catering to teachers, while men dominate in cooperatives serving transport workers. Women's cooperatives generally tend to be smaller in capital, membership, and business volume, and they may require stronger connections to cooperative movements and support structures. Gender disparities in literacy levels, skills, land ownership, access to credit, and information can also impede women's participation in cooperatives (CICOPA, 2016).

Cooperatives play a significant role in promoting health and ensuring access to healthcare services. They contribute to healthy lives by establishing the necessary infrastructure for delivering healthcare, offering financing options for healthcare, and providing home-based healthcare services to individuals with conditions such as HIV/AIDS (e.g. Zimbabwe).

Cooperatives operating under the fair trade label in Africa, such as the Oromia Coffee Farmers Cooperative Union in Ethiopia, utilise fair trade rebates to provide public health and healthcare services in remote areas. In addition, cooperatives in Africa, Tanzania, Lesotho, and parts of Asia offer home-based care services for individuals affected by HIV/AIDS.

Healthcare cooperatives come in various forms, including worker cooperatives that provide health services, patient or community cooperatives that the users own, and hybrid multistakeholder cooperatives. These cooperatives can offer various services, from home care to fully equipped hospitals.

According to the International Health Cooperative Alliance and UN reports, over 100 million households receive healthcare services through cooperatives worldwide. There are various global examples showing those activities, as in the case of Canada, where more than 100 healthcare cooperatives primarily focus on home care and cater to over a million people across eight provinces. Colombia has examples of health cooperatives supporting a large portion of the total population, while Japan has over 125 medical cooperatives serving nearly three million patients. In the United States, healthcare cooperatives are popular forms of healthcare insurance owned by policyholders (MacKay, 2007).

Cooperatives also contribute to food security by assisting small farmers, fishermen, livestock keepers, forest holders, and other producers to overcome various challenges they face in food production. Agriculture is a sector where the cooperative business model is widely used, with cooperatives holding an estimated 32% of the global market share. Small agricultural producers often need help accessing market information, quality inputs, credit, and infrastructure in rural areas. Agricultural cooperatives address these challenges by providing services such as group purchasing and marketing, collective access to credit through warehouse receipt systems, and establishing input shops for joint purchases. Cooperatives also enhance producers' skills, knowledge, and innovation capabilities, solidify them in decision-making processes, and amplify their collective voice to influence policy-making.

Furthermore, cooperatives have played a role in preserving indigenous food crops, such as indigenous potatoes in Argentina, thereby enhancing food security. Additionally, diversifying household food supply through initiatives such as dairy cooperatives has improved nutrition and increased income.

Cooperative identity, types, and areas of health provision

The insurance services offered by cooperative insurers have experienced an upward trend. In the 19th century, cooperative and mutual involvement primarily revolved around social security initiatives, including limited healthcare and social care provisions, mainly driven by the cooperative consumer movement in Western, Northern, and Central Europe. During the early 20th century, certain European countries witnessed social security collaboration between the public sector and cooperative and mutual insurance enterprises. Retail cooperatives played a significant role in enhancing nutrition, while housing cooperatives contributed to improved sanitation, making notable societal impacts. However, their involvement in health service delivery remained limited, with the cooperative consumer movement focusing more on forms of social care.

The 1920s and 1930s saw an expansion of cooperative engagement in health service delivery across various parts of the world. In Japan, both agricultural and consumer cooperative movements were involved in providing health services. Farmers' organisations played a crucial role in early experiments with user-owned cooperatives in the United States. In Canada, agricultural cooperative movements supported community-based health services. In Israel, joint trade unions and cooperative enterprise-based health services were integrated, while in Eastern Europe, rural user-owned and community-based health cooperative systems emerged and expanded significantly. Asian countries described in the monograph used various rural cooperatives for health service delivery.

During the same period, government-cooperative/mutual partnerships continued to grow, particularly in European countries where welfare state elements were gradually established. In the United States, there were also developed rural cooperatives.

Consequently, at the outset of WWII, significant cooperative activities in health and social care were observed in various parts of Asia, Europe, and North America. These cooperatives were predominantly user-owned, either as health cooperatives or consumer-owned retail and housing movements, along with their associated cooperative insurance enterprises (mutuals), which were similarly user-owned.

The International Cooperative Alliance (ICA) plays a vital role globally as the custodian of the statement on the Cooperative Identity, encompassing the values and principles of the cooperative movement. In 1995, the ICA adopted a revised version of this statement, including the definition of a cooperative, the values underlying cooperatives, and the seven cooperative principles. The ICA also provides detailed guidance through the Guidance Notes on the Cooperative Principles and Values, assisting cooperative enterprises in practical application. A cooperative is an independent association of individuals who voluntarily unite to meet their everyday economic, social, and cultural needs and aspirations through a jointly owned and democratically controlled enterprise.

Cooperatives are grounded in values such as self-help, self-responsibility, democracy, equality, equity, and solidarity. Following the ethical principles of honesty, openness, social responsibility, and concern for others, cooperative members embrace these values in their actions.

The cooperative principles guide cooperatives to embody their values in practice. These principles include voluntary and open membership, democratic member control, member economic participation, autonomy and independence, education, training, information, cooperation among cooperatives, and concern for the community (ICA. 1995). By adhering to these principles, cooperatives exemplify the cooperative identity, fostering their members' well-being and contributing to their communities' sustainable development.

The characteristic that sets cooperatives apart from shareholder-owned and joint-stock investor-owned companies is the democratic control of its members. In cooperatives, customers, investors, workers, and managers are not separate entities but rather part of the same democratic organisation. Cooperatives are established, owned, and operated by their members to fulfil their everyday economic, social, and cultural needs and aspirations. As cooperatives grow in size and diversity, they may need to develop new structures for democratic control that are suitable for their specific scale and organisation. However, it is crucial to ensure that the essence of the second principle, which is democratic member control, is maintained. Without genuine and effective democratic member control, an essential aspect of the cooperative identity is lost.

While not necessarily the most important, the third principle of cooperatives is the most sensitive and challenging. It is primarily a financial translation of the cooperative identity and the financial implications of the second principle of member democratic control. However, it is important not to interpret this principle in isolation and reduce cooperatives to their economic dimension alone as just one aspect of cooperative identity. Therefore, examining this principle in conjunction with the other components of the definition of cooperative identity, values, and principles in the Alliance's Statement on the Cooperative Identity is worthwhile.

While the economic dimension is mentioned first, the shared social and cultural aspirations and needs hold equal importance. This reflects the intentions of the founders of the cooperative movement, who aimed to bring about societal transformation and viewed cooperatives as more than just economic enterprises. Social and cultural needs and aspirations are integral to all cooperatives, alongside their economic dimension. This affirms that cooperatives are enterprises driven by the commitment and participation of their members, making them an economic, social, and cultural reality. Furthermore, cooperatives can have other dimensions and purposes, such as social or cultural cooperatives that may not engage in market activities. In such cases, the economic dimension serves as a means to an end for the cooperative's activities (ICA, 2013a).

The fifth principle focuses on education, training, and information. It emphasises that cooperatives should provide education and training to their members, elected representatives, managers, and employees, enabling them to contribute effectively to the development of their cooperatives. Furthermore, cooperatives are encouraged to inform the general public, especially young individuals and opinion leaders, about the nature and benefits of cooperation. Various cooperative enterprises, business groups, secondary and tertiary-level cooperative organisations, and international cooperative movement organisations have significantly emphasised disseminating information about cooperatives to fulfil this objective. They aim to highlight the potential and opportunities for cooperative organisational forms in emerging sectors and widely disseminate health and social care information. This dissemination occurs through various channels, from simple newsletters to different Internet communication tools usage. Some cooperative organisations even establish subsidiaries or affiliated enterprises such as newspapers, radio stations, or television stations. For instance, in Singapore, the national trade union movement has supported establishing a cooperative radio station owned and operated by individual trade unions.

Additionally, many enterprises adopt a cooperative structure within the media sector regardless of their type. These can include worker-owned cooperatives comprising journalists and entire newspapers, radio stations, and television broadcasting stations. In addition, cooperative organisations may occasionally operate alongside or affiliate with existing media outlets to fulfil their objectives.

9 Health cooperatives and international organisations

International Cooperative Alliance (ICA) and International Health Cooperative Organisation (IHCO)

The ICA is a global organisation that brings together, represents, and serves cooperatives worldwide. Established in 1895, it is one of the oldest non-governmental organisations with a significant membership base of one billion cooperative members worldwide. The first International Cooperative Congress was held in the Hall of the Society of Arts in London in August 1895, where resolutions were announced to prepare a Constitution for the ICA. Through those resolutions, an ICA was created to promote cooperation and profit-sharing in all its forms. The resolutions from the inaugural International Cooperative Congress held in 1895 served as the Guiding Principles for the development of statutes and the operation of the Alliance (ICA, 1895).

Today, with an estimated three million cooperatives globally, the ICA acts as the apex body, advocating for the interests and success of cooperatives and providing a platform for knowledge sharing, expertise, and coordinated action. The organisation is crucial in promoting and advancing the cooperative movement internationally. It facilitates cooperation among cooperatives by fostering business relationships and partnerships, organising regional and international events for knowledge exchange, providing support tools and disseminating know-how, and facilitating training programs and publications in collaboration with cooperative development agencies (ICA, 2023a). A key focus of the ICA is promoting the distinctiveness of cooperatives. It works towards establishing minimum cooperative standards and protecting the cooperative identity through engagement with national regulations. The organisation represents and promotes the cooperative sector in various contexts, including media and multilateral organisations such as the United Nations, International Labour Organisation (ILO), food and Agriculture Organisation (FAO), International Fund for Agricultural Development, the International Accounting Standards Board, and the B20. Through its advocacy efforts, the ICA aims to create a supportive political, legal, and regulatory environment for cooperatives to thrive. It actively

DOI: 10.4324/9781003183068-9

engages in relevant discussions at the United Nations through its consultative status with the United Nations Economic and Social Council (ECOSOC). It maintains partnerships with the FAO and ILO. The organisation is a founding member of the Committee for the Promotion and Advancement of Cooperatives (COPAC), a global partnership promoting and advocating for people-centred cooperative enterprises.

Also, the cooperatives play a significant role in advancing the United Nations' Sustainable Development Goals (SDGs). They contribute to SDG1 (poverty eradication) by empowering individuals to create economic opportunities. SDG2 (zero hunger) is supported by agricultural cooperatives assisting smallholder farmers in accessing resources and markets. Cooperatives also contribute to SDG5 (gender equality) by promoting women's participation and access to resources, and examples of this contribution are mentioned within the monograph in cases of African countries and Indian cooperatives, among others.

Furthermore, they are pertinent to SDG8 (decent work and economic growth) as they offer employment and resilience during crises. In general, the ICA serves as an economic tool for individuals and communities, empowering them to influence their local areas and contributing to global development by creating wealth, democracy, and sustainability. The organisation acknowledges the United Nations SDGs as a strategic priority, aligning its efforts with the global development agenda (ICA, 2013a).

The Cooperatives for 2030 campaign aims to educate cooperatives about the United Nations SDGs and foster active participation in accomplishing these objectives (ICA, 2023a). As the global representative of the cooperative movement, the ICA is dedicated to supporting cooperative enterprises in responding to the UN's call to action and documenting the contributions of cooperatives to the 2030 Agenda.

Within the Coops for 2030 campaign, the ICA has identified SDG targets that are relevant to cooperatives. These targets are categorised into three main action areas: eradicating poverty, enhancing access to essential goods and services, and safeguarding the environment. Considering these goals, there is a significant impact on the population's health from various perspectives. Specifically, in the food and agriculture sector, cooperatives receive dedicated support from the FAO of the United Nations.

The FAO acknowledges the crucial role of inclusive and efficient cooperatives and producer organisations in assisting small agricultural producers and marginalised groups, including youth and women (ICA, 2023b). These cooperatives provide economic and social empowerment to their members while establishing resilient business models that can withstand economic and environmental challenges, thereby creating sustainable rural employment. In collaboration with cooperatives and producer organisations, the FAO offers services to support small farmers, fisherfolk, livestock keepers, and forest users in developing countries. These services encompass improving access to and management of natural resources, facilitating market access for inputs and outputs, enhancing information and knowledge sharing, and enabling the participation of small producers in policy-making.

The FAO collaborates with cooperatives and producer organisations by helping establish a supportive environment through regulatory and legal frameworks, promoting their effective participation in policy dialogues, enhancing their capacity development, and sharing knowledge through various resources. Within each action area, the Coops for 2030 campaign identifies relevant targets, proposes pledges for cooperatives to achieve those targets, and provides indicators to monitor progress. Through active participation in this campaign, cooperatives can contribute substantially to the SDGs and positively impact sustainable development.

When considering health-focused cooperatives, an entire ICA sector, known as the IHCO, supports this field. IHCO was established in 1996 and consists of national apex organisations and cooperative businesses engaged in various aspects of healthcare, including primary and specialised healthcare, hospital management, health insurance, socio-healthcare, health promotion, health literacy, and pharmacy distribution. IHCO aims to present cooperatives as a viable alternative to private and public healthcare systems (COOP, 2022). According to historical records from the League of Nations, in 1923, Dr Gavrilo Kojić, a pioneer of the health cooperatives movement in Serbia, addressed the requirement for forming the IHCO in 1923. After several other attempts, IHCO was ultimately established in 1996, with the ESPRIU Foundation playing a pivotal role in its establishment.

IHCO's primary focus is to emphasise the global reach and impact of the cooperative business model in the healthcare sector, raising awareness about its added value. It advocates for a people-centred approach that prioritises meeting the population's health needs, promoting high-quality healthcare services, and ensuring ethical working conditions for healthcare professionals. The services provided by IHCO include cooperatives that cater to groups requiring care, such as home care for older people or assistance for individuals with limited mobility. It also encompasses cooperatives that aim to enhance citizen welfare, improve health outcomes, and prevent the onset of diseases.

The achievement of Universal Health Coverage is closely linked to the effective implementation of healthcare systems, which involves making prudent decisions on resource allocation. Given the labour-intensive nature of the healthcare industry, the role of health professionals becomes crucial in driving positive changes. By pooling resources and creating better working conditions for health professionals, health cooperatives enable improvements in healthcare provision. These cooperatives leverage workers' skills and financial resources to address market failures and deliver services and products that may otherwise be inaccessible.

IHCO has an essential role in the global coordination of the work and progress of health cooperatives, considering their activities in various healthcare sectors. The first sector is primary and specialised healthcare, where cooperatives formed by doctors and healthcare professionals provide treatment and disease care services. Another sector is the management of hospitals, health centres, and facilities, where cooperatives allow members to provide themselves with the necessary resources for healthcare or the facilities required to carry out their work. Health cooperatives also play a significant role in health insurance by offering policies that provide direct healthcare services or financial compensation for specific diseases and treatment costs.

Additionally, socio-healthcare cooperatives cater to groups in need, such as providing home care for older adults or individuals with mobility difficulties. Promotion, prevention, and health literacy cooperatives focus on improving the well-being and health of citizens while preventing diseases. Furthermore, pharmacy cooperatives distribute medicines and health products, ensuring access to medications even in rural or challenging areas. They add value to pharmacists and promote equity in patient access to medicine. Worker cooperatives generate employment opportunities, enhance working and economic conditions for health professionals, and prioritise professional judgement freedom.

In the production sector, cooperatives owned by individuals producing similar goods or services, such as pharmacists, ensure services and equitable access to medicine. User cooperatives are formed in response to specific groups' lack of healthcare provision, access difficulties, or care failures. Members of these cooperatives provide themselves with the necessary resources for care. Lastly, multi-stakeholder cooperatives are owned and controlled by multiple membership classes, including patients, doctors, nurses, paramedics, non-health workers, and public authorities, ensuring a diverse representation and collaboration in decision-making processes.

The IHCO, a voluntary association of consumer, producer, and multi-stakeholder health cooperatives, aims to provide high-quality, cost-effective community healthcare based on freedom of choice, integrated services, and ethical working conditions. As a Sectoral Organisation of the ICA, the IHCO has several objectives. Firstly, it provides a platform for member organisations to discuss and exchange relevant issues. Secondly, it disseminates information about the nature and role of health cooperatives to international agencies, national governments, the media, and the public. Thirdly, it promotes the development of health cooperatives. Additionally, the IHCO collaborates with ICA Regional Organisations, Thematic Committees, and other Sectoral Organisations. Finally, it also carries out functions and activities that align with the ICA's mission.

Membership in the IHCO is open to cooperative organisations that are full members or associated members of the ICA, or members of full or associated members of the ICA. To be eligible, organisations must have the primary objective of providing healthcare to their members, offering self-employment opportunities for health professionals, integrating consumer and producer cooperatives, or promoting health cooperatives through education or research.

International Labour Organization (ILO) and health cooperatives

Since its establishment in 1919, the ILO has remained the sole tripartite agency within the United Nations. Its mission is to bring together governments, employers, and workers from 187 Member States to develop policies, establish labour standards, and create programmes that promote fair employment for all individuals, irrespective of gender. The ILO was formed due to the Treaty of Versailles, which signified the conclusion of WW I and acknowledged the necessity of social justice as the basis for global and enduring peace (ILO, 2023). The Labour Commission, headed by Samuel Gompers, the leader of the American Federation of Labour, devised the ILO Constitution in early 1919. Representatives from nine countries – Belgium, Cuba, Czechoslovakia, France, Italy, Japan, Poland, the United Kingdom, and the United States – played a part in establishing the ILO as a tripartite organisation, distinct in its composition of government, employer, and worker delegates. Various factors, encompassing security, humanitarian concerns, political considerations, and economic realities, propelled the establishment of the ILO. Nevertheless, the founders acknowledged the importance of social justice in ensuring peace, particularly in response to the prevalent exploitation of workers during industrialisation.

Furthermore, an increasing recognition of the interdependence of the global economy emerged, highlighting the need for cooperation in establishing comparable working conditions among nations engaged in market competition. The Preamble of the ILO Constitution encapsulates these ideals, emphasising the indispensability of social justice in attaining enduring peace. It acknowledges the existence of labour conditions that give rise to injustice, hardship, and deprivation for numerous individuals, ultimately endangering global harmony. The Preamble stresses the urgency of ameliorating these conditions, acknowledging that the failure of any nation to embrace humane labour standards hinders the progress of other nations striving to improve their circumstances. Furthermore, the Preamble identifies areas of improvement that remain pertinent today, including regulating working hours and labour supply, preventing unemployment, and providing equitable wages. It underscores the significance of social protection for workers, children, young people, and women. Additionally, the Preamble highlights principles such as equal remuneration for the work of equal value and the right to freedom of association. It also recognises the importance of vocational and technical education, among other crucial principles, in fostering sustainable and inclusive development.

The International Labour Conference, called by the Governing Body of the International Labour Office, approved the Promotion of Cooperatives Recommendation during its 90th session on June 20, 2002. The Recommendation acknowledges the significance of cooperatives in job creation, resource mobilisation, investment generation, and their overall contribution to the economy. It recognises that cooperatives, in their various forms, encourage active participation in economic and social development. Moreover, the Recommendation recognises the challenges and opportunities presented by globalisation. It highlights the necessity for stronger human solidarity at national and international levels to ensure a fairer distribution of its benefits.

The Recommendation serves as a framework for governments, employers and workers' organisations, cooperative organisations, and international cooperation to establish a conducive environment for cooperatives and promote their development. It signifies a commitment to advancing the principles and values of cooperatives to foster sustainable economic and social progress. Cooperatives operate in various sectors of the economy, and this Recommendation is applicable to all types and forms of cooperatives.

A "cooperative" is a self-governing association of individuals who voluntarily come together to meet their daily economic, social, and cultural needs through jointly owned and democratically controlled enterprises. Promoting and strengthening the cooperative identity based on cooperative values and ethical principles is essential. Cooperative values encompass self-help, self-responsibility, democracy, equality, equity, and solidarity, while ethical values include honesty, openness, social responsibility, and concern for others. Furthermore, the cooperative principles developed by the international cooperative movement play a pivotal role. These principles include voluntary and open membership, democratic member control, member economic participation, autonomy and independence, education, training, and information, cooperation among cooperatives, and concern for the community.

Measures should be adopted to unleash the potential of cooperatives in all countries, regardless of their level of development. The objective is to assist cooperatives and their members in various aspects. This involves creating and developing income-generating activities and sustainable decent employment, enhancing human resource capacities and knowledge of the cooperative movement, fostering business potential and entrepreneurial skills, strengthening competitiveness and gaining access to markets and finance, increasing savings and investment, improving social and economic well-being while eliminating discrimination, contributing to sustainable human development, and establishing a viable and dynamic sector that addresses the social and economic needs of the community. Special measures should be encouraged to enable cooperatives, as enterprises are driven by solidarity to address the needs of their members and society, including achieving social inclusion and supporting disadvantaged groups.

The ILO's strategy for achieving universal access to healthcare focuses on bridging gaps in coverage and reducing financial barriers. The aim is to establish robust and efficient social health protection systems that prevent individuals from experiencing financial hardship and an elevated risk of poverty when seeking essential healthcare. This strategy is rooted in recognising the human right to health and social security while highlighting the importance of social health protection in work and employment. The ILO's strategy is relevant in achieving these global objectives by directly aligning with the Millennium Development Goals and implementing the Decent Work Agenda.

On the other hand, care provision is experiencing significant and transformative changes due to demographic shifts, such as an ageing population and increasing non-communicable diseases. Care work encompasses various services, including childcare, elder care, and support for individuals with disabilities and chronic illnesses. Unfortunately, care work is predominantly undertaken by women, both in paid and unpaid roles. While the expanding and diverse care needs present substantial employment potential for the future, the care economy globally lacks essential benefits, protections, fair wages, and compensation, leaving care workers vulnerable to physical, mental, and sometimes even sexual harm.

To address those challenges, the ILO has also prepared a report on healthcare cooperatives, addressing the challenges and providing solutions in the care sector on two fronts: redefining the nature and delivery of care services and improving the terms and conditions for care workers (ILO, 2016). Additionally, to bridge the limited understanding of how the cooperative model operates within the care economy, both as a care provider and an employer of care workers, the ILO Cooperatives Unit (COOP) and the Gender, Equality and Diversity Branch have undertaken a joint initiative: a global mapping of care provision through cooperatives. This report highlights that cooperatives are emerging as innovative care providers, particularly when viable public or private options are lacking. Cooperatives also offer enhanced terms and conditions of work in the care sector, including access to benefits, increased bargaining power, and more regular working hours, which are particularly beneficial for female employees.

Furthermore, cooperatives offer care in distinct and preferred ways compared to public, private, and non-profit providers. By prioritising equitable inclusion and democratic decision-making throughout the care process, cooperatives promote interdependence in providing care. This enables care workers, beneficiaries, their families, and other stakeholders to have a say in shaping the services offered and the overall functioning of the care organisation. Despite these advantages, cooperatives in the care sector face challenges that impede their sustainability and viability. Limited access to capital and start-up funding, a lack of cooperative expertise and knowledge gaps within the care sector, and other obstacles hinder the full potential of cooperatives. Opportunities to overcome these challenges include sharing knowledge, implementing targeted training initiatives, and establishing strategic alliances and partnerships within the care chain and the cooperative movement.

United Nations and health cooperatives

Since its establishment, the United Nations has recognised the significance of establishing a mutually beneficial partnership with the international cooperative movement. During its first session in 1945–1946, the General Assembly granted the ICA the highest category of consultative status with the Economic and Social Council of the United Nations. Since then, the United Nations and the ICA have collaborated on various issues of common concern. Throughout the years, the General Assembly has adopted ten resolutions, starting from 1950, that call for the continued support of the cooperative movement worldwide by Member States and the United Nations system. Similarly, the Economic and Social Council has adopted 11 resolutions on the same theme, including resolutions addressing agriculture and entrepreneurial development. In 1987, the Interregional Consultation on Developmental Social Welfare Policies and Programs held in Vienna endorsed the Guiding Principles for Developmental Social Welfare Policies and Programs. These principles, subsequently endorsed by the General Assembly in resolutions 42/125, 44/65, and 46/90, emphasise promoting the broadest possible participation of all individuals in social welfare policies as a fundamental principle and objective (UN, 1997).

In resolution 44/58, dated December 8, 1989, the General Assembly acknowledged the role of cooperatives in implementing the Guiding Principles and called for close monitoring of national experiences in promoting cooperatives. Furthermore, the Secretary-General was requested to encourage international cooperation, in collaboration with interested governments and organisations, to support the cooperative movement as a vital instrument for economic and social development and to implement the Guiding Principles.

The Secretary-General was requested to encourage international cooperation, in collaboration with interested governments and organisations, to support the cooperative movement as a vital instrument for economic and social development and to implement the Guiding Principles. Regional commissions and specialised agencies were also invited to further their efforts in promoting cooperatives.

The Copenhagen Declaration on Social Development, adopted at the World Summit for Social Development in Copenhagen in March 1995, committed heads of state and government to prioritise social development and recognise the importance of social welfare policies and programs in achieving sustainable development and reducing poverty.

The commitment of states and governments to allocate and utilise resources more efficiently for social development includes recognising and maximising the potential and contribution of cooperatives.

In response to the General Assembly's requests, the United Nations Secretariat, primarily through the Department for Policy Coordination and Sustainable Development, has undertaken a program that involves liaising with the international cooperative movement, particularly the ICA. The program also includes the United Nations' representation on the Committee for the Promotion and Advancement of Cooperatives and the preparation of a biennial report by the Secretary-General on the status and role of cooperatives in changing economic and social conditions, which is submitted to the General Assembly.

By the end of 1995, cooperative business enterprises represented and served 760 million individual members globally. In resolution 47/90 of December 16, 1992, the General Assembly requested the Secretary-General to maintain and enhance the support provided by the United Nations to the programs and objectives of the international cooperative movement. In the subsequent resolution 49/155 of December 23, 1994, the Assembly called for the ongoing support of the programs and objectives of the international cooperative movement.

Both resolutions highlight the significant contribution of cooperatives in addressing major economic and social challenges. Resolution 49/155 also recognises that cooperatives, in their various forms, play an essential role in the economic and social development of all countries, facilitating the participation of all population groups, including women, youth, disabled persons, and older people, in the development process. Furthermore, the Assembly encourages governments to fully consider the potential of cooperatives in solving economic, social, and environmental problems when formulating national development strategies.

The United Nations General Assembly adopted Resolution No. 56/114 during its 57th session on December 19, 2001. The resolution acknowledges previous resolutions and the request made to the Secretary-General to seek the views of governments on draft guidelines aimed at creating a supportive environment for cooperative development. It recognises that cooperatives, in their various forms, contribute to the economic and social development of all individuals, including marginalised groups, and are becoming significant factors in overall development.

The resolution takes note of the Secretary-General's report on "Cooperatives in Social Development." It draws the attention of Member States to the draft guidelines for their consideration when developing or revising national cooperative policies. Governments are encouraged to review the legal and administrative provisions governing cooperatives to ensure a supportive environment and protect their potential to achieve their objectives. It also urges collaboration among governments, international organisations, specialised agencies, and cooperative organisations to acknowledge and utilise the role of cooperatives in implementing and following up on the outcomes of various global conferences and summits.

The resolution calls for the full utilisation and development of cooperatives to achieve social development goals such as poverty eradication, productive employment generation, and social integration. It emphasises the importance of facilitating the establishment and development of cooperatives, particularly for people living in poverty or vulnerable groups. Governments are invited to establish effective partnerships with the cooperative movement and develop programs to strengthen cooperative education and leadership. Additionally, it encourages the observation of the International Day of Cooperatives, celebrated annually on the first Saturday of July.

After the previous resolution, United Nations also provided the resolutions as 58/131 of December 22, 2003, 60/132 of December 16, 2005, 62/128 of December 18, 2007, 64/136 of December 18, 2009, 65/184 of December 21, 2010, 66/123 of December 19, 2011, related to the cooperatives work. Furthermore, in resolution 64/136, the General Assembly designated 2012 as the International Year of Cooperatives. Subsequent resolutions have encouraged Member States, the United Nations, and other relevant stakeholders to share and continue the best practices identified during the International Year.

Through multiple resolutions developed through time, the significance of involving individuals and groups in social welfare policies and programs is emphasised. This can be achieved through new partnerships that enable beneficiaries to have a more significant say in decision-making regarding their needs and the implementation of programs, including community-based initiatives. Also, integration with social welfare activities is crucial to effectively meet health needs, especially those of the most vulnerable. This involves medical and paramedical practitioners, community workers, and health workers trained in prevention and promotion techniques. Health costs can be managed while providing effective care in a community context by placing less emphasis on institutional treatment and prioritising ambulatory healthcare, along with coordinated efforts with other welfare activities.

As social welfare is not solely the responsibility of governments but also involves numerous other sponsors such as non-governmental and voluntary organisations, trade unions, cooperatives, and community and social action groups that play a significant role in sponsoring social welfare programs, all those stakeholders should be acknowledged, supported, and consulted.

In addition, the diversity of sponsors and approaches brings advantages such as better identification of needs, innovative strategies, broader participation, and the involvement of more resources. However, it also requires improved coordination and more precise delineation of responsibilities and functions to achieve optimal results. The global agenda and Guiding Principles recognise the need to strengthen the role and contribution of non-governmental and voluntary organisations, private entities, and individuals in enhancing social services, well-being, and development within the framework of national laws.

During the Covid-19 pandemic and after, the United Nations has actively engaged with the cooperative health sector, recognising cooperatives as entities that have actively responded to the crisis and played a role in mitigating its impact on countries and communities (UN, 2021). The UN acknowledges the need to strengthen the profile of cooperatives through law and policy, acknowledging their self-identification, the diverse nature of their enterprises, and their central role in sustainable development. Equal treatment of cooperatives compared to other forms of enterprise is essential, and a certified profile provides clarity for business partners and facilitates the application of laws, including tax and labour laws, respecting the specific characteristics of cooperatives. UN considers it crucial for all actors, particularly cooperatives and governments, to continuously implement the recommendations and guidelines of the ICA statement on the cooperative identity, the draft guidelines for creating a supportive environment, and ILO Recommendation No. 193. These actions will enable cooperatives to significantly contribute to socio-economic development and the 2030 Agenda for Sustainable Development. The United Nations system continues to provide policy analysis, technical support, and capacity-building assistance to cooperatives and national governments to promote the ongoing growth of cooperatives for the effective implementation of the 2030 Agenda (UN, 2021).

The International Year of Cooperatives successfully drew attention to the cooperative enterprise form and achieved many of its objectives. Member States continue to share the lessons learnt during the International Year, enhancing the contribution of cooperatives to sustainable development. To further promote the cooperative enterprise model for a better recovery from the Covid-19 pandemic and accelerate actions for implementing the 2030 Agenda, the General Assembly may consider the following recommendations for the governments to develop policies and programs to leverage the cooperative enterprise model for a more inclusive and resilient recovery. This includes expanding cooperative healthcare services to cover more people, focusing on underserved communities, such as informal sector workers, and addressing the inequalities exposed during the pandemic and additionally, promoting the role of cooperatives in providing financial services to underserved groups and communities, such as young people, persons with disabilities, older persons, women, and indigenous communities. In addition, National Governments should continue improving legislative and regulatory frameworks in alignment with the draft guidelines for creating a supportive environment which includes recognising cooperatives in national constitutions where they still need to be done and ensuring their equal treatment in policies and laws. Governments should also consider passing a general law applying to all categories of cooperatives to avoid fragmentation and increase efficiency, in line with a single policy document on joint promotion, including secondary and tertiary cooperatives provisions.

World Health Organization (WHO) and health cooperatives

Established in 1948, the WHO is a specialised agency of the United Nations dedicated to fostering global collaboration among nations, partners, and individuals. Its mission is to advance health, ensure global safety, and assist vulnerable populations, with the ultimate goal of enabling everyone, regardless of location, to achieve optimal health and well-being.

Planning for the WHO began in early 1946 under the Economic and Social Council of the emerging United Nations organisation. Andrija Štampar, elected Vice President of the Council, was appointed to the Technical Preparatory Committee responsible for formulating a Constitution and initial agenda for the yet-to-be-named international health organisation. One of his most notable contributions was his instrumental role in establishing the WHO as he significantly drafted the Constitution, particularly its renowned Preamble, often called the "Magna Carta of Health." The WHO Constitution was provisionally adopted during an International Health Conference held in New York City in the summer of 1946. Concurrently, an Interim Commission was established to manage the WHO's functions until the formal ratification of its Constitution. Štampar chaired the Interim Commission until the first World Health Assembly convened in the summer of 1948 upon the Constitution's ratification. He presided over the inaugural Assembly meeting as the unanimously elected president. Štampar remained actively involved with the WHO until he passed away on June 26, 1958 (Sigerist, 1939).

Considering the significance of the work of Yugoslav expert Dr Štampar for WHO and International Health, we connect the historical links from his work on establishing health cooperatives globally. Namely, Dr Andrija Štampar occupied a full-time post at the Health Organization of the League of Nations, where he worked extensively from 1931 to 1933, travelling across Europe and the United States. From 1933 to 1936, he continued his travels in China. Upon returning to Europe in 1936 and 1937, he compiled an official report on European schools of public health and studied effective maternal and child protection methods. In 1938 and 1939, he toured the United States and Canada, lecturing on hygiene and social medicine at prominent universities. In the country overview-related chapters of this monograph, his presence in China, the United States, Yugoslavia, and other countries is seen in activities related to the opening and developing health cooperatives. His experience from Yugoslavia was significantly spread thanks to his global position at WHO to numerous countries worldwide; therefore, we can consider him as one of the protractors of health cooperatives globally. Of course, this is considered only one form of knowledge transfer by the WHO regarding the historical impact on the development of health cooperatives. The others were related not only to theoretical frameworks but also to practical contributions.

As the WHO established the view on the cooperative enterprise, considering that in its various forms, it plays a crucial role in combating poverty and promoting health and social well-being by improving the overall material and social conditions of communities, cooperatives indirectly contribute to the objective of enhancing health and social care. However, there are cases where cooperatives are specifically established to address health issues. In collaboration with the

WHO, the ICA has supported the development of cooperative enterprises in northern Zambia. The primary goal is to examine the effectiveness of cooperative ventures in empowering migratory women fish traders to protect themselves against the transmission of the human immunodeficiency virus. These efforts demonstrate how cooperatives can effectively improve health outcomes and safeguard vulnerable communities while supported by international apex organisations.

The objectives of the WHO closely align with those of cooperatives in the health and social care sectors. Both emphasise promoting healthy living, preventive programs, and community participation. For example, in 1977, the World Federation of Public Health Associations, in collaboration with WHO and UNICEF, developed a position paper representing the views of non-governmental organisations on primary healthcare. The paper highlighted the potential for self-sustainable healthcare by integrating the healthcare system with community development programs such as fishing and farming cooperatives, credit unions, and insurance schemes (UN, 1997).

In 1992, WHO focused on two relevant initiatives as part of its technical and economic support to countries and communities in need, particularly the least developed countries. These initiatives aim to enhance local enterprises. One approach involved strengthening links between healthcare and other community programs and fostering self-sustainability.

In addition, the WHO has pursued two approaches to strengthening local enterprises in the healthcare field. The first approach involved collaborating with United Nations Development Program (UNDP) and the World Bank to support the establishment of provider-owned community health cooperatives in Benin. These cooperatives were initiated by recently graduated health professionals facing unemployment. The aim was to explore innovative ways of utilising health personnel effectively through local non-governmental organisations, particularly cooperatives. The second approach focused on identifying existing cooperatives with solid managerial capabilities and assessing their interest in incorporating health components into their current activities. WHO recognised cooperatives of all types as potentially beneficial organisational forms for promoting health and expanding health services. Moreover, as employment and income-generating enterprises, cooperatives had the potential to finance and manage their healthcare development. Therefore, WHO believed it was worth exploring the role cooperatives could play in developing their health services and serving their members and their families.

In addition to WHO involvement, UNDP and the World Bank also supported the development of provider-owned health cooperatives in Benin. Also, UNESCO, the United Nations Educational, Scientific and Cultural Organization, supported the ACOGIPRI cooperative, which focused on rehabilitating young persons with disabilities in El Salvador.

Over the 1990, there has been a growing recognition among governments worldwide of the crucial importance of community-based primary health services that involve active citizen participation. Moreover, governments have realised that such services are essential for improving health and social well-being. This recognition has been reflected in various international declarations, strategies, and guidelines. Furthermore, international organisations like WHO and UNICEF have actively supported and promoted these community-based health initiatives. As a result, governments have increasingly acknowledged these services' significance in enhancing public health and well-being.

According to WHO and UNICEF guidelines, community participation is essential for establishing and sustaining primary health services. Both user-owned, and provider-owned health cooperatives emphasise the integration of high-quality curative treatments with a comprehensive preventive approach to healthcare. This approach involves individuals, families, and communities actively working towards adopting healthy lifestyles and creating a supportive environment for health. While non-profit community institutions can offer programs and facilities, only a cooperative organisational structure guarantees the necessary level of community commitment to ensure the effective functioning of such institutions (UNICEF, 2020).

Establishing permanent and formal channels of collaboration with government agencies in charge of health matters is crucial for exchanging perspectives, developing standard guidelines, and planning operational cooperation. Moreover, regular communication and coordination with regional and national offices and programs of WHO and UNICEF should also be a crucial responsibility of the tertiary organisation overseeing the engagement of health and social care cooperatives.

In Sweden, the experiment conducted in the early 1990s, which aimed to promote both user-owned and provider-owned cooperatives with the involvement of local government authorities, national cooperative housing organisations, and insurance enterprises (such as Riksforbund and Folksam) and their local members, did not have significant progress. Some initiatives remained at the planning stage and faced challenges. In 1994, local government policies regarding establishing provider-owned daycare cooperatives changed, leading to minimal further development in that cooperative model. By early 1996, there was even a backlash, with certain recently formed cooperatives, particularly provider-owned ones, facing pressure to revert to the public sector.

In the work of WHO, considerable potential was noted in establishing a dedicated global cooperative organisation that represents and supports health cooperatives, in line with the broader goals of the international cooperative movement, to improve health outcomes in the communities they serve. Integration as a specialised entity within the ICA was identified as likely the most suitable and practical approach, and this is why (among others) IHCO was generated. The area of work for IHCO at the international level is to carry out functions similar to those proposed for national-level organisations, including establishing partnerships with international representatives of key stakeholders and further securing permanent consultative status with WHO and UNICEF would be of utmost importance, as it would enable meaningful collaboration and participation in shaping health policies and initiatives.

10 Conclusion

This research monograph focuses on health cooperatives' historical development and modern aspects. Examining the historical evolution of health cooperatives in 20 countries across five continents analyses the growth and emergence of these unique organisational forms. The research covers the 19th century to the present, incorporating multidimensional approaches from medical history, legal, sociological, and economic perspectives. The monograph emphasises the contributions of international apex organisations. These organisations have played essential roles in health cooperatives' establishment and ongoing operations worldwide. The research also identifies pivotal historical landmarks and knowledge transfer among nations facilitated by visionary individuals, shedding light on the development of health cooperatives across different regions. The monograph acknowledges the inflexibility of current healthcare systems and argues that health cooperatives, with their community engagement, democratic decision-making, and ethical principles, can offer innovative solutions. It addresses various challenges healthcare systems face, such as the climate crisis, conflict-affected regions, socio-economic disparities, lack of access to medicines, and substandard medical products. By promoting health in the face of climate change, improving access to healthcare, and addressing these challenges, health cooperatives can contribute to a more equitable and sustainable future. Health cooperatives have diverse business models and revenue sources, including contracts with the state, individual and provider billing, insurance systems, and donations or grants. Their flexibility in financing enables them to adapt to different contexts and provide accessible healthcare services. Cooperatives also play a crucial role in achieving sustainable development goals by reducing poverty and exclusion and promoting gender equality. They empower members, provide economic opportunities, and facilitate social inclusion and women's participation in local economies and leadership positions.

In the previous chapters, we explored development determinants and the context of the cooperative movement in the health and social care sectors, considering different types of societies and their impact on the configuration of

DOI: 10.4324/9781003183068-10

cooperative enterprises. We also examined the benefits a cooperative organisational structure offers stakeholders in these sectors. Furthermore, we discussed the organisational procedures and institutional arrangements required to facilitate comprehensive, integrated, and effective engagement by the cooperative movement in health and social care. The context of healthcare systems, their challenges, and the historical development of health cooperatives with modern examples of practice were displayed.

Healthcare systems and their challenges

The modern healthcare systems globally are complex and interconnected with various sectors such as education, industry, and agriculture. Over the centuries, these systems have evolved through beliefs, scientific advancements, commercial influences, and social forces. Different economic views, including capitalism and socialism, have shaped healthcare models, but there is a growing recognition of the need for patient-centricity and a holistic approach to healthcare.

Historically, health cooperatives have been successful in various societies, offering holistic models that address medical needs and socio-economic and cultural aspects. The healthcare system encompasses different components within educational institutions, workplaces, communities, and various sectors. Its objective is to improve overall health, reduce disparities, and provide access to healthcare services. However, there are significant disparities in healthcare expenditure globally, with OECD countries spending much more per capita than other nations. Public health is crucial in preventing diseases, prolonging life, and improving physical health through community efforts. It has developed alongside economic globalisation and faces challenges related to global trade and public health priorities. Trade agreements like TRIPS impact access to affordable medicines and medical devices. The availability of generic drugs after patent expiration is important for affordability, but regulations and legislation at national and international levels play a significant role in this regard. Also, preventive care and public health surveillance are essential in enhancing overall health and preparedness for future health crises. However, only a tiny portion of overall health expenditure is allocated to prevention activities The relationship between global trade and public health requires adequate representation of public health concerns and consideration of sustainable economic development. Health economics is a growing field that addresses healthcare-specific issues, health policy, and system development. The globalisation of healthcare has led to employee migration in the sector, benefiting developed countries but raising ethical and economic concerns. Technological advancements have improved healthcare quality but also present complex challenges. The global challenges faced by healthcare systems include the climate crisis, which threatens both the planet and human health, and conflicts that hinder healthcare delivery in affected regions. Addressing these challenges requires collective efforts and political interventions.

The modern healthcare systems globally are influenced by various factors and face significant challenges. Patient-centricity, holistic approaches, and health cooperatives' involvement can improve healthcare delivery. Addressing disparities in healthcare expenditure, focusing on preventive care and public health, considering the impact of global trade, and addressing emerging challenges are crucial for the future of healthcare systems worldwide.

The impact of human activities on the environment poses risks to human health and strains healthcare systems. Climate change worsens these risks, necessitating adaptations in healthcare systems to mitigate the effects. Vulnerable populations, especially in low- and middle-income countries, face additional challenges due to weaker healthcare systems and limited resources.

Cooperatives are crucial in achieving sustainable development goals, particularly in reducing poverty and exclusion. They empower disadvantaged individuals, provide economic opportunities, and facilitate access to assets and affordable supplies. Cooperatives also promote gender equality by enhancing women's economic and social engagement and offering self-employment opportunities. In the healthcare sector, cooperatives contribute to health provision and financing. They establish infrastructure, offer healthcare services, and provide insurance options. Cooperatives in agriculture address challenges faced by small farmers and enhance food security by providing services such as collective purchasing, credit access, and skill development.

Considering many options cooperatives keep within their settings, and many of those were presented in this research monograph, we see the substantial potential of those organisational forms in future healthcare system settings in solving many of the current and future challenges.

The historical evolution

The period before the 19th century was presented in this monograph for each country overviewed. It contains information about early community engagement models that vary across the globe and cultures. While in some countries family cooperatives have been established for centuries (Eastern Europe, Latin America, etc.), in others Church played a vital role, including the guilds and different societies. Mutuals also showed early development forms, transferring this model across the continents. Asian countries also had early societies with their own specifics compared to the other geographical clusters.

In the 19th century, the development of health cooperatives and mutuals focused primarily on social security measures. The Rochedale Pioneers in the United Kingdom played a significant role in shaping modern cooperative organisations. Also, some countries as Japan followed Raiffeisen cooperative model for developing health cooperatives. In addition, the development of health cooperatives gained momentum after the Rochdale Pioneers and the International Cooperative Alliance (ICA)'s first Congress in 1895.

Initial modern cooperatives based on the established principles started their initiatives first in Serbia and Japan. Public-private partnerships and cooperative engagement expanded during the late 19th and early 20th centuries, emphasising social care provision more effectively.

During the period between WWI and WWII, health cooperatives witnessed global expansion. Countries, including Japan, the United States, Canada, Israel, and Eastern Europe, developed user-owned and community-based health cooperative systems. Rural community-based cooperative health service delivery experiments were also conducted in India, Sri Lanka, and China. Government–cooperative partnerships further developed in European countries with established welfare states, while socialist systems hindered cooperative engagement in China, Poland, and the former Kingdom of Yugoslavia. The post-WWII era brought mixed developments for health cooperatives. Western European countries absorbed existing cooperative enterprises as comprehensive welfare states were established.

In contrast, the United States and Japan continued to experience cooperative expansion. Provider-owned health service delivery cooperatives emerged in Latin America during the late 1960s and expanded in the 1970s. Environmental concerns and a focus on preventive health initiatives in the 1980s led to the involvement of consumer-owned retail cooperatives, agricultural cooperatives, and housing cooperatives. Opportunities for cooperative enterprises increased as public sectors underwent restructuring, deregulation, and privatisation.

Health cooperatives were facing many challenges in history, showing amplitudes of growth in different periods and across regions. Also, competition from the private for-profit sector was significant in early development (between WWI and WWII), and it was noted in many observed countries. For example, there was significant resilience in Serbia because of the accusations for dumping prices set by the private sector in healthcare equipment and hygiene production. In the United States, there was also noted opposing attitude of the medical chamber to the development of health cooperatives. Another early developmental challenge was noted in Poland but applied to many countries and was related to the neglecting of the healthcare movement by the state, especially in terms of creating an adequate legal framework.

Recently, many of the challenges were addressed in efforts by international and national organisations addressing obstacles to health cooperatives' development. With the growing challenges healthcare systems face globally, healthcare cooperatives are being recognised for their potential to address affordability issues and information imbalances. Mutual aid societies and cooperatives have historically played a role even within countries with universal public health systems, demonstrating the relevance of health cooperatives across different healthcare contexts. To revitalise health cooperatives, healthcare authorities and stakeholders must better understand their role and potential.

From a historical perspective, individual initiatives of people engaged in real-world situations within each community were bringing success to the developmental goals. Reasonable adjustments in the organisation of the health and social care sectors, such as changes in the extent of public-sector responsibility and the effectiveness of public-sector delivery, offer opportunities for expanded engagement. The potential formulation of comprehensive strategies to enhance cooperative engagement in health and social care, taking into account recent trends in informal and formal discussions within the cooperative movement and preliminary activities that can serve as a foundation for policy development and operational collaboration among relevant cooperative components. The current capacity of tertiary-level institutions within the cooperative movement would bring together interested parties to formulate a comprehensive strategy. Key considerations include the existence of a national cooperative apex organisation, sector-specific apex organisations capable of engaging in health and social care (e.g. agriculture, retail, insurance, health, and social care), structures facilitating collaboration or interaction between different components in the absence of a national apex organisation, the state of cooperative development finance institutions, and the status of research and development institutions, cooperative media, education, and training. Additionally, the positions of governments and other stakeholders regarding the potentially expanded role of cooperatively organised enterprises in these sectors are crucial.

Health cooperatives and international apex organisations

There are significant prospects for a selective approach in engaging with health and social care, focusing on favourable conditions and potentially successful experiments. Regional and international cooperative organisations can be crucial in promoting involvement in these sectors, especially in areas where national apex organisations are underdeveloped. To maximise success, integration at the global level with both non-governmental and governmental health sector organisations is essential. The International Labor Organization (ILO) has already initiated a program centred on health and social care cooperatives and related insurance cooperatives, which could be complemented by a broader strategy encompassing agriculture, fisheries, housing, community development, savings, and credit movements. The ILO recognises the importance of cooperatives in job creation, resource mobilisation, and overall economic contribution. Cooperatives, in their various forms, encourage active participation and foster social and economic development. ICA is a global organisation representing and serving cooperatives worldwide. With over one billion cooperative members, the ICA acts as an advocate for cooperatives, promoting cooperation and profit-sharing. It fosters business relationships, organises events for knowledge exchange, and provides support tools and training programs. The ICA also works to establish minimum cooperative standards and protect the cooperative identity.

Within the healthcare sector of ICA, the International Health Cooperative Organization (IHCO) focuses on showcasing cooperatives as a viable alternative to private and public healthcare systems. IHCO represents cooperatives engaged in various aspects of healthcare, including primary and specialised healthcare, hospital management, health insurance, and pharmacy distribution. It promotes a people-centred approach to healthcare, emphasising high-quality services and ethical working conditions. IHCO collaborates with the ICA and other organisations to discuss relevant issues, disseminate information about health cooperatives, and promote their development. It encompasses various types of health cooperatives, such as those providing treatment and disease care services, managing healthcare facilities, offering health insurance, and promoting health literacy and prevention.

The United Nations has recognised the importance of partnering with the cooperative movement. Since 1945, the General Assembly has adopted multiple resolutions supporting cooperatives and acknowledging their significant contribution to economic and social development. These resolutions encourage governments to consider the potential of cooperatives in addressing economic, social, and environmental challenges recognising health cooperatives as valid organisational forms contributing to the healthcare systems.

The World Health Organization (WHO), established in 1948, aims to foster global collaboration to improve health and well-being worldwide. WHO recognises the role of cooperatives in combating poverty, promoting health, and improving overall community conditions. Cooperatives can be crucial in providing health services and empowering vulnerable communities. WHO has supported the development of cooperative enterprises in various countries to address health issues and improve health outcomes.

The ILO and WHO emphasise community participation, preventive programs, and healthcare integration with other community development initiatives. They recognise the potential of cooperatives in providing sustainable healthcare and financing health services. Governments worldwide increasingly recognise the importance of community-based primary health services and the need for active citizen participation. Guidelines and support from international organisations like WHO and UNICEF have further promoted the significance of community-based health initiatives and the role of cooperatives in enhancing public health. By promoting cooperative values and principles, such as democracy, equity, and solidarity, these organisations strive to achieve sustainable economic and social progress while improving health outcomes and safeguarding vulnerable communities.

Based on the presented role of the international apex organisations in their work and promotion of health cooperatives, there is noticed symbiotic view on the previous achievements and potential health cooperatives might have in future in addressing numerous challenges.

Contemporary and prospective views on the health cooperatives

Like any other cooperatives, cooperative enterprises operating in the health and social care sectors have a fundamental obligation to achieve financial viability in the market. To thrive, they must generate income that exceeds their expenditures. This necessitates efficient management practices to ensure their success. Historically, there were many challenges with cooperatives in achieving financial sustainability, and in cases of governmental support, there were examples of corruption and misuse of the funds. On the other hand, there should be no generalisation in this respect, as these malfunctions are present in all types of organisational structures, including charitable and other NGO organisations and even the private sector.

Learning from historical examples, modern health cooperatives are thriving to demonstrate good organisation, a continuous search for innovative interventions to meet social needs, and the willingness to assume associated risks and responsibilities. With their highly democratic nature and accountability to the community, the risk of deviating from their original goals or failing to adapt to new conditions is minimised. Due to their business experience, they often outperform charitable organisations, voluntary associations, and other non-profit entities.

Consequently, they are frequently more efficient than public-sector entities engaged in similar activities, moving away from the standardised, non-innovative, and inefficient approach often found in public services. The unique organisational structure of cooperative enterprises in the health and social care sectors gives them advantages over public and for-profit enterprises. The participation of customers, such as users, clients, and patients, in setting goals and designing operations is precious in these sectors. Cooperative organisations can fully utilise this resource, whereas the structures of public agencies and for-profit enterprises could be more conducive to effective citizen participation in goal-setting and management. Meaningful dialogue between users and providers, patients and doctors, clients and social workers is essential for the successful operation of enterprises in the health and social care sector. While the motivation for such dialogue is minimal in the public and private for-profit sectors, it is an inherent feature of the cooperative organisational structure. This collaboration pays off in successful operations and provides both provider and user satisfaction.

Moreover, cooperative enterprises, deeply rooted in their communities, can leverage community resources, including volunteers and community support. They form effective partnerships with other citizens' organisations and local government authorities. The cooperative organisational structure empowers purely social associations economically, increasing the likelihood of turning aspirations into reality. By controlling their business enterprises, groups of citizens no longer have to rely solely on uncontrollable public agencies or for-profit enterprises that require payment for their services. However, this requires a knowledgeable population involved in cooperative activities. Also, commitment to sustainability and a continued presence sets cooperative enterprises apart from investor-driven entities that can quickly close or relocate, detached from community interests.

For all these reasons, cooperative enterprises have a crucial role in the future development of mixed health and social care sectors in various societal contexts. This holds for developed market economies adjusting the roles and shares of public, private, non-profit, and for-profit sectors. It is also the case for transitional economies rebuilding their health and social care sectors after the retreat of the former state and parastatal monopolies. Similarly, developing economies adjusting the roles and shares of public, communal, mutual, non-profit, and for-profit sectors can benefit from cooperative enterprises. Those might not be dominant healthcare system entities, but they can be supportive. While varied structures will likely be the norm in most countries, there is no doubt that the unique characteristics of cooperative enterprises, with their immense potential, will lead to a significant role analogous to the primary significance of cooperatives in developed market economies. The challenge remains in finding the most effective means to realise this clear potential within the shortest possible time frame fully.

Cooperatives are not part of a monolithic system capable of easy local, national, or global coordination. However, the cooperative movement already possesses significant institutional resources to promote health and social care progress vigorously. There are numerous examples of best practices, important initiatives, and a highly favourable environment to enter and expand innovative approaches.

Also, one of the models seen more frequently is health cooperatives supporting the public domain, which is shown as applicable in different economic models. Adjustments in the public sector are likely to occur further, but the implications for increased cooperative engagement may vary. Italy and, to some extent, the United Kingdom have experienced significant opportunities for private-sector expansion, including cooperative enterprises, in social care. However, in Sweden, the public sector has not significantly withdrawn, resulting in fewer opportunities for the private sector, including cooperatively organised development than initially anticipated. Also, cooperative insurance and housing enterprises have negotiated with local governments to transfer certain functions from the public to the cooperative sector. Italy already has well-established partnerships in certain regions. In France, mutualité has been a long-standing partner of the public sector at the national level.

In addition, expanded opportunities in the public sector for private-sector development may not necessarily translate into more excellent prospects for cooperative enterprises. Citizens and enterprises may prefer other forms of mutual aid; private for-profit enterprises, which possess more excellent capital resources and advertising capabilities, may seize most of the newly created opportunities. Nevertheless, in most of these societies, there are substantial opportunities for expansion beyond the public sector, presenting significant prospects for cooperative participation in the emerging market. The challenge lies in identifying specific niches where cooperatives are the most appropriate and likely to succeed, ensuring a steady rate of expansion rather than rapid transformation.

Also, retail and housing cooperatives have established themselves well in various countries. Retail cooperatives have gained significant experience in improving nutrition and preventive health. In contrast, housing cooperatives have served as a foundation for social care cooperatives and can be further developed into user-owned health cooperatives. Cooperative banks and savings institutions are well-positioned to finance expansion in these sectors for all cooperative enterprises. They can also serve as distributors for health insurance provided by cooperative insurers. Worker-owned cooperatives have ample opportunities to manufacture goods and provide services in the health and social care sectors, including labour-contracting cooperatives. Additionally, there is potential for establishing secondary cooperative networks owned by health and social care enterprises, particularly cooperatively organised networks that provide support services. Some of the examples are shown in this monograph in France for example.

In Latin American countries, cooperative enterprises have opportunities for expanded engagement in the health and social care sectors. Most countries are moving towards improving their health and social care systems, and national social security systems are being introduced to provide a wide range of services. Health cooperatives owned by providers are accredited under these systems, ensuring a significant customer base.

Efforts are being made to improve services for the disadvantaged population, including reconstructing overwhelmed religious and philanthropic hospitals and social care institutions. Following the Italian model, this presents considerable potential for developing health and social care cooperatives in collaboration with cooperative insurance enterprises, trade unions, and mutual associations.

In middle-income countries in Asia, there is a need to revise public-sector responsibility as resources are insufficient to meet the growing needs and aspirations of the population. Private for-profit provision is likely to cater to the upper-income minority. Cooperative forms of the organisation effectively address the majority population's health and social care needs.

Currently, the base of cooperatively organised health and social care activity could be more robust in most of these countries. However, well-developed cooperative organisations in other sectors, such as agriculture and fisheries, can serve as a foundation for expansion. In least-developed countries, the health and social care sectors have been severely disrupted due to economic, environmental, and political issues. In some countries, cooperative movements are still recovering from past exploitation and distortion. However, opportunities are emerging through deregulation and privatisation.

Governments have often shown a positive stance towards cooperative health and social care engagement. They are increasingly open to opportunities as cooperatives successfully fill the void left by the public sector. Partnerships between the public and cooperative sectors are seen as viable solutions to address resource limitations and introduce innovative approaches. While some caution exists regarding privatisation, particularly in healthcare and social services, there is no significant opposition to experiments in public–cooperative partnerships.

Trade unions, farmers' associations, self-employed worker associations, women's organisations, and environmental organisations are reorganising and gaining strength, contributing to the strengthening of civil society. There is a potential for partnerships between these organisations and the cooperative movement, as they are interested in improving conditions in areas such as health and social care. These alliances are starting to emerge in several countries. Considering the constraints imposed by the economic conditions of many countries, professionals may be open to affiliating with user-owned health cooperatives and cooperative insurance enterprises. Membership in provider-owned cooperatives operating within a broader cooperative system may also be rewarding. Partnerships between health cooperatives and health professionals, primarily employed in the public sector, have been successful in some cases, with no known opposition. Private enterprises also find affiliated health cooperatives more suitable for improving labour conditions and community well-being than establishing their facilities. The dismantling of state-controlled and enterprise-based health and social care systems in transitional countries presents significant opportunities for cooperatively organised engagement, even in the face of the rapid expansion of private for-profit enterprises. Health and social care cooperatives can act as catalytic centres, leveraging local resources rather than relying on external funding. They offer advantages over externally promoted organisational forms in terms of mobilisation and empowerment. While some countries are still restructuring former parastatal collectives, early experiments in genuine cooperatives have already occurred in agriculture, savings and credit, banking, and housing. In those countries (e.g. Eastern Europe), health and social care cooperatives and cooperative pharmacies are currently limited in number, but surviving medical cooperatives or health departments within cooperative enterprises could be revitalised. Hence, significant opportunities exist for a selective approach, starting where conditions are relatively favourable and experiments have a higher chance of success.

The climate for cooperative organisations in the health and social care sectors has become more favourable. These sectors are undergoing a complete transformation, which is unfamiliar territory for governments in most countries. Also, housing cooperatives continue to hold a significant position in many countries. In contrast, savings and credit cooperatives have shown considerable ability to attract members and expand quickly since the transition began in many of these countries. Leveraging these cooperatives as a foundation, introducing innovation in the organisation of health and social care cooperatives, and establishing linkages with insurers for their members and communities are feasible. Research and development, media, education and training, and national-level apex organisations within these new cooperative movements are still in the early stages of development if they exist at all. However, these weaknesses are compensated by substantial technical assistance from cooperative movements in other parts of Europe and North America. Despite the rapid growth of private for-profit enterprises, the potential of health and social care cooperatives as catalysts for organising local resources rather than relying on externally funded services is becoming increasingly favourable. Cooperatives have distinct advantages in mobilisation and empowerment compared to other externally promoted organisational forms.

The transformation of the health and social care sectors presents opportunities and challenges for cooperative organisations. Governments in most countries need to familiarise themselves with the new landscape, making it difficult for them to oversee the establishment of multistakeholder health and social care systems. This unfamiliarity may make absorbing new cooperative elements and those already under consideration challenging.

Social care cooperatives owned by multiple stakeholders have promising prospects in some countries, with a positive reputation based on their contributions to the well-being of vulnerable groups. Establishing user-owned health cooperatives depends on local circumstances and requires a supportive environment characterised by familiarity with cooperatives as practical means of mutual assistance. Strengthening civil society, which cooperatives can contribute to in the long term, is crucial. International efforts to support civil society may be persuaded to endorse user-owned cooperatives, as they address a clear need and serve as an example of the benefits of mutual assistance at the community level.

Bibliography

Abeldaño, R. A. (2017). Análisis del gasto de los hogares en salud en Argentina, como componente de la cobertura universal de salud. *Cien Saude Colet*, 22, 1631–1640.

Agnell, A.-L. (1950). Översikt av det svenska sjukhusväsendets utveckling till 1900-talets mitt [Overview of the development of the Swedish hospital sector until the mid-20th century]. *In Svenska sjukhus – En översikt av det svenska sjukhusväsendets utveckling till 1900-talets mitt. Tredjedelen [Swedish Hospitals – An Overview of the Development of the Swedish Hospital Sector until the Mid-20th Century. Part Three].* Stockholm, Sweden: Gothia.

Akrong, F. (2021). The role of cooperatives in improving health care delivery: A review. *Journal of Health and Medical Sciences*, 4(2), 117–123.

Allen, J. (2009). Social enterprise in healthcare: Promoting collaborative working between the NHS and the third sector. *Social Enterprise Journal*, 5(2), 125–142.

Almeida, C. M. (1981). *A assistência médica ao trabalhador rural: FUNRURAL, a história de uma política social* [Dissertação]. Rio de Janeiro: Instituto de Medicina Social, Universidade Estadual do Rio de Janeiro.

Almeida, M. H. (1996). Federalismo e políticas sociais. In: Affonso, R. B. A. de, & Silva, P. L. B. (Eds.), *Federalismo no Brasil: descentralização e políticas sociais* (pp. 13–40). São Paulo: Fundap.

Alvarez, A. (2008). Malaria and the emergence of rural health in Argentina: An analysis from the perspective of international interaction and cooperation. *Canadian Bulletin of Medical History*, 25(1), 137–160. https://doi.org/10.3138/cbmh.25.1.137. PMID: 18831146.

Andrews, B., & Bullock, M. B. (Eds.). (2014). *Medical Transitions in Twentieth-Century China*. Indiana University Press. www.jstor.org/stable/j.ctt16f992b

Anell, A. (1996). The monopolistic integrated model and health care reform: the Swedish experience. *Health Policy*, 37, 19–33.

Anell, A., & Claesson, R. (1995). *Svenska sjukhus förr och nu – Ekonomiska aspekter på struktur, politik och framtida förutsättningar* [*Swedish Hospitals: An Economic Perspective on Historical Developments and Future Conditions*]. Lund: Institute for Health Economics.

Anell, A., Glenngård, A. H., & Merkur, S. (2012). Sweden: Health system review. *Health Systems in Transition*, 14(5), 1–159.

Angus, D. E., & Manga, P. (1990). *Co-op/Consumer Sponsored Health Care Delivery Effectiveness.* Canadian Co-operative Association.

Archer, J. H. (1980). *Saskatchewan: A History.* Saskatchewan Archives Board. Manitoba, Canada.

Avsec, F., & Štromayer, J. (2015). Development and socioeconomic environment of cooperatives in Slovenia. *Journal of Cooperative Organization and Management,* 3(1), 40–48. https://doi.org/10.1016/j.jcom.2015.02.004

Babinet, E. (2017). Cooperatives in France: The driving force of the economy. *Euricse Research Paper Series,* 74, 1–36.

Bajpai, N., & Dholakia, R. (2011). Improving the performance of accredited social health activists in India (Working Paper No. 1). Columbia Global Centers/South Asia, Columbia University , Mumbai, India, https://doi.org/10.7916/D8988G63

Bărbulescu, C. (2018). *Physicians, Peasants and Modern Medicine: Imagining Rurality in Romania, 1860–1910.* Central European University Press. www.jstor.org/stable/10.7829/j.ctvh8qz91

Barr, R. (2004). *Las Obras Sociales en la Argentina.* www.idelcoop.org.ar/sites/www.idelcoop.org.ar/files/revista/articulos/pdf/2004_90529605.pdf

Bauchner, H., Fontanarosa, P. B., & Thompson, A. E. (2015). Professionalism, governance, and self-regulation of medicine. *JAMA,* 313(18), 1831.

Bello, A. H., & Bonilla, M. L. G. (2008). Vulnerability and exclusion: Life conditions, health situation, and access to health services of the population displaced by violence settled in Bogotá – Colombia, 2005. *Gerencia y Políticas de Salud,* 7(14). https://revistas.javeriana.edu.co/index.php/gerepolsal/article/view/2685

Belmartino, S. (1991). *XXVIII meeting of the advisory committee on health research, contribution of the social sciences to research on health systems and services.* PAHO & WHO. https://iris.paho.org/bitstream/handle/10665.2/39091/ACHR28_91_11.pdf?sequence=1&isAllowed=y

Benenden Health. (n.d.). *About Us.* www.benenden.co.uk/about-benenden

Bilsen, J., Drieskens, S., Demarest, S., & Van der Heyden, J. (n.d.). *Health Interview Survey 2018: Health Status and Determinants.* Brussels: Sciensano.

Biocoop. (2021). *Biocoop – CA 2020.* www.calameo.com/biocoop/read/0070337975 1a41a15eed7

Borsay, A., & Hunter, B. (2014). *Healthcare and English Society: From the Restoration to the Revolution.* Routledge.

Borzaga, C., Bodini, R., Carini, C., Depedri, S., Galera, G., & Salvatori, G. (2014). Europe in transition: The role of social cooperatives and social enterprises. *SSRN Electronic Journal.* https://doi.org/10.2139/ssrn.2436456

Braga, J. C., & Paula, S. G. (1981). *Saúde e previdência: estudos de política social.* São Paulo: Cebes/Hucitec.

Britannica, T. Editors of Encyclopaedia. (2023, March 20). *Traditional Chinese Medicine. Encyclopedia Britannica.* www.britannica.com/science/traditional-Chinese-medicine

Brown, S. (2001). Monastic medicine: A theological perspective. *Journal of Religion and Health,* 40(1), 75–86.

Brown, T. M., & Fee, E. (2006). Andrija Stampar: Charismatic leader of social medicine and international health. *American Journal of Public Health,* 96, 1383. https://doi.org/10.2105/ajph.2006.090084

Burke, B., & Finan, T. (2017). *Cooperatives, Grassroots, Development, and Social Change*. Tucson: The University of Arizona Press.

Cadiai Social Cooperative. (n.d.). https://stories.coop/cooperatives/cadiai-social-coop erative

Cami. (2023). *Noticias CAMI*. www.rascomra.com.ar/noticias/cami-50.html

Care Cooperative. (2023). *Cooperative Housing: Beyond Traps of Ownership and Renting for Profit*. www.carecooperatives.eu/blog/stories-and-cases/cooperative-hous ing-beyond-traps-of-ownership-and-renting-for-profit/

Carnell, E., et al. (2019). Modelling public health improvements as a result of air pollution control policies in the UK over four decades – 1970 to 2010. *Environmental Research Letters*, 2019, 1–2.

CECOP – CICOPA Europe. (2016). *Spodbujanje delavskih, socialnih in storitvenih zadrug v Republiki Sloveniji* [*Promoting Worker, Social, and Service Cooperatives in the Republic of Slovenia*]. https://skupnostobcin.si/wp-content/uploads/2016/ 06/poroc%CC%8Cilo-cicopa-spodbujanje-delavskih-socialnih-in-storitvenih-zad rug-v-.pdf

CFC (2002). Conselho Federal de Contabilidade. Resolução CFC 944/2002 – Entidades Cooperativas de Assistência à Saúde. Aprova a Norma Brasileira Contábil das cooperativas do ramo saúde (NBC T 10.21). Retrieved from www1.cfc.org.br/sisweb/ sre/detalhes_sre.aspx?Codigo=2002/000944

CFC (2005). Conselho Federal de Contabilidade. Resolução CFC 1.013/2005 – Entidades Cooperativas. Esclarece a interpretação técnica do Conselho de Contabilidade sobre critérios e procedimentos específicos de avaliação, de registro das variações patrimoniais e de estrutura das Demonstrações Contábeis e de informações mínimas a serem incluídas em notas explicativas, relativas à NBC T 10.8 – Entidades Cooperativas. Retrieved from www1.cfc.org.br/sisweb/sre/detalhes_sre.aspx?Codigo=2005/001013

CHCA. (2023). *Care Solutions*. www.chcany.org

CKGM. (2023). *Poland*. http://ckgm.pl/asp/pl_start.asp?typ=13&menu=5&dzialy= 5&akcja=artykul&artykul=159

Commonwealth Fund. (2009). *Cooperative Healthcare: The Way Forward?* www. commonwealthfund.org/blog/2009/cooperative-health-care-way-forward

Compton, R. E., & Schlackman, N. (1998). The evolution of health insurance in the United States. *The Geneva Papers on Risk and Insurance. Issues and Practice*, 23(86), 123–140. www.jstor.org/stable/41952406

Confecoop. (n.d.). *Cooperativism in the world: United States*. https://confecoop.coop/coo perativismo/en-el-mundo/estadosunidos/#:~:text=Rese%C3%B1a%20Hist%C3%B3r ica&text=Hoy%20en%20d%C3%ADa%20las% 20cooperativas, las%20casas%20 perdidas%20por%20incendios

Coomeva. (2023). *History*. https://stories.coop/stories/a-brief-history-of-coomeva/

COOP. (2022). *Identity IHCO*. https://identity.coop/ihco/

Cooperativas de las Americas. (2020). *Analysis of the Legal Cooperative Framework within the ICA-EU Alliance National Report for Brazil*. https://coops4dev.coop/sites/ default/files/2021-03/Legal%20Framework%20Analysis%20-%20Brazil.pdf

Co-operatives Secretariat. (1999). *Health Care Co-operatives Start-up Guide*. Government of Canada.

coops4dev. (2017). *Cooperatives, Grassroots, Development, and Social Change*. https:// coops4dev.coop/en/4devamericas/brazil coops4dev. (2020). *Mapping: Key Figures National Report: United States of America.* https://coops4dev.coop/sites/default/files/2021-01/USA%20-%20Key%20Figu res%20Report.pdf

coops4dev. (2023a). *Colombia.* https://coops4dev.coop/en/4devamericas/colombia

coops4dev. (2023b). *Key Figures Brazil.* https://coops4dev.coop/en/4devamericas/brazil

coops4dev. (2023c). *Legal Cooperative Framework Analysis within the ICA-EU Convention National Report for Colombia.* https://coops4dev.coop/sites/default/files/ 2021-03/Legal%20Framework%20Analysis%20-%20Colombia.pdf

coops4dev. (2023d). *Poland.* https://coops4dev.coop/en/4deveurope/poland

coops4dev. (2023e). *USA key figure.* www.coops4dev.coop/en/4devamericas/usa#general

Corens, D. (2007). Belgium: A health system review. *Health Systems in Transition,* 9(2), 1–172. European Observatory on Health Systems and Policies. www.euro.who.int/__ data/assets/pdf_file/0007/96442/E90059.pdf

Côrtes, S. V. (2009). Fórum. Sistema Único de Saúde: espaços decisórios e a arena política de saúde. *Cad Saúde Coletiva,* 7, 1626–33.

Craddock, T., & Vayid, N. (2004). *Health Care Co-operatives in Canada.* Agriculture and Agri-Food Canada: Co-operatives Secretariat.

Croatian Cooperative Union. (2023). http://hzs.hr/povijest-zadrugarstva/

Croatian Health Insurance Fund (CHIF). (2013). *CHIF Guide for the New Revenue Model for Primary Health Care.* Zagreb: Croatian Health Insurance Fund. www.cezih. hr/dokumenti/

Croatian Health Insurance Fund (CHIF). (2014). *CHIF Exits the State Treasury on January 1, 2015.* Zagreb: Croatian Health Insurance Fund. www.hzzo.hr/izlazak-hzzo-a-iz-drzavne-riznice-nuzan-je-preduvjet-stvaranja-boljeg-odgovornijeg-pametni jeg-i-odrzivog-zdravstvenog-sustava-za-sve-nas/

Croatian Health Insurance Fund (CHIF). (2020). *Business Report of the Croatian Health Insurance Fund for 2019.* Zagreb: Croatian Health Insurance Fund. https://hzzo.hr/ wp-content/uploads/2020/07/IZVJE%C5%A0%C4%86E-O-POSLOVANJU-HZZO-a-za-2019.pdf

Croatian Health Insurance Fund (CHIF). (2023). https://hzzo.hr/o-nama/povijest

Cummings, M. (2019). *The healthcare industry is a major source of harmful emissions.* Yale News, Yale University. https://news.yale.edu/2019/08/02/healthcare-industry-major-source-harmful-emissions

Cuzović, S., Cuzović, Dj., & Stamenović, M. (2019). *Globalizacija – Savremeni aspekti ekonomije, trgovine i zdravstva.* Ekonomski Fakultet, Univerzitet u Nišu, Novi Sad, P205-2011.

Cylus, J., Richardson, E., Findley, L., Longley, M., O'Neill, C., Steel, D., ... & Stuckler, D. (2015). United Kingdom: Health system review. *Health Systems in Transition,* 17(5), 1–126.

De Conto, M. (2019). *Legal Aspects of the Brazilian Healthcare Cooperatives.* Aydin University. www.un.org/development/desa/dspd/wp-content/uploads/sites/22/2019/ 06/Brazil.pdf

De Jongh, M., & Bester, J. (2011). Health cooperatives: Key contributors to the health sector. *African Journal of Primary Health Care & Family Medicine,* 3(1), Art. #263.

Decadoo. (2023). *Digital Health Engagement Platform (DHEP).* www.dacadoo.com/

Deller, S., Hoyt, A., Hueth, B., & Sundaram-Stukel, R. (2009). Research on the economic impact of cooperatives [digital version].

Development of Cooperatives in Latin America. (1941). *Monthly Labor Review*, 52(4), 810–816. www.jstor.org/stable/41817646

Domínguez A. P., y S., Pinilla K. F. & García F. G. (2017). Health regulation in Colombia: A problem of hijacked information. *Papel Político*, 22(1), 105–125. https://doi.org/10.11144/Javeriana.papo22-1.rscp

Donati, M., Capo, E., & Albanese, F. (1990). Agricultural Co-operatives and Unions: Competitions and connivances in Co-operatives and Farmers' Unions; in Western Europe. *Collaboration and Tensions (Just)*. Esbjerg: South Jutland University Press.

Dragić, M. (1975). Health cooperatives in Serbia. *Archives for the history of health culture of Serbia, Belgrade*.

Duarte, C. M. (2001). UNIMED: história e características da cooperativa de trabalho médico no Brasil [UNIMED: History and characteristics of a Brazilian medical cooperative]. *Cad Saude Publica*, 17(4), 999–1008. Portuguese. https://doi.org/10.1590/s0102-311x2001000400034. PMID: 11514881.

Dugac, Z. (2011). *Health, Hygiene and Eugenics in Southeastern Europe to 1945*. New York (p. 230). Central European University Press.

Džakula, A. (2005). Health care based on priorities is lost in decentralisation. *BMJ*, 331(7510), 235.

Eckelman, M. J., et al. (2020). Healthcare pollution and public health damage in the United States: An update. *Health Affairs*, 39(12). www.healthaffairs.org/doi/10.1377/hlthaff.2020.01247

ECyT-ar. (2017). *Cooperatives in Argentina*. https://cyt-ar.com.ar/cyt-ar/index.php/Cooperativas_en_Argentina

Egdell, V., & Dutton, M. (2016). Devolution and healthcare in the UK: A critical juncture in health policy? *Policy & Politics*, 44(4), 537–554.

Engel, A. (1972). *Om det svenska lasarettsväsendets utveckling från Serafimerlasarettets tillkomst till regionsjukvårdsplanen* [*About Development of Swedish Hospitals from the Serafimer Hospital to the Regional Health Plan*]. Stockholm: Sydsvenska medicinhistoriska sällskapets årsskrift.

EPHEU. (2013). OPHACO. https://epheu.eu/ophaco/

Equal Care Co-op. (n.d.). www.equalcare.coop

Equal Care Co-op: A UK Social Care Platform (Shareable, 2019). https://letschangetherules.org/map/equal-care-coop#:~:text=Founded%20in%202018%2C%20Equal%20Care%20Co-op%20%28Eccoo%29%20is,the%20Upper%20Calder%20Valley%20in%20Calderdale%2C%20West%20Yorkshire.

Espriu Foundation. (n.d.). *Espriu Foundation*. www.espriu.es

EU 2021/522 of the European Parliament and of the Council of 24 March 2021. *EU4Health programme 2021–2027 – a vision for a healthier European Union*. https://health.ec.europa.eu/funding/eu4health-programme-2021-2027-vision-healthier-european-union_en

EURICSE, IHCO. (2018). *The cooperative health report: Assessing the worldwide contribution of cooperatives to healthcare*. https://euricse.eu/wp-content/uploads/2018/04/IHCO_Executive-summary_new-format.pdf

European Economic and Social Committee. (2012). *The role of cooperatives and social enterprises in the implementation of the European Pillar of Social Rights*. www.eesc.europa.eu/sites/default/files/resources/docs/executive-summary-for-publication_en.pdf

Ferre, F., de Belvis, A. G., Valerio, L., Longhi, S., Lazzari, A., Fattore, G., Ricciardi, W., & Maresso, A. (2014). Italy: a health system review. *Health Systems in Transition*, 16(4), 1–168. PMID: 25471543.

Fisher, G. M. (1938). The Cooperative Movement in Japan. *Pacific Affairs*, 11(4), 478–491. www.jstor.org/stable/2751318

Framework Law no. 195/2006 on decentralisation, published in the *Monitorul Oficial al României, Part I*, no. 453 of May 25, 2006.

França, G. V. A., Restrepo-Méndez, M. C., Maia, M. F. S., Victora, C. G., & Barros, A. J. D. (2016). Coverage and equity in reproductive and maternal health interventions in Brazil: impressive progress following the implementation of the unified health system. *International Journal of Equity in Health*, 15, 149.

France, G., Taroni, F., & Donatini, A. (2005). The Italian healthcare system. *Health Economics*, 14(Suppl 1), S187–S202. https://doi.org/10.1002/hec.1035

Gabriele, A. (2006). Social services policies in a developing market economy oriented towards socialism: The case of health system reforms in Vietnam. *Review of International Political Economy*, 13(2), 258–289.

Gavrilo Kojić, Address to the League of Nations (1923). Museum of Science and Technology, collection of the Museum of the Serbian Medical Society, personal fund of Dr Gavrilo Kojić, uninventoried material.

GCO (Groupes Cooperateurs en Oncologie). (n.d.-a). *Charter of collaboration between GCO and industry* [PDF]. www.gco-cancer.org/attachments/article/38/Charter%20of%20collaboration%20between%20GCO%20and%20industry.pdf

GCO (Groupes Cooperateurs en Oncologie). (n.d.-b). *Ethics charter* [PDF]. www.gco-cancer.org/attachments/article/38/Ethics%20charter.pdf

GCO (Grupos Cooperativos en Oncologie). (n.d-c). *Hogar* [Home]. www.gco-cancer.org/en

Gerkens, S., & Merkur, S. (2020). Belgium: Health system review. *Health Systems in Transition*, 22(5), i–237.

Girard J. P. (2003). Revolution within revolution. *Making Waves, Canada's Community Economic Development Magazine*, 14(3).

Girard, J. P. (2014). *Better Health and Social Care. How Are Co-ops & Mutuals Boosting Innovation & Access Worldwide? Volume 1: Report*. International Summit of Cooperatives, 6–9 October 2014. LPS Productions.

Girard, V. (2014). *Health Cooperatives and Mutuals: Overview and Assessment*. International Labour Organization.

Giribaldi, C. (2007). *Experiencias de las cooperativas de salud de América: El caso de Argentina. Número 175 / Año 2007*. www.idelcoop.org.ar/sites/www.idelcoop.org.ar/files/revista/articulos/pdf/2007_38201810.pdf

Gmeinder, M., Morgan, D., & Mueller, M. (2017). *How much do OECD countries spend on prevention?* OECD Health Working Papers, No. 101. OECD Publishing. Paris. https://doi.org/10.1787/f19e803c-en.

Government of Canada. (n.d.). *Health cooperatives in Canada*. https://open.canada.ca/data/en/dataset/f241c519-a250-456b-8b1d-a1d483308c20

Government of Kerala. (1998). *The Study Report of the Committee on Cooperative Hospitals and Dispensaries*. Trivandrum, India: Registrar of Cooperative Societies.

Greengross, P., Grant, K., & Collini, E. (1999). *The Histor and Development of the UK National Health Service 1948–1999 (Second Edition Revised July 1999)*. DFID Health Systems Resource Centre.

Grijpstra, D., Broek, S., Buiskool, B. J., & Plooij, M. (2011). *The role of mutual societies in the 21st century*. Policy Department A: Economic and Scientific Policy Directorate General for Internal Policies, 231 European Parliament. www.europarl.europa.eu/document/activities/cont/201108/20110829ATT25422/20110829ATT25422EN.pdf

Grijpstra, D., Broek, S., Buiskool, B.J. & Plooij, M. (2011). The role of mutual societies in the 21st century. Policy Department A: Economic and Scientific Policy, Directorate General for Internal Policies, 231 European Parliament. Available at: http://www.europarl.europa.eu/document/activities/cont/201108/20110829ATT25422/20110829ATT2 5422EN.pdf.

Grijpstra, S., Merkur, S., & McKee, M. (2011). Private health insurance in Italy: A transitional market in an evolving health system. *Health Policy*, 103(2–3), 218.

Gruending, D. (1974). The first ten years. Retrieved from: www.saskatooncommunityclinic.ca/wp-content/uploads/2017/03/the-first-ten-years.pdf

Guerrero R., Gallego A. I., Becerril-Montekio V., & Vásquez J. (2011). Sistema de salud de Colombia [The health system of Colombia]. *Salud Publica Mex*. 53(2), s144–55. Spanish. PMID: 21877080.

Guinnane, T., & Martínez-Rodríguez, S. (2011). Cooperatives before cooperative law: Business law and cooperatives in Spain, 1869–1931. *Revista de Historia Economica – Journal of Iberian and Latin American Economic History*, 29(1), 67–93. https://doi.org/10.1017/S0212610911000012

Haddad, F. S. (2010). Michael Abraham Shadid: A Lebanese precursor of prepaid and cooperative medical care. *Journal of Medical Liban*, 58(1), 45–49.

Hadžović, S. (1997). Pharmacy and the great contribution of Arab Islamic science to its development. *Med Arch*, 51(1–2), 47–50.

Ham, C. (2020). The challenges facing the NHS in England in 2021. *BMJ*, 371, m4973. https://doi.org/10.1136/bmj.m4973

Han, N. P. (1991). Strengthening the cooperative medical system actively. *Chinese Health Economics*, 4, 12–14.

Harrison, M. I., & Calltorp, J. (2000). The reorientation of market-oriented reforms in Swedish health care. *Health Policy*, 50, 219–240.

Health and Global Policy Institute. (2018). Historical overview. *Japan Health Policy NOW*. http://japanhpn.org/en/historical/

Healthcare movement – *Health*. (1934). Zdravlje – Zdravstveni pokret: Association of Health Cooperatives and the Yugoslav Society for the Protection of Public Health. Eds. Vid. Gaković & K. Schneider; Bojan Pirc. ISSN 2560-5038, (12), Belgrade, Serbia.

Hollis, A., & Sweetman, A. (1998). Microcredit: What can we learn from the past? *World Development*, 26(10), 1875–1891.

Hopton, J., & Heaney, D. (1999). Towards primary care groups: Developing local healthcare cooperatives in Scotland. *BMJ*, 318(7192), 1185–1187.

Hughes, R., et al. (2011). State boards of health: Governance and politics. *Journal of Law, Medicine & Ethics*, 39(1), 37–41. www.cambridge.org/core/journals/journal-of-law-medicine-and-ethics/article/abs/state-boards-of-health-governance-and-politics/D0A5420F35F6B4171A9D90EF9C46B881

Hyden, G. (1988). Approaches to cooperative development: Blueprint versus greenhouse. In Attwood, D. W. & Baviskar, B. S. (Eds.) *Who Shares? Cooperatives and Rural Development* (pp. 149–171). New Delhi: Oxford University Press.

ICA. (1895). *Report of the First International Cooperative Congress*. London.

ICA. (1995). *Cooperatives Identity*. www.ica.coop/en/cooperatives/cooperative-identity/

ICA. (2013a). *Blueprint for Cooperative Decade.* www.ica.coop/sites/default/files/2021-11/ICA%20Blueprint%20-%20Croatian.pdf

ICA. (2013b). *Guidance Notes to the Cooperative Principles.* https://ica.coop/sites/defa ult/files/2021-11/ICA%20Guidance%20Notes%20EN.pdf

ICA. (2020). *Mapping: Key Figures National Report: Colombia ICA – EU Partnership.* https://coops4dev.coop/sites/default/files/2020-10/Colombia%20-%20Key%20Figu res%20Report.pdf

ICA. (2021). www.coops4dev.coop/sites/default/files/2021-03/Legal%20Framew ork%20Analysis%20-%20USA.pdf

ICA. (2023a). *About ICA.* www.ica.coop/en/about-us/international-cooperative-alliance

ICA. (2023b). *Cooperatives for 2030 Campaign.* www.ica.coop/en/whats-co-op/ co-ops-for-2030

ICA. (2023c). *History Cooperative Movement.* www.ica.coop/en/cooperatives/history-cooperative-movement

IHCO. (2015). *Unimed Brasil – A Model of Cooperative Governance.* https://ihco.coop/ 2015/05/25/unimed-brazil-a-model-of-cooperative-governance-2/

IHCO. (2017). *International Health Cooperative Organization (IHCO) – Report 2017 Executive Summary and Part 1.* https://euricse.eu/wp-content/uploads/2018/03/IHCO-Report-2017-Executive-summary-and-Part-1-1.pdf

IHCO. (2018a). The Cooperative Health Report: *Assessing the Worldwide Contribution of Cooperatives to Health-Care.* https://euricse.eu/wp-content/uploads/2018/04/IHC O_Executive-summary_new-format.pdf

IHCO. (2018b). *Health Cooperative Report.* www.fundacionespriu.coop/sites/default/ files/documentos/cooperative-health-report-2018.pdf

ILO. (2002). *R193 – Promotion of Cooperatives Recommendation, 2002 (No. 193).* www.ilo.org/dyn/normlex/en/f?p=NORMLEXPUB:12100:0::NO::P12100_ILO_C ODE:R193

ILO. (2016). *Providing Care through Cooperatives: Survey and Interview Findings /* Lenore Matthew, Simel Esim, Susan Maybud, & Satoko Horiuchi; International Labor Office, Cooperatives Unit (COOP), Gender, Equality and Diversity Branch (GED) – Geneva.

ILO. (2023). *History of ILO.* www.ilo.org/global/about-the-ilo/history/lang--en/ index.htm

International Cooperative Alliance. (2021). *History of Cooperatives.* www.ica.coop/en/ what-co-operative/history-cooperatives

International Health Cooperative Organization (IHCO). (2018). *Report on Health Cooperatives.* https-//previewihco.files.wordpress.com/2018/03/cooperative-health-report-2018.pdf

International Labour Organization (ILO). (2018). *Advancing Cooperation among Women Workers in the Informal Economy: The SEWA Way.* Geneva. www.ilo.org/wcmsp5/gro ups/public/---ed_emp/---emp_ent/---coop/documents/publication/wcms_633752.pdf

Jadovno. (2014). *Sokolske zdravstvene zadruge.* https://jadovno.com/sokolske-zdravstv ene-zadruge/?lng=lat#.YNG3YlQzaUk

JCA. (2018). *Statistics on Cooperatives.* www.japan.coop/study/pdf/211018_01en.pdf

Jelisavac Trošić, S. Todić, & D. Stamenović, M. (2018). *Svetska trgovinska organizacija – Životna sredina i sistem zdravstvene zaštite.* Beograd: Institut za međunarodnu politiku i privredu.

Jhabvala, R., & Bali, N. (1993). *My Life My Work: A Sociological Study of SEWA's Urban Members* (Working Paper No. 2). Ahmedabad: SEWA Academy.

Johansen, A., West, R., & Vracko, P. (2020). *Integrated, Person-Centred Primary Health Care Produces Results: A Case Study from Slovenia.* Copenhagen: WHO Regional Office for Europe. https:// apps.who.int/iris/bitstream/handle/10665/336184/ 9789289055284-eng.pdf

Johnston Birchall. (2011). *People-centred Business Cooperatives Cooperatives and the Idea of Membership.* UK: Palgrave Macmillan.

Jonsson, K., & Ekman, I. (2002). *The Swedish health care system.* Health policy, 62(3), 291–304.

Karahasanović, A. (1977). Health care in Bosnia and Herzegovina during the time of the Turks (1463–1878). *The First Congress of Doctors of Bosnia and Herzegovina, held in Sarajevo in 1977, proceedings*, 19–21.

Karan, A., Yip, W., & Mahal, A. (2017). Extending health insurance to the poor in India: an impact evaluation of Rashtriya Swasthya Bima Yojana on out-of-pocket spending for healthcare. *Social Science & Medicine, 181*, 83–92.

Kavita, A. (2017). Case study: Effectiveness of CRM strategies in the global era (with special reference to retail markets of India). *Advances in Management*, 10(9), 14.

Kojić, G. (1922). *Minutes from the II Congress of Health Cooperatives, May 14.* Museum of Science and Technology, collection of the Museum of the Serbian Medical Society, personal fund of Dr Gavrilo Kojić, uninventoried material.

Kojić, G. (1923). *Address to the League of Nations.* Museum of Science and Technology, collection of the Museum of the Serbian Medical Society, personal fund of Dr Gavrilo Kojić, uninventoried material.

Kosanović, R., & Anđelski, H. (2015). Osnovni pravci razvoja zdravstvenog osiguranja u Republici Srbiji (1922–2014). *Zdravstvena zaštita*, 44(3), 48–70. https://doi.org/ 10.5937/ZZ1503048K

Kyzomirski, K. (1927). *Jakim celom służy spółdzielnia zdrowia.* Warszawa: nakł. Związku Spółdzielni Rolniczych i Zarobkowo-Gospodarczych R P.

Land Crops. (n.d.). *Biocoop: a cooperative company committed to organic farming.* www.calameo.com/biocoop/read/00703379751a41a15eed7

Legacoop. (n.d.). *Legacoop | Associazione Italiana delle cooperative e mutual.* www. legacoop.coop

legifrance.gouv.fr. (2009). *LAW No. 2009-879 of July 21, 2009, reforming hospitals and relating to patients, health and territories.* www.legifrance.gouv.fr/dossierlegislatif/ JORFDOLE000019674897/

Lemma, T. (2008). Growth without structures: The Cooperative Movement in Ethiopia. In: Develtere, et al. (Eds.), *Cooperating Out of Poverty: The Renaissance of the African Cooperative Movement* (pp. 128–152). Geneva: ILO.

Leow, R. (2014). China's health transitions. *The Lancet*, 384(9945), 738–739. https://doi. org/10.1016/S0140-6736(14)61427-6

Ley 11.388, 10 de Diciembre de 1926. *Boletín Oficial, 27 de Diciembre de 1926.* Derogada. Id SAIJ: LNN0026259.

Liu, D., & Tsegai, D. (2011). The new cooperative medical scheme and its implications for access to health care and medical expenditure: Evidence from rural China. *ZEF Discussion Papers on Development Policy*. Bonn: Center for Development Research.

Liu, X., & Cao, H. (1992). China's cooperative medical system: Its historical transformations and the trend of development. *Journal of Public Health Policy,* 13(4), 501–511.

Lopez, M., & Moreno, L. (2014). Cooperatives and healthcare services in Catalonia: An analysis of the economic and social impact. *CIRIEC-Spain, Public, Social and Cooperative Economy Magazine,* 80, 123–148.

Lopez, M., & Villanueva, F. (2017). The role of cooperatives in the development of Catalonia's health sector. *REVESCO: Magazine of Cooperative Studies,* 124, 78–103.

López, R. (2004). el cooperativismo en salud, una presencia necesaria. *Revista Idelcoop – Año 2004 – Volumen 31 – N° 157.* www.idelcoop.org.ar/sites/www.idelcoop.org.ar/files/revista/articulos/pdf/2004_90529605.pdf

Ma, J., Xu, J., Zhang, Z., & Wang, J. (2016). New cooperative medical scheme decreased financial burden but expanded the gap of income-related inequality: evidence from three provinces in rural China. *International Journal for Equity in Health,* 15, 72. https://doi.org/10.1186/s12939-016-0361-5.

Machado, C. V. (2018). Políticas de Saúde na Argentina, Brasil e México: diferentes caminhos, muitos desafios. *Cien Saude Colet,* 23, 2197–2212.

MacKay, L. (2007). Health cooperatives in BC: The unmet potential. *British Columbia Medical Journal,* 49(3), 139–142.

Marshall, C. (2020). Benenden Health boss Marc Bell on the mutual's drive into digital health. *Health Investor UK.* www.yorkpress.co.uk/news/13587443.marc-bell-chief-executive-benenden/ress

Mašić, I. (2004). *Roots of Medicine and Healthcare in Bosnia and Herzegovina.* Sarajevo: Avicenna.

Mašić, I. (2010). *Medieval Arab Medicine.* Sarajevo: Avicenna. (2010:296). ISBN: 978-9958-720-40-6.

Médici, A. C. (1990). Financiamento e contenção de custos nas políticas de saúde: tendências atuais e perspectivas futuras. *Planej Polít Públicas,* 4, 83–98.

Mandić, O. (1974). "Rodbinske zajednice u evolucionoj šemi društvenih odnosa", *Sociologija sela* (Zagreb), br. 2, Available at: https://hrcak.srce.hr/file/176883

Meng Q. et al. (2015). People's Republic of China health system review. *Health Systems in Transition,* 5(7), 1–75.

Ministério da Saúde. (2006). Secretaria Executiva. Departamento de Apoio à Descentralização. *Diretrizes operacionais dos Pactos pela Vida, em Defesa do SUS e de Gestão.* Brasília-DF: O Ministério.

Ministerio de Educación. (2009). *La medicina en los tiempos de la Independencia.* El diario de salud. Bogota. Colombia.

Ministerio de Salud y Protección Social. (2018). *Indicator of Affiliation to the General Health Social Security System.* Colombia potentia de la vida. Bogota. Colombia. www.minsalud.gov.co/proteccionsocial/Regimensubsidiado/Paginas/coberturas-del-regimen-subsidiado.aspx

Ministry of Health and Family Welfare (MoHFW). (1983). *National Health Policy 1983.* New Delhi, India: Ministry of Health and Family Welfare, Government of India.

Ministry of Health and Family Welfare (MoHFW). (2002). *National Health Policy 2002.* New Delhi, India: Ministry of Health and Family Welfare, Government of India.

Ministry of Health and Welfare Medical Bureau. (1976). *100 Years of Medical Administration.* Gyosei. 54–56, 271, 589, 788–792, Ministry of Health, Tokyo. http://id.ndl.go.jp/bib/000001340737.

Ministry of Health, Ministry of Finance, & Ministry of Civil Affairs. (2012). *Announcement of the Development of New Rural Cooperative Medical Scheme in 2012*. China.

Ministry of Health of China. (2003). *Establishment of a New Rural Cooperative Medical System Guo Ban Fa [2003] No. 3*. www.gov.cn/zwgk/2005-08/12/content_21850.htm

Miranda, A. S. (2007). Intergovernmental health policy decisions in Brazil: Cooperation strategies for political mediation. *Health Policy Plan, 22,* 186–192.

Mladenatz, G. (2003). *História das doutrinas cooperativistas* (J. C. Castro, M. G. Leal, & C. Potiara Castro, Trans.). Brasília: Confebras.

Montes, A. (1974). Orígenes de la Asociación Cooperativa en la Provincia de Santa Fe. *Revista de Idelcoop, Año 1974, Vol. 1, Historia y doctrina*. www.idelcoop.org.ar/sites/www.idelcoop.org.ar/files/revista/articulos/pdf/74010201.pdf

Mushkin, S. J. (1958). Toward a definition of health economics. *Public Health Reports (1896–1970),* 73(9), 785–793. https://doi.org/10.2307/4590242

Nayar, K. R. (2000). Decline of cooperative medical services in Kerala, India. *Economic and Political Weekly,* 35, 519–521.

NCBA CLUSA. (2023). *State Cooperative Statute Library*. https://ncbaclusa.coop/resources/state-cooperative-statute-library

Nieddu, M. (2017). Social and solidarity economy in France: From early beginnings to new development policies. *Annals of Public and Cooperative Economics, 88*(3), 361–384. https://doi.org/10.1111/apce.12151

Noronha, A. V. (1976). *Cooperatives. Guarulhos,* Brazil: Cúpulo.

OECD/European Observatory on Health Systems and Policies. (2019). *Italy: Country Health Profile 2019*. State of Health in the EU, OECD Publishing, Paris/European Observatory on Health Systems and Policies, Brussels..

OECD. (2020). *How Resilient Have European Health Systems Been to the COVID-19 Crisis?* OECD Publishing, Paris. https://doi.org/10.1787/85e4b6a1-en.

European Observatory on Health Systems and Policies. (2009). *Health systems in transition: Sweden*. Copenhagen: WHO Regional Office for Europe.

OECD/European Observatory on Health Systems and Policies. (2021a). *Romania: Country Health Profile 2021, State of Health in the EU*. Paris/European Observatory on Health Systems and Policies, Brussels: OECD Publishing.

OECD/European Observatory on Health Systems and Policies. (2021b). *Poland: Country Health Profile 2021, State of Health in the EU*. Paris/European Observatory on Health Systems and Policies, Brussels: OECD Publishing.

Official Gazette of the RS 16/2018. JP Službeni glasnik. Belgrade. Serbia Available at: Službeni glasnik RS-Prosvetni glasnik, broj 16, od 17.09.2018. (paragraf.rs)

Official Gazette of the RS, No. 25/2019. JP Službeni glasnik. Belgrade. Serbia. Tekstovi usvojenih zakona ("Sl. glasnik RS'", br. 25/2019) | PROPISI.NET | Svi propisi Republike Srbije online

Official Gazette of the RS, no. 112/2015. JP Službeni glasnik. Belgrade. Serbia . https://www.paragraf.rs/glasila/rs/sluzbeni-glasnik-republike-srbije-112-2015.html.

Ogata, K. (1923). *The Cooperative Movement in Japan*. London: Butler and Tanner (p. 6).

Oklahoma Historical Society. (2023). *The Encyclopedia of Oklahoma History and Culture*. www.okhistory.org/publications/enc/entry.php?entry=SH001

Palme, J. et al. (2002). *Welfare in Sweden: the balance sheet for the 1990s, Ds 2002:32, Translation of Part 1 of the final report of the Welfare Commission [Kommittén Välfärdsbokslut] SOU 2001:79.* Stockholm, Fritzes.

Panayotof-Schaan, L. (2009). An overview of health cooperatives: A case-study perspective using Canadian and international examples. *BCICS Occasional Paper Series*, 3(1).

Panikkar, P. G., & Soman, C. R. (1984). *Health Status of Kerala: Paradox of Economic Backwardness and Health Development.* Trivandrum, India: Center for Development Studies.

Parker, D. S. (2007). Civilizing Argentina: Science, medicine, and the modern state. *Social History of Medicine*, 20(3), 624–625. https://doi.org/10.1093/shm/hkm089

Parker, F. (1943). Developments in the cooperative movement in 1943. *United States Department of Labor, No. 768.* Washington.

Pasqualini, C. D. (1987). La historia de la inmunología en la Argentina [History of immunology in Argentina]. *Medicina (B Aires)*, 47(6), 673–8. PMID: 3333080.

Patton, K. (1928). *Kingdom of Serbs, Croats and Slovenes: A Commercial and Industrial Handbook.* Washington: US Government Printing Office (pp. 129–131).

PisRS. (2009). *Zakon o zaposlovanju, samozaposlovanju in delu tujcev (Zakon o zaposlovanju)* [Law on employment, self-employment, and the work of foreigners (Employment Act)]. *Zakon o zadrugah* (Uradni list RS, št. 97/09 – uradno prečiščeno besedilo in 121/21).

Planalto. *Law no. 9.867/99, Article 1.* www.planalto.gov.br/ccivil_03/Leis/L9867.htm

Portillo, G. (1998). *Ley de Cooperativas N° 20.337: Jurisprudencia y Doctrina* (Rosario, FAS, 1998).

Preston, L. (2018, March 12). *A mutual relationship with the NHS: the future of healthcare?* www.thenews.coop/97175/sector/mutual-relationship-nhs-future-hea lthcare

Prętki, K. (2011). *Spółdzielnia zdrowia jako koncepcja rozwoju opieki zdrowotnej na wsi w okresie II Rzeczypospolitej* [Health cooperative as a concept for the development of healthcare in rural areas during the Second Polish Republic]. *Miscellanea Historico-Iuridica*, 10. https://repozytorium.uwb.edu.pl/jspui/bitstream/11320/1599/1/Miscel lanea_T-10_9.pdf

Puljiz, V. (1977). *Eksodus Poljoprivrednika [Exodus of Farmers].* Zagreb: Centar Za Sociologiju Sela.

Quevedo V., E., Pérez R., G. E., Miranda C., N., Eslava C., J. C., Hernández A., M., et al. (2008). *Historia de la Medicina en Colombia: De la Medicina Ilustrada a la Medicina Anatomoclínica (1782–1865)* (Vol. II). Colombia: Tecnoquímicas.

Rabrenović, M., & Stamenović, M. (2018). Pravno-ekonomski aspekti globalizacije u zdravstvu. *Pravni život*, 3–4, 85–95.

Rabrenović, M., Stošić, S., & Stamenović, M. (2016). Značaj strategijskog upravljanja za klinička ispitivanja. *Pravni život*, 9/2016; 401–407.

Rainhorn, J. D. (2003). Paradoxes et dilemmes d'un système de santé en crise: l'exception vietnamienne. In Maurer, J. L. & Gironde, C. (Eds.), *Le Vietnam à l'aube du XXIe siècle – Bilan et perspectives politiques, économiques et sociales* (pp. 325–345). Geneva: IUED–CRAM-Karthala, Modern Asia Research Center.

Rajasekharan Nayar, K., & Razum, O. (2003). Health cooperatives: review of international experiences. *Croatian Medical Journal*, 44(5), 568–575.

Ramírez, A. (2007). *Historia de la medicina en Santa Marta*. Bogotá: Universidad Cooperativa de Colombia.

Rands, S. (1994). *Privilege and Policy – A History of Community Clinics in Saskatchewan. Community Health Cooperative Federation*. www.saskatooncommunityclinic.ca/wp-content/uploads/2017/03/0000-privilege-and-policy.pdf

Revista de la Cooperativa de Trabajo Idecoop. (1997). *El cooperativismo médico argentino en la década del noventa: Evaluación y perspectivas* [Argentine medical cooperativism in the 1990s: Evaluation and perspectives], 97(5), 21–24. www.idelcoop.org.ar/sites/www.idelcoop.org.ar/files/revista/articulos/pdf/97052101.pdf

Roberts, J. (2016, February 4). Mutual relationship: Is the NHS the future of healthcare? *Cooperative News*. www.thenews.coop/97175/sector/mutual-relationship-nhs-future-healthcare/

Constante Beitia C (2015). El Plan de Salud de Cataluña: instrumento transformador del sistema de salud [The Health Plan for Catalonia: an instrument to transform the health system]. Med Clin (Barc). 2015 Nov;145 Suppl 1:20-6. Spanish. doi: 10.1016/S0025-7753(15)30033-6. PMID: 26711057.

Sakamoto, H., Rahman, M., Nomura, S., Okamoto, E., Koike, S., Yasunaga, H., ... Ueda, P. (2018). Japan health system review. *Japan Health System Review*, 8(1). World Health Organization. Regional Office for South-East Asia. https://apps.who.int/iris/handle/10665/259941

Saltman, R. B., Bankauskaite, V., & Vrangbæk, K. (Eds.). (2007) *Decentralisation in Health Care: Strategies and Outcomes*. European Observatory on Health Systems and Policies. UK: Open University Press McGraw-Hill Education McGraw-Hill House

Scottish Office Department of Health. (1999). *Towards a Healthier Scotland: A White Paper on Health*. Edinburgh: Stationery Office.

Selvaraj, S., Karan, K. A., Srivastava, S., Bhan, N., & Mukhopadhyay, I. (2022). *Indian Health System Review*. New Delhi: World Health Organization, Regional Office for South-East Asia.

SEWA. (2000). *Annual Report – 2000*. Ahmedabad: SEWA.

Shimazaki, K. (2013). *The Path to Universal Health Coverage–Experiences and Lessons from Japan for Policy Actions*. National Graduate Institute for Policy Studies.

Sicard, E. (1944). The South Slavic Zadruga in the evolution of the domestic group. *Zadruga in Serbian Literature, 1750–1912*.

Sigerist, H. E. (1939). Andrija Štampar. *Bulletin of the History of Medicine*, 7, 138–147.

Solarz, I. (1938). *Spółdzielnie Zdrowia* [*Health Cooperatives*]. Warszawa: Związek Spółdzielni Rolniczych i Zarobkowych RP.

Sowada, C., Sagan, A., & Kowalska-Bobko, I. (2022). *Poland: Health System Summary, 2022*. WHO Regional Office for Europe on behalf of the European Observatory on Health Systems and Policies. Copenhagen.

Stamenović, M. (2018). Challenges of economic globalisation in healthcare considering healthcare cooperatives as response. *Economic and Social Development (Book of Proceedings), 30th International Scientific Conference on Economic and Social*, p. 243–248, www.esd-conference.com/past-conferences.

Stamenović, M. (2019a). Biotehnološka i farmaceutska industrija kao razvojna šansa Republike Srbije. In *Strane direktne investicije – novi pogledi* (pp. 169–187). Institut za međunarodnu politiku i privredu. https://doi.org/10.5281/zenodo.3595613

Stamenović, M. (2019b). Challenges of healthcare cooperatives on territory of Serbia 1918–1949. Zdravstvena zaštita, 48(2), 25–31. https://doi.org/10.5937/ZZ1902025S

Stamenović, M. (2019c). Health cooperatives – a forgotten treasure. *Matica Srpska Social Sciences Quarterly 2019*, 169, 19–36. https://doi.org/10.2298/ZMSDN1969019S

Stamenović, M. (2019d). Post-transition status and selected challenges of the healthcare system of Serbia. *Revizor*, 22(85), 31–47.

Stamenović, M. (2020). *Zdravstvene zadruge-srpski koreni globalnog razvoja i moderne iniciajtive [Health cooperatives – Serbian roots of global development and modern initiatives]*. Novi Sad: Prometej.

Stamenović, M. (2021a). Challenges of health care systems and health cooperatives in international and national context. *Matica Srpska Social Sciences Quarterly*, 178, 225–243. https://doi.org/10.2298/ZMSDN2178225S

Stamenović, M. (2021b). Countries' Approach to Compulsory Licensing in the Time of the COVID-19 Pandemic. *International Organizations and States' Response to COVID-19*, p. 19. https://doi.org/10.18485/iipe_response2covid19.2021.ch19

Stamenović, M. (2021c, August 29). *The Health Cooperatives as Response to Healthcare Challenges and COVID-19 Pandemic*. Paper presented at the First International Scientific Conference "Covid-19 and Challenges of the Business World," Belgrade, Serbia. https://doi.org/10.5281/zenodo.5326421

Stamenović, M. (2021d). Quantitative analysis of biotechnology patents nexus to national economies and policies. *Auditor*, 22(89–90), 7. https://doi.org/10.5937/Rev2090007S

Stamenović, M. (2023). Revolutionizing the future of new drug discovery: use of AI by industry giants and case study of Abbvie. *Revizor*, 26(101), 11–21.

Stamenović, M., & Ćuzović, S. (2018). Innovation in biomedical and pharmaceutical industry in a light of globalization of the market within the region. *In The Sixth International Academic Conference, University of Business Studies Banja Luka: University for Business Studies* (pp. 103–111). ISSN: 2566-3178.

Stamenović, M., & Dobraca, A. (2017). Benefits of outsourcing strategy and IT technology in clinical trials. *Acta Informatica Medica: AIM: Journal of the Society for Medical Informatics of Bosnia & Herzegovina: casopis Drustva za medicinsku informatiku BiH*, 25(3), 203–207. https://doi.org/10.5455/aim.2017.25.203-207

Stamenović, M., Dobraca, A., & Smajlovic, M. (2018). Contemporary Aspects of Marketing in Clinical Trials Including Segments of IT and Technology Transfer. *Acta Informatica Medica: AIM: Journal of the Society for Medical Informatics of Bosnia & Herzegovina: casopis Drustva za medicinsku informatiku BiH*, 26(1), 67–70. https://doi.org/10.5455/aim.2018.26.67-70

Stamenović, M., Gulan, B., & Dragaš, B. (2017). *Srbija Danas – savremeni aspekti neoliberalizma, ekonomije, demografije, zdravstva, bezbednosti i tranzicije*. Novi Sad: Prometej.

Stamenović, M., & Sevarlić, M. (2020). *Dr Milorad Stamenovic's initiative for the re-establishment of health cooperatives/proposal for public hearing in the National Assembly of the Republic of Serbia submitted on January 27, 2020*. No. 06-140/20/ Initiative for reopening health cooperatives in the Republic of Serbia. Zenodo. https://doi.org/10.5281/zenodo.4007497

Stamenović, M., & Trosic, S. J. (2023). Cross-sectional analysis of the countries and corresponding trips flexibilities for pharmaceuticals. *Economic and Social Development: Book of Proceedings*, 325–334.

Štampar, A. (1939a). *Zdravlje i društvo* [Health and society]. Hrvatska naklada, Zagreb.

Štampar, A. (1939b). *Zdravlje i društvo* [Health and society]. (p. 132). Hrvatska naklada. Zagreb.

Statista. (2022a). *Health care in Japan – statistics & facts.* www.statista.com/topics/5035/health-care-in-japan/#topicOverview

Statista. (2022b). *Health in Colombia.* www.statista.com/topics/8753/health-in-colombia/#topicOverview

Statista. (2022c). *State of health in China – statistics & facts.* www.statista.com/topics/7433/state-of-health-in-china/#topicOverview

Stojisavljevic, B. (1973). *Povijest sela.* Prosvjeta. Zagreb.

Sugita, Y. (2012). The 1922 Japanese Health Insurance Law. *Harvard Asia Quarterly,* 14, 36–43.

Sun, X., Jackson, S., Carmichael, G., & Sleigh, A. C. (2009). Catastrophic medical payment and financial protection in rural China: Evidence from the New Cooperative Medical Scheme in Shandong Province. *Health Economics,* 18(1), 103–119.

Sung, H., et al. (2021). Global Cancer Statistics 2020: GLOBOCAN Estimates of Incidence and Mortality Worldwide for 36 Cancers in 185 Countries. *CA: A Cancer Journal for Clinicians.* Advance online publication. https://doi.org/10.3322/caac.21660

Swedish Competition Authority. (2010). *Omregleringen av apoteksmarknaden – redovisning av ett regeringsuppdrag* [Re-regulation of pharmacies. Report]. Stockholm, Konkurrensverket.

Swedish National Institute of Public Health (2023). *Public health objectives.* www.fhi.se/en/

Takakazu, Y. (2011). War and health insurance policy in Japan and the United States – World War II to postwar Reconstruction. *The Johns Hopkins University Center.* Baltimore, USA (pp. 22–25).

Centers for Disease Control and Prevention (CDC. (1999). Ten Great Public Health Achievements—United States, 1900–1999. *Morbidity and Mortality Weekly Report,* 48(12), 241-243..

Thatcher, M. (1985). Facing the New Challenge. In: Ungerson, C. (eds), *Women and Social Policy.* Women in Society. Palgrave, London. https://doi.org/10.1007/978-1-349-17956-5_23

The Miroslav Krleza, lexicography Institute. (n.d.). www.enciklopedija.hr/Natuknica.aspx?ID=67025

The Ontario Cooperative Association (OCA). (2018). *Information on the Cooperative Sector.* https://ontario.coop/sites/default/files/Innovative%20Co-ops.pdf

Thomson, S., Osborn, R., Squires, D., & Reed, S. J. (2011). *International Profiles of Health Care Systems 2011: Australia, Canada, Denmark, England, France, Germany, Iceland, Italy, Japan, the Netherlands, New Zealand, Norway, Sweden, Switzerland, and the United States.* New York: The Commonwealth Fund.

Tikkanen, R. (2020). *International Health Care System Profiles Japanese.* Commonwealth Fund. www.commonwealthfund.org/international-health-policy-center

Toh, C. H., & Haynes, R. (2022). The Health and Care Act 2022: Challenges and priorities for embedding research in the NHS. *Lancet,* 400(10349), 343–345. https://doi.org/10.1016/S0140-6736(22)01195-3.

Trevisan, A. (2009). *Cooperativas, una alternativa de alivio en épocas de crisis.* facultad de ciencias económicas y jurídicas universidad del aconcagua. http://bibliotecadigital. uda.edu.ar/objetos_digitales/363/seminario-3762-cooperativas.pdf

Tulibacki, T. (2005, December 10). Kazimierz Wyszomirski. *Gazeta Wyborcza Częstochowa,* p. 5.

UN. (1997). *Cooperative Enterprise in the Health and Social Care Sectors.* UN. New York

UN. (2001). *Resolution No. 56/114 adopted by the United Nations General Assembly at its 57th session,* 19th December, 2001.

UN. (2021). Seventy-sixth session Item 27 (b) of the provisional agenda – social development, including questions relating to the world social situation and to youth, ageing, persons with disabilities and the family: *Cooperatives in social development. Report of the Secretary-General.* UN. Geneva.

UNDP. (1997). *Human development report.* New York: Oxford Oxford University Press. https://hdr.undp.org/system/files/documents/hdr1997encompletenostatspdf.pdf

UNICEF. (2020). *Community-based health care, including outreach and campaigns, in the context of the COVID-19 pandemic.* World Health Organization and the United Nations Children's Fund (UNICEF), 2020.

Unimed. (2023). *Our history.* www.segurosunimed.com.br/nossa-historia

United States Department of Labor. (1943). *Monthly Labor Review.* Vol. 56. Washington: Government Printing Office.

Unschuld, P. U. (1999). The past 1000 years of Chinese medicine. *The Lancet,* 354 *(Special Issue, SIV9),* December. https://doi.org/10.1016/S0140-6736(99)90352-5

USA Public Law 95-351. (1978). *Public Law 95-351, 95th Congress.* https://uscode. house.gov/view.xhtml?path=/prelim@title12/chapter31&edition=prelim)

USDA. (2000). *USDA's Understanding Cooperatives: Co-op History Section, developed by Leesa Witt.* http://nfu.org/images/stories/Cooperatives-History-from-NFU-Curric.pdf

USDA & Rural Business/Cooperative Service, R. Business-Cooperative Service. (2001). *Strategic Planning in Farmer Cooperatives.* www.rd.usda.gov/sites/default/files/ RR184.pdf

U.S. Government Printing Office. (1943). *Monthly Labor Review, 909–911.*

Vlădescu, C., Scîntee, S. G., Olsavszky, V., Hernández-Quevedo, C., & Sagan, A. (2016). Romania: Health system review. *Health Systems in Transition,* 18(4), 1–170.

Voinea, A. (2015). *Why 20 million Brazilians rely on a cooperative for healthcare.* www. thenews.coop/97242/sector/health/20-million-brazilians-rely-co-operative-healthcare/

Vyas, J. (1992). Banking with poor self-employed women. *Savings and Credit: The NGO Factor.* Bangalore, India: ActionAid.

Wang, X., He, X., Zheng, A., & Ji, X. (2014). The effects of China's New Cooperative Medical Scheme on accessibility and affordability of healthcare services: An empirical research in Liaoning Province. *BMC Health Services Research,* 14, 388.

WEF. (2020). *WHO Healthcare Challenges.* www.weforum.org/agenda/2020/02/who-healthcare-challenges-2020s-climate-conflict-epidemics/

Weissert, C. S., & Weissert, W. G. (2006). *Governing Health: The Politics of Health Policy* (3rd ed.). Baltimore, MD: Johns Hopkins University Press.

Wolz, A., Möllers, J., & Micu, M. M. (2020). Options for agricultural service cooperatives in a postsocialist economy: Evidence from Romania. *Outlook on Agriculture,* 49(1), 57–65. https://doi.org/10.1177/0030727019861973

World Bank. (2023). *Current health expenditure per capita (current US$) – Myanmar.* https://data.worldbank.org/indicator/SH.XPD.CHEX.PC.CD?locations=MM

World Bank. (n.d.-a). *Current health expenditure (% of GDP) – France.* https://data.worldbank.org/indicator/SH.XPD.CHEX.GD.ZS?locations=FR

World Bank (n.d.-b). *Current health expenditure (% of GDP) – Italy.* https://data.worldbank.org/indicator/SH.XPD.CHEX.GD.ZS?locations=IT

World Bank. (n.d.-c). *GDP (current US$) in France* [Data file]. https://data.worldbank.org/indicator/NY.GDP.MKTP.CD?locations=FR

World Bank. (n.d.-d). *Population, total – Sweden.* https://data.worldbank.org/indicator/SP.POP.TOTL?locations=SE

World Health Organization. (2019). *Healthy Environments for Healthier Populations: Why Do They Matter, and What Can We Do?* (No. WHO/CED/PHE/DO/19.01). World Health Organization.

Wyszomirski, K. (1939). Spółdzielnia Zdrowia w walce o zdrowie wsi. *Zdrowie Publiczne, 2,* 76.

Xu, J., Gorsky, M., & Mills, A. (2019). Historical roots of hospital centrism in China (1835–1949): A path dependency analysis. *Social Science & Medicine, 226,* 56–62. https://doi.org/10.1016/j.socscimed.2019.02.025.

Yamauchi, T. (2015). The agricultural ethics of Ninomya Sontoku. *Taiwan Journal of East Asian Studies,* 12(2), 235–257. https://doi.org/10.6163/tjeas.2015.12(2)235

Zadružna zveza Slovenije. (2023). *Zgodovina* [History]. www.zadruzna-zveza.si/o-zvezi/zgodovina

Zadružni savez Srbije. (2023). *Iz istorije zadrugarstva.* www.zssrbije.org/zadruzni-savez-srbije/iz-istorije-zadrugarstva/

Zarko, C. (2006). El movimiento de cooperativas de salud en España y en el mundo. *Mediterráneo Económico, 32,* 257–273. ISSN 1698-3726. www.publicacionescajamar.es/publicacionescajamar/public/pdf/publicaciones-periodicas/mediterraneo-economico/32/22.pdf

Zdravstveni dom Ljubljana. (n.d.). *ZDL History.* www.zd-lj.si/en/index.php?option=com_k2&view=item&layout=item&id=263&Itemid=1558

Zdravstveni pokret – Zdravlje. (1934) *Healthace Movement – Health.* Belgrade: Yugoslav Society for the Protection of Public Health..

Zdravstveni pokret – Zdravlje. (1936) *Healthace Movement – Health.* Belgrade: Yugoslav Society for the Protection of Public Health.

Zenkyoren. (2020). *Annual Report 2020.* www.ja-kyosai.cr.jp/about/annual_report/pdf/2020annual.pdf

Zhang, L., Li, S., Yi, H., d'Intignano, L. M., & Ding, Y. (2016). Correlation between new cooperative medical scheme policy design and catastrophic medical payment: Evidence from 25 counties in rural China. *Asia-Pacific Journal of Public Health, 28,* 26–38. https://doi.org/10.1177/1010539515612907

Zhou, S. Q. (1987). The consolidation and development of the cooperative medical system and health insurance. *Chinese Rural Health Administration,* 12, 58–66.

Index

Note: Page numbers in **bold** refer to tables, and those in *italics* refer to figures.

For Product Safety Concerns and Information please contact our EU
representative GPSR@taylorandfrancis.com
Taylor & Francis Verlag GmbH, Kaufingerstraße 24, 80331 München, Germany